PUBLICATIONS
OF THE GREGORIAN RESEARCH CENTRE
ON CULTURES AND RELIGIONS

EDITED BY

ARIJ A. ROEST CROLLIUS, S.J.

INTERRELIGIOUS AND INTERCULTURAL
INVESTIGATIONS

VOLUME 5

PONTIFICIA UNIVERSITÀ GREGORIANA
CENTRO CULTURE E RELIGIONI

INTERRELIGIOUS AND INTERCULTURAL INVESTIGATIONS

VOLUME 5

SABURO SHAWN MORISHITA

TEODORI: COSMOLOGICAL BUILDING AND SOCIAL CONSOLIDATION IN A RITUAL DANCE

EDITRICE PONTIFICIA UNIVERSITÀ GREGORIANA
ROMA 2001

EDITRICE PONTIFICIA UNIVERSITÀ GREGORIANA
Piazza della Pilotta, 35 - 00187 Roma

TABLE OF CONTENTS

LIST OF ILLUSTRATIONS

INTRODUCTION

Dance is a mode of communication affiliated with the qualities explicitly inherent in human beings—that of expressing abstract ideas. Exposing concepts by using the body as the medium of expression is part and parcel of human activity. Animals, too, are known to dance but their actions are grounded in their biological features, and not for, as with human beings, expressing ideas. In other words, dance always involves human movement that reveals human experience through the body, this being the prime instrument (Lange 1975). To put it briefly, "to dance is human, and humanity almost universally expresses itself in dance" (Hanna 1987, 3). Since it is one means through which human beings are able to express thoughts into form, it is not surprising to find dance as a vehicle for spiritual activities. One of the earliest publications to treat sacred dances comparatively asserts that the origin of dance itself is rooted in its profound sacred character and other forms of dance have derived from such use (Oesterley 1923). Often cited as examples to uphold this theory are dances that were performed by the ancient Greek civilization. For them, dance was a direct creation of the gods that were revealed to humans who in turn taught it to others. A large part of Greek dances, in fact, can be traced back to varying religious rituals to honor various divinities (Lawler 1985, 13). The moving human body, then, recreates and channels symbolic ideas not only to the gods who were honored but to those who danced and observed them as well.

Different in tone and character to these Greek dances, yet nevertheless through use of the same components of the human body, the Teodori, literally "hand dance," is a ritual dance which focuses on the expression of the body and hands. Members of a Japanese new religion called Tenrikyo communally perform the Teodori, translated as "the dance with the hand movements." Tenrikyo, "the teachings of divine wisdom," was founded by a Japanese woman named Nakayama Miki (1798–1887) in 1838. According to its doctrine, Miki received a divine revelation from God the Parent and became its living shrine on earth to teach people the way to live the Joyous Life, the purpose of humankind's very own creation. Among the rituals that were taught by the foundress to express this joy is the Teodori. It is performed as a means of faithful communal practice in Tenrikyo local churches.

This study aims to uncover the meanings and dynamics of the Teodori. It intends to do so by relying on the analytical insights provided by Clifford Geertz, an interpretive anthropologist, who advocates a semiotic approach. Two reasons why this particular method has been chosen are worth mentioning. Many dance scholars agree that the general notion of dance is a cultural and social phenomenon (Hanna 1987; Hodgens 1988; Kaeppler 1978; Kealiinohomoku 1979; Lange 1975; Royce 1977; Spencer P. 1985). The Teodori is not an exception. The main objective here is to render the Teodori to others as a phenomenon that will amplify the "universe of human discourse" (Geertz 1973, 14) by emphasizing its sociocultural meanings. The second reason for applying an anthropological approach to the Teodori is to touch upon the mechanics of how religion and culture interrelate with one another. Many consider Tenrikyo to be construed by and for a particular people and should therefore confined to its own terrain. An anthropological account on one of the main facets of a new religious movement like Tenrikyo—a movement that advocates its intrinsic cultural value in the missions—may be helpful in distinguishing its true universal message from its cultural values. In other words, the ritual dance as a religious phenomenon viewed systematically through a set of anthropological lens will not only help others understand the mechanics of a ritual dance but will also be fruitful for members of the Tenrikyo community in uplifting their own comprehension of this ritual dance.

Tenrikyo services that are mentioned below are based on the *Mikagura-uta*, the songs for the service. This scripture is a normative one since it was written by Nakayama Miki and divided into two parts: the songs for the Kagura and the songs for the Teodori. This study intends to analyze the ritual dance based on the latter part. The performance of the Teodori in a monthly service context always assumes the accompaniment of nine musical instruments. Further, the combination of singing and dancing to the songs for service, with the playing of the musical instruments, constitute a complete performance of the Teodori. It is relevant to note that the performance of the Teodori during a monthly service for most Tenrikyo followers is the source for which to rejoice. For our own analytical purposes, however, we shall argue that the Teodori is an integral "text" composed of both verbal and nonverbal symbolic patterns. As such, then, the Teodori as a text can be decoded without the associated musical instruments that accompany the Teodori during a typical monthly service performance. The primary focus of the inquiry will rely on the combination of these symbols that are produced by the verbal and nonverbal symbolic patterns. Before further elaboration, a few words should be made on acute Tenrikyo distinctions interconnected with the Teodori that will assist us in taking a step forward in understanding the

2

overall background.

Various Tenrikyo Services

For Tenrikyo followers, *tsutome* is a term that means "service" and this alone possesses a number of referents. The most important of such referents is the *Kagura zutome*, or the Kagura Service. This service is the masked dance that is performed around the Kanrodai where Church Headquarters—located in Tenri City, Japan—is situated. This will be explained in detail in chapter two. All other services that we describe below are performed at each local church, including Church Headquarters. The Tenrikyo daily service consist of an *asa zutome*, or morning service, and a *yū zutome*, or evening service. Such services are held at different times at each local church. The five instruments that are lined across in front of the altars at a Tenrikyo church are played to the text of the seated service.[1] Immediately after the performance, two songs from the Teodori are usually danced. Afterwards, scriptures are read out aloud by the members of the congregation. Another type of service is the *onegai zutome*, a prayer service or a petition service. This is a type of service that asks distinctively for God the Parent's intervention for a specific purpose. The most common form of a prayer service is when a community makes an appeal or petition to God to save a person from a particular illness. Other forms of a prayer service is that of asking God that a particular church activity, such as a spiritual retreat, a pilgrimage trip, or even a church association event that involves recreation, goes well. The prayer service is performed together with two instruments on the upper dais—the wooden clappers and the counter—with the other members of the congregation praying from the worship hall.

The perplexity concerning a Tenrikyo service emerges when one speaks of a monthly service, a grand service, a memorial service, or a new year's service. The Japanese word for monthly service is *tsukinamisai*, literally, a regular or recurring monthly festival. The reason for inserting the word "service" perhaps originates from the religious services held by Christian denominations in the West. Of note, then, is that the explicit meaning of festivity in a *tsukinamisai* therefore loses some of its original import. The monthly service at Church Headquarters is given highest priority since the Kagura Service, the masked dance referred to above, is performed. What completes a monthly service at Church Headquarters is the performance of the Teodori, the hand dance, which is accompanied by nine musical instruments. Therefore, the seated service, derived from the text for the

---

[1] These five instruments are the small gong, cymbals, wooden clappers, a counter, and a drum. They are situated horizontally on top of the upper dais and in this particular order from left to right. The text of the seated service can be found in chapter two.

Kagura Service, together with the performance of the Teodori, are considered major components of a local church's monthly service.

In contrast to a regular or recurring monthly service is the grand service. Once again, the Japanese original, *taisai*, has been eclipsed since it literally means "grand festival." There are two types of grand services: the spring grand service held in January and the autumn grand service held in October. Where the former commemorates the withdrawal of the physical life of the foundress, the latter commemorates the founding of Tenrikyo. Both services are performed in the same manner as a monthly service yet with emphasis on their distinct import. The new year's service, or *gantansai*, is one which is performed on the first day of the year. The procedure is performed exactly in the same manner as a monthly service yet its attention is focused on asking God the Parent that a beneficial productive year lays ahead of the community of believers. Two memorial services, or *mitamasai*, are held annually. These services consist of a monthly service like gathering with the performance of the Teodori and are held to recall the dedicated efforts of predecessors.

One final note on the service. We have briefly stated the different forms of the service without mentioning much on the reason for its performance. There are four basic doctrinal reasons for the performance of a Tenrikyo service. First, the service is a means to ask God the Parent through ritual behavior that blessings are received, not only in terms of a particular illness as in the prayer service, but an invocation that salvation be realized. Secondly, the service is a means to thank God the Parent for the blessings already received. Tenrikyo doctrine emphasizes that humankind and the world would not exist if it were not for the constant protection from God. Therefore, it is a liturgy for which one demonstrates gratitude to God the Parent for guidance. Thirdly, and at an individual level, the service is a means by which a person is able to purify him/herself of self-centered attitudes s/he has accumulated. Seen in this way, the service is a kind of ritual behavior in the reflexive order. Finally, the service is a means by which the community of believers demonstrate their unity of minds as well as to portray the joy in which they have come to know the teachings of Tenrikyo. These socially formulated perceptions of the service are what we aim at uncovering in this study.

General Orientation

We have divided the study into four chapters. The first chapter consists of two parts that explores methodological questions. We begin the first part with a review of Clifford Geertz's approach to the anthropological study of religion. Geertz perceives that any such study must be seen in light of a cultural system and thus we begin by examining his meaning of culture. We seek to develop this idea so that it will become clear why an application of this approach will be a pivotal factor in unraveling the ritual dance. The second part is a reflection on how native anthropologists are doing research in their own respective countries. This section attempts to answer the question of objectivity and intrinsic with this study: "How does being a missionary of this particular religious community alter the outcome of the writing despite its reliance on an anthropological approach?" We propose that an answer can be found in reflexivity, a process of objectifying the self so that it is able to become an object to itself. These assumptions cast a framework for which the rest of the study will be based.

Chapter two focuses on the text. In the field of semiotics, a text is a combination of signs (Thwaites et al. 1994, 67). As is true of any written text, a combination of signs is transmitted by a sender to a receiver through a medium of a code or a group of codes. Once the receiver has acknowledged this as a text, then, s/he interprets it according to the disposed set of code or codes (Scholes 1982), whereby a receiver encodes a text. Likewise, we regard the Teodori as an integral text in the sense that it is constituent of a combination of signs and therefore suggests, by definition, to be open for interpretation. In eliciting the text, we have divided this chapter into three parts. The first part will be dedicated to the writer of the text, namely the foundress of Tenrikyo, Nakayama Miki. We attempt to draw up an historical account of the woman who not only had a special message to convey but an aesthetical way of expressing it. The second part concerns a description of the text itself with two subdivisions: the verbal and nonverbal symbolic patterns of the Teodori. Finally, the third part describes how the text is given life and actualized. That is, in this section we describe how the text is performed during a typical Tenrikyo monthly service and underline other recurring events that arise from such an occasion.

Chapter three concerns itself with the intertext of the Teodori. A sweeping generalization of an intertext is when references are made from within one text to other texts. These other texts are the intertexts of the text itself (Manning 1987). Scholars have used the word "genre"—a literary device—to combine texts and their intertexts into one category (Thwaites et al 1994, 88). That is, when one particular text interrelates with other texts, the constituents of the particular text can be traced in these other texts. The common principle of an intertext is that, like a sign that may refer to another sign instead of an object, a text can also refer to other texts. Consequently, an intertext is a hidden text within a text that informs the reader about the text itself with or without the knowledge of the author (Scholes 1982). In short, we intend in this chapter to examine the Teodori's intertextuality so as to unravel its world view and to render its *model of* cosmic reality.

Chapter four is dedicated to context. Context is the social and psychological world of the speaker and the hearer, an important element for any sort of communication to take place (Manning 1979). For our purposes, we use the word context in all of its conventional meanings. Such being the case, we shall be using the word "setting" and "context" interchangeably. Particular attention is given to the Japanese context for we believe that this particular social setting is the source from which the ritual dance emerges and therefore enhances our description with deeper meaning. This chapter, as a result, is written in two parts. The first part is an investigation that stands on the cross section between intertext and context. We examine dance and pilgrimage within the context of its own religious tradition. In this sense, we suggest that these two religious motifs are factors that have shaped the character of the Teodori. At a further level, then, the drive is to demonstrate how context imparts persuasive dispositions that are salient in rendering a *model for* social reality. This chapter also emphasizes on perceiving the Teodori as a ritual dance that imparts social boundaries and confines. The *uchi/soto* dichotomy, the inside/outside principle, will aid us in seeking how the Teodori creates lines of social import. Social factors are mapped out that emerge during the performance of the Teodori. Such social derivatives, we suggest, construe a common ethos for the community of Tenrikyo believers. Finally, we concentrate on the embodiment of the *uchi* factor, the inside factor, by indexing a cosmology with the given context. In the hopes to appropriate these quadrants satisfactorily, the context-centered work of anthropologist Mary Douglas is incorporated in the study. There are two basic drives for this choice. One lies in her notion of social form and boundaries that other anthropologists have argued are compatible with the Japanese context (Valentine 1990). The other reason lies in her way of correlating the relationship between how a group perceives the physical body with the construction of the social body. In retrospect, then, the chapter ends with a Tenrikyo mode concerning the heart of Douglas's theoretical contribution, one grounded in the relationship between physical and social bodies.

The special focus of these chapters is to portray the cultural meaning and social dynamics of this ritual dance through use of an anthropological framework known as interpretive anthropology. That is, we intend to underscore and grasp the sense in which the Teodori is an expressive form of cosmological building and social consolidation. One of its tenets is to remain in the proximity of an experience-near account of the material under question. Using the semiotic codes of text–intertext–context, we aim at uncovering the cognitive elements and evaluative components—a world view and ethos—of the community of Tenrikyo believers who get together from time to time in communal practice for the Teodori. In a modest way, the endeavor simply touches the tip of an iceberg: analysis of this sort is intrinsically incomplete and the more so the deeper one goes (Geertz 1973, 29). Suitable for our final chapter, then, are suggestions that can be taken into account to "better inform and better conceptualize" (Geertz 1973, 27) the ritual dance for future research. A Tenrikyo bibliography is extracted from the general bibliography consulted for this study in the hope of facilitating readers to Tenrikyo sources, studies, and statements.

CHAPTER ONE

THE METHOD

The Work of Clifford Geertz

"Religion as a Cultural System," first published in 1966 in a collage of essays called *Anthropological Approaches to the Study of Religion* (Banton 1966), acknowledged Geertz as formulating the most influential anthropological definition of religion to have appeared in years. The same article was later reprinted in his widely acclaimed *The Interpretation of Cultures* (Geertz 1973). It is this article for which we shall employ for our own propositions. Other publications by Geertz help refine the formulated synthesis found in this article and we shall resort to Geertz's other writings from time to time so as to map out a version of his conceptual schemes.[1]

What is most important from the start is the term " culture."[2] At the onset of his article, Geertz claims that the anthropological study of religion is inert and suggests that by redefining the concept of culture one may revive the anthropological study of religion that borrows much when unpacking a religion. Geertz elsewhere has noticed that the definitions of culture were so broad in the 1950s that it gave hunting licenses to search for culture everywhere (Geertz 1973, 37–43). Geertz then makes his own contribution to

---

[1] Besides his well-acclaimed *The Interpretation of Cultures* (Geertz 1973) a collection of further essays in *Local Knowledge* (1983) has proved fruitful in clarifying issues put forward in his previous publication. In the introduction he says: "When . . . I collected a number of my essays and rereleased them under the title . . . *The Interpretation of Cultures*, I thought I was summing things up;. . . . But, as a matter of fact, I was imposing upon myself a charge. In anthropology, too, it so turns out, he who says A must say B, and I have spent much of my time since trying to say it. The essays below are a result" (Geertz 1983, 3). In *Works and Lives* (Geertz 1988) his concern is less toward a framework on cultural analysis than a concern on how various anthropologist have been conditioned by their own historical contexts—thus providing a means to "observe the observer" and ways in which anthropologists are authors in their own right in a special way. A more recent publication, *After the Fact* (Geertz 1995) portrays himself as the subject of the volume since it is mainly on his own life as anthropologist after four decades of work. All such essays, however, underline the importance of his interpretive approach.

[2] We believe that the term "culture" can be a very ambiguous term. Taking advantage of Geertz's cultural dimension of religious analysis we attempt here to briefly explain what he means by the term so that confusion, which has been a very predominant when trying to define the term, will not result (De Napoli 1987).

the concept of culture by cutting it down to size. Since the foundation of his formula on religion rests on his definition of culture, we shall provide a documentation of what Geertz exactly means by it.

Geertz retains that "man is an animal suspended in webs of signification he himself has spun and takes culture to be those webs" (Geertz 1973, 5). Against a definition of culture to be that which lies somewhere in the hearts and minds of men or seen as complexes of concrete behavior patterns—customs, usages, traditions, habit clusters—Geertz says that a better view of culture is seen as a set of control mechanisms—plans, recipes, rules, instructions—for the governing of behavior (Geertz 1973, 44). This account would treat culture as a discourse and not as a super-organic entity or a psychological structure ingrained in the hearts and minds of individuals. In short, Geertz perceives culture as one lying *among* and *between* people. Culture for Geertz, then, is:

> A historically transmitted pattern of meaning embodied in symbols, a system of inherited conceptions expressed in symbolic forms by means of which men communicate, perpetuate, and develop their knowledge about attitudes toward life (Geertz 1973, 89).

Geertz argues that the concept of culture is essentially a semiotic one (Geertz 1973, 24). To study culture, he retains, is to study a shared code of meanings. Claiming a resemblance between the literary critic and the anthropologist, culture is an "assemblage of texts" (Geertz 1973, 448) and anthropology is a matter of interpretation and not one of decipherment. From this assertion, we note off hand that social activities can be read for meanings just as written and spoken words are commonly read: culture is in and of the world and should be perceived as a traffic in significant symbols. It is seen in public which means it lies in the house yard, the market-place, the town square (Geertz 1973, 45) It is inquired through particular situations of fieldwork, artifacts, documents and any other evidence of human expression and consequently becomes an ensemble of text which an anthropologist must decode. Culture shapes and is shaped by the world it flourishes and culture is a kind of context, or limiting condition, molding the way people perceive themselves, others, society, and the universe.

From this perspective, culture is in action that embodies symbolic expression. Rather than governing what each and every human does it defines and limits choices. It becomes a matter of connecting the action to sense rather than the behavior to its determinants. The analysis of culture, then, is sorting out the structures of signification and determining their social ground and import (Geertz 1973, 9). Ethnographies that are derived from such analysis, those he calls "thick description," are interpretations of the interpretations yielded by the natives. Anthropologists begin their own interpretations of what their informants are up to, or think they are up to, and systematize those. Cultural analysis consists of guessing at meaning, assessing the guesses, and drawing explanatory conclusions from the better guesses.

Geertz goes on to recognize religion itself to constitute a cultural system, just as he suggests that art, ideology, and common sense are constituents of a cultural system.[3] Geertz's main postulate is that sacred symbols serve to consolidate a people's ethos and world view. At the interface of any sacred symbol will be these two blending factors.

An ethos, he says, is the tone, quality, character of a people's life, its moral and aesthetic style and mood. The ethos in a religious belief is made consciously reasonable to represent a way ultimately adapted to the actual state of affairs the world view describes. The world view is the picture a group or community has of the way things in sheer actuality are, their most comprehensive ideas of order. The world view is rendered emotionally persuasive by being presented as an image of the actual state of affairs which is well-organized to accommodate that particular way of life. On the one hand, a world view objectifies moral and aesthetic preferences as mere common sense given the fixed shape of reality. On the other hand, a world view endures these beliefs about reality by calling out moral and aesthetic feelings as evidence for their truth.

Religious symbols formulate a basic congruence between a particular style of life, an ethos, and a particular metaphysic, a world view, which sustain each other with the borrowed authority of the other. These two aspects, ethos and world view, are joined together in sacred symbols and are experienced by individuals in rituals and often play a role in everyday life. It follows that sacred symbols also provide the same individuals who partake in the religious ritual with a specific religious perspective so that they may adopt it from time to time to confront the problem of meaning.

This is not, Geertz continues, a novelty for it happens all the time. Given that it happens all the time, however, little has been elaborated on this matter empirically. His intention is how to uncover the fusion of ethos and world view which takes place in a given sacred symbol. Geertz begins his inquiry with a definition of religion he claims will provide for a useful orientation to unpack and extend the investigation. Religion is:

---

[3] *Ideology as a Cultural System* can be found in (Geertz 1973, 193–233). Further, *Common Sense as a Cultural System* as well as *Art as a Cultural System* can be found in (Geertz 1983, 73–93) and (Geertz 1983, 94–120), respectively.

a system of symbols which acts to establish powerful, pervasive, and long-lasting moods and motivations in men by formulating conceptions of a general order of existence and clothing these conceptions with such an aura of factuality that the moods and motivations seem uniquely realistic (Geertz 1973, 90).

Emphasis is placed on the word symbol. For Geertz, symbol is used for any object, act, event, quality, or relation that serves as a vehicle for a conception (Geertz 1973, 91). The conception here refers to the symbol's meaning. Symbols, he continues, are "tangible formulations of notions, abstractions from experienced fixed in perceptible forms, concrete embodiments of ideas, attitudes, judgments, longings, or beliefs." (Geertz 1973, 91). Cultural acts—the fabrication, grasping, and usage of symbolic forms—are social events like any other. They are as public as marriage and as observable as agriculture. Such systems of symbols, or cultural patterns, will be key terms for the analogy.

Cultural Patterns: A *Model Of* and *Model For*

Cultural patterns are sets of symbols whose relations to one another model other relations. They are processes in systems both physical and metaphysical in corresponding, copying, or disguising others. Geertz would say that there is a *model of* and a *model for* import, although they constitute two sides of the same coin and are needed for his elaboration.

A *model of* reality is the manipulation of symbol structures so as to bring them into parallel with a pre-established nonsymbolic system as when grasping how damns work with a hydraulic theory or with a flow chart. Geertz maintains that a theory or flow chart models concrete connections as to make them understandable. On the other hand, a *model for* reality is the orchestration of the nonsymbolic systems in terms of the connection expressed in the symbolic as when building a damn according to the theory or conclusions drawn from the flow chart. The theory of hydraulics or flow chart organizes the actual physical relationships for reality. The important analogy here is that an association is made between the social and the psychological (Geertz 1973, 93), and it attempts to show that rituals construct in some manner the existing tangible relationships of people of a given society who perform them. The double aspect of a cultural pattern, then, is that a system of symbols give meaning—objective conceptual form to reality in both the social and psychological sense—by shaping themselves to reality and shaping reality to themselves (Geertz 1973, 93). Geertz goes on to say that this twofold aspect sets true symbols from other sorts of meaningful forms.

A question is then posed: how do concrete symbols or systems of symbols express the world's climate and shape the world as we have mentioned? The answer is that reality is shaped by inducing in a person a notable distinctive set of disposition (capacities, propensities, skills, habits, liabilities, proneness) which give an inborn character to the course of his activity and the quality of his encountering (Geertz 1973, 95). The term disposition is not an activity as such but a probability of an activity being occurred or performed during a certain circumstance. An example is to be devout does not mean that a person is devout in the present tense but is liable to perform acts of devotion. Concerning the trait of such disposition, especially with respect to religious activities, Geertz claims that there are two types of disposition that are important, namely moods and motivations (Geertz 1973, 96).

A motivation is a persisting tendency, a habitual inclination to perform certain sorts of act, and experience certain sorts of feeling in certain sorts of situations. Motivations are not, again, acts or feeling as such but a capacity to perform certain classes of acts or to have notable classes of feelings. Moods, on the other hand, are quite clear. As in the case of motivations, a mood is not the act itself but simply, as the word suggests, a propensity to act. The major difference between moods and motivations is that while moods are made meaningful with regard to the situation from which they are established, motivations are made meaningful with regard to the ends toward which they are established to arrive at. Moods have a scalar quality and motivations have vectorial qualities. In the final analysis, then, motives are interpreted in terms of their consummation and moods are interpreted in terms of their sources (Geertz 1973, 97).

A second question can be postulated: how do these dispositions come into being? The answer is simply because a human being is able to create a general order of existence by definition. In other words, dispositions spring from a conception of cosmic order that man himself has created. If sacred symbols did not at one and same time induce dispositions and compose general ideas of order, then a set of religious activity or religious experience would not exist. What any religion affirms, Geertz continues, is that it affirms something (Geertz 1973, 98–99).

This affirmation of something is part of the overall powers of conception that is innate in human beings. The ability to generate, to perceive, and to use symbols may fail us but if it were to fail, man would be simply inept. The thing about symbols is that we need symbols to be humans for we would be "a formless monster with neither sense of direction nor power of self-control, a chaos of spasmodic impulses and vague emotions" (Geertz 1973, 99). Human beings depends upon symbols and symbol systems with a dependence so great as to be decisive for his or her being. As a result, his or her awareness to even small evidence that symbols may prove unable to deal with an aspect of experience raises worry within him or her.

Furthermore, the power of conception is one contrary to chaos. As mentioned earlier, if humankind did not depend so much on symbols s/he would be in complete chaos and disorder. Perfectly familiar things simply become disorganized. This example goes to prove just how preoccupation is created within us when things are not classified or conceived. Most important, then, is a general order of orientation and conception in order for survival (Geertz 1973, 100). Dwelling upon the notion of what chaos threatens to break upon man, Geertz suggests three salient limitations within the realm of how sacred symbols work: (1) the limit of analytic capacity, (2) the limit of his power of endurance, and (3) the limit of man's moral insight.[4]

The Religious Perspective

At this point, a third question can be posed: how does the religious man move from a troubled perception of experienced disorder to a more or less settled conviction of fundamental order? A clue to the answer lies in belief and with any particular belief there exists a foregoing acceptance of

---

[4] Most people cannot leave unclassified problems as such and a strange or odd experience must be reconciled, however peculiar or silly it may be, with ordinary experience. Anxiety and disquiet arises when the standard for which a given people attempt to outline their empirical world no longer functions as such. This standard—one's explanatory apparatus—is one's common sense, science, philosophical speculation, myth, and religion. Although the system of symbols is jeopardized it does not disappear nor does it change. People explain phenomena within the framework provided a system of symbols: however strange or uncanny the event may be it is nevertheless explained. Analytical limitations therefore threaten the most general ability to understand the world, raising uncomfortable questions of whether beliefs about nature are workable and whether the standard of truth people use are valid (Geertz 1973, 101–102).

The second challenge is the problem of suffering (Geertz 1973, 103). The two basic subdivision of this factor is what we call illness and mourning. This being the case, however, meaningfulness of suffering lies not in avoiding suffering and mourning but teaches us *how to suffer* and *how to mourn*. Religion has probably agitated men as much as it has reassured them and forced people into a confrontation of the fact that they are born to trouble as often as it has enabled them to defy such confrontation. Geertz argues that by illustrating someone "how" to suffer it gives the person salient vocabulary to express themselves. As religion fastens the power of conception of our symbolic means for formulating analytical ideas in a valid conception of the altogether shape of reality, the other side fastens the power of our symbolic means for expressing in a similar conception of its pervasive inclination, its inherent manner, and nature.

The problem of suffering passes easily into the problem of evil (Geertz 1973, 105). Where the problem of suffering deals with jeopardizing the ability to put our "undisciplined squads of emotions" into order, the problem of evil deals with threats to our capacity to make moral judgments (Geertz 1973, 106). It is the adequacy of the symbolic resources to furnish a feasible set of ethical measures, normative guides to direct our action. This would mean that like bafflement and suffering, the problem of evil is the formulation of such a genuine order of the world that will render, and even applaud, the discerned ambiguities and inconsistencies of human experience. What is important to a religious man is that such elusiveness be accounted for and the problem of meaning is a matter of affirming, or at least recognizing the inevitable ignorance, pain and injustice while at the same time denying that these irrationalities are characteristic of the world (Geertz 1973, 108). It is in terms of religious symbolism that both affirmation and denial are made.

authority that alters experience (Geertz 1973, 109). As we have already suggested, it is the existence of bafflement, pain and moral paradox that leads one to belief in general. Yet this is not the basis for belief but the most important range of it: with belief there is an acceptance of authority. When speaking of a religious perspective a man must first believe in order to know (Geertz 1973, 110).

The special character of a religious perspective is that unlike the common sense perspective, it moves beyond the realities of everyday life to broader standpoints, correcting and completing them, and its concern is not action upon those broader realities but faith in them. Rather than aloofness, a religious perspective is commitment and rather than dissection, an engagement. It is in light of what Geertz calls the "really real" upon which the religious perspective rest and symbolic activities thus are devoted to heightening and rendering sacrosanct the conflicting disclosures of secular experience (Geertz 1973, 112). It is the fusing of a certain complex of symbols with an effective authority that is the sum and substance of religious action. This brings us to the notion of religious ritual—the location where what has been mentioned thus far comes together in a single performance.

For Geertz, ritual is consecrated behavior. He adds that it is in ritual where one finds a portrayal of the world view and ethos:

> It is in some ceremonial form that the moods and motivations which sacred symbols induce in men and the general conceptions of the order of existence which they formulate for men meet and reinforce one another. In a ritual, the world as lived and the world as imagined, fused under the agency of a single set of symbolic forms, turn out to be the same world (Geertz 1973, 112).

All religious rituals involve this symbolic blending of world view and ethos. It is the more detailed rituals in which metaphysical conceptions and a broad range of moods and motivations of are combined to shape the religious awareness of a people (Geertz 1973, 113). They represent not only the point at which the conceptual and dispositional aspects of religious life converge for the believer, but also the point at which the mixing between them can be examined by a detached observer. For the observer a ritual can be presentations of a particular religious perspective and thus artistically appreciated or scientifically investigated but for the participants, however, they are in addition "enactments, materializations, realizations of not only models of what they believe, but also models for the believing of it" (Geertz 1973, 114). In rituals people realize their faith as they depict it. The religious perspective flows from the enactment of the ritual itself since the acceptance of authority is embodied in ritual. An enactment of a religious ritual makes the *model of* and *model for* aspects of religious belief reflections for one another by inducing world view and an ethos by way of a single set of symbols.

No one is able to live in the world of religious symbols all the time and the majority of men live in it only for the moment. The common-sense world—where the "paramount reality of human experience" takes place—is the place where we are most solidly rooted. Dispositions derived from religious rituals have their most important results outside the confines of the ritual itself for they reflect the individual's conception of the established world of reality (Geertz 1973, 119). Religious belief in the midst of ritual and religious belief in the recalled reflection of it are never the same. For this reason, then, religion is sociologically interesting because it molds social order and not because it stands to describe such an order.

The movement back and forth between the religious perspective and the everyday ordinary perspective is actually one of the more visible occurrences in the social scenes and yet one of the most neglected by anthropologist (Geertz 1973, 119). Yet it is the placing of acts in an ultimate context that makes religion socially authoritative. It alters the panorama of common sense in such a way that the moods and motivations induced by religious practice seem themselves supremely practical. The ritual performer is transformed when returning to the common-sense world after jumping into the framework of meaning that religious conceptions define. Since the performer is changed, the common-sense world also changes: the common-sense world is now seen as but the partial form of a broader reality, correcting and completing it (Geertz 1973, 122). Certainly, the common-sense world is not perceived the same everywhere. It is in a particular trait and specific disposition induced in the believer by a specific conception of cosmic order that organizes such distinctions. Geertz concludes:

> For an anthropologists, the importance of religion lies in its capacity to serve for an individual or for a group, as a source of general, yet distinctive conceptions of the world, the self, and the relation between them, on the one hand—its model of aspect—and of rooted no less distinctive "mental" dispositions—its model for aspect—on the other (Geertz 1973, 123).

Geertz concludes that the anthropological study of religion is therefore a two-stage operation according to the above-mentioned theoretical guidelines: an analysis of the system of meanings embodied in the symbols that make up the religion proper and relating these systems to social-structural and psychological processes (Geertz 1973, 125). Although he does not demonstrate specifically how this is done, we can draw a few conclusions from his approach to religion. Before going any further, however, a simple illustration will assist us in conceptualizing what has been said thus far.

Figure 1. World view and ethos

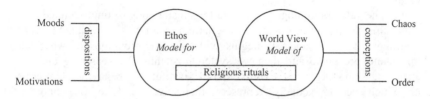

Thick Description

After presenting Geertz's approach on the study of religion we now take a look into the way in which this theoretical framework becomes concordant with his actual anthropological style. For Geertz, it is in what he describes as "thick description" that one goes about in discovering the cultural other and rendering it in some systematic order. It is this process that he has become well known—as an ethnographer rather than a theorist—imposing a new order in the way of doing anthropology.

The aim of interpretive anthropology is one that enlarges the realm of the universe of human discourse (Geertz 1973, 14). It consists of tracing the curve of social discourse that aids us in gaining access to the conceptual world in which our subject lives so that we can converse with him or her. Geertz proposes a model concerned primarily of asking the import of what subjects say and determining the social ground for that particular import. Behavior must be attended to because it is here that cultural form finds expression for to disregard action is to render analysis empty. Geertz retains that coherence is not the test of validity but that a good interpretation is one that takes us into the heart of it. This signifies that a good interpretation must bring us in touch with the lives of strangers and such an interpretation will certainly expose the normality of a culture. When normality of a culture is exposed, it becomes logically more accessible. Interpretive formulations of other peoples symbol systems therefore must be actor-oriented, from the native's point of view and is at the heart of his "thick description" (Geertz 1973, 3–30).

An anthropologist goes into a culture and discovers something, a ritual for example, which stirs his or her attention. The anthropologist then makes his or her way into specific descriptive elaborations so as to advise readers from his or her own culture about meanings in the culture being outlined.

This description, "thick description," is at one extreme a conversation across cultural codes and at the other, a written form of the public speaker adjusting style and content to the knowledge of an audience. Geertz stresses upon the levels of degrees of approximation and open-endedness as favorable characteristics of interpretation, although he tends to think of the interpreter as being a certain length from the objective of interpretation, as a reader might engage in a text.

The value of ethnography lies not against a body of uninterpreted data but against the power of scientific imagination in conversing with the lives of a stranger. Cultural analysis begins with our interpretations of what our informants are up to and then we systematize those by searching out and analyzing symbolic forms—words, images, institutions, behaviors—in terms of which people actually represent themselves and to one another. Anthropological writings, then, are second and third order "fiction" in the sense that they are made of something, fashioned to construct casually, actor-oriented descriptions—yet one which always concerns a making (Geertz 1973, 15).

The Method Used for this Study

For our study, then, a fourth question concerning a method arises: how do we go about analyzing the Teodori in such a way as to see it as a mode of cosmological building and a process of social consolidation? In other words, what will the making consist of and how do we go about construing such anthropological writings? The paradigm of world view and ethos becomes pertinent in this case. As mentioned, a particular world view is a *model of* belief and not gene-like in character. It is a *model of* belief which is a world as lived—the sheer actuality of reality—an assumed structure of belief. A distinct ethos, on the other hand, is a *model for* belief and gene-like in character. It is a *model for* belief which, to stick with a different analogy, is a blueprint, a template, a source of information which is also complimentary to a particular world view. Ritual, which is in actuality a cluster of symbols being simultaneously utilized, is the act most obvious where one can discover what is known about living in the particular people partaking in a particular performance. Harmony between world view and ethos can be observed in ritual since meanings and values of the participants are most clearly expressed for both the observer as well as for the observed.

This does not mean, however, that such religious performances are taken to be the same for observer and the observed. For the visitor, the performance can only be presentations of a particular religious perspective and thus aesthetically appreciated or scientifically dissected. For the participant, religious performances are not only realizations and enactments of ritual but a *model of* and a *model for* what they believe in as well. For us,

18

then, we shall aim to demonstrate an analysis of the religious ritual in question by grasping the "native's point of view" and reformulating it in terms more familiar to the reader. In short, we shall utilize the above-mentioned Geertzian formulation of dispositions and conceptual schemes to render the Teodori—the text—as thick as possible.

In this particular mode we shall endeavor to unfold the Teodori as a mode of cosmological building and as a process of social consolidation. As the above outline of Geertz's approach to religion stresses, our point of departure is the religious ritual. Through a thorough description and analysis of the ritual this study intends to elaborate the conceptual and dispositional categories found among Tenrikyo believers. Throughout the underlying structure of the study we shall make continuous reference to the classifications salient to Geertz's approach. In other words, what this study aims at is an outline of social discourse where we make clear a *model of* cosmic belief and a *model for* social reality of Tenrikyo believers. When this outline becomes apparent, then, it is further hoped that such becomes the foundation for a conversation across religious boundaries.

Yet other methodological constructs are at stakes on a different level. At the root of such examinations, however, lie the fact that a personal biography is at stake.[5] We have mentioned a few words concerning the

---

[5] I was born the sixth child of nine in a Tenrikyo church established on the west coast of the United States. Both of my parent's primary objective in sailing to a foreign country was, and continues to be, spreading the teachings of Tenrikyo to as many people possible. From my childhood years, then, I had no choice but to become a member of the church and naturally—and almost mindlessly—I performed a ritual dance called the Teodori. This has become a major focus in this thesis's inquisitive since, as early as I can remember, I was singing and dancing to a dance that did not incorporate well with conceptions imparted upon me outside the religious premise. School, conversations with friends, and children's television programs never evolved around the importance to dancing to a religious text. Something, it seemed, never fit in. More precisely, it appeared to be that such dancing and singing—"joy" which was the objective—highly contrasted with the everyday life surrounding its performance. The strangeness of the ritual itself has been the basic incentive for asking the question, "What does this all mean?"

The world view and ethos of the church community, then, clashed interests in many respects with the values and norms of the community in which the church was situated. I remember many times, while playing with neighborhood friends, how I would abruptly end the playful recreation so that a weightier performance could take place, that of the ritual dance for an evening service. At the same time, friends and folks would ask, "What are your singing and dancing for and why do you do it?" Unfortunately, an adequate reply was never given for I, myself, could not satisfy my own curious yearnings. What made matters dim was the fact that both parents never mastered the English language and communication was made all the more difficult between us. Likewise, my attitude of not wanting to learn the Japanese language during my youth also contributed to this communicative dilemma.

Since I was brought up with religious ideals and was taught that changes in the world can be actualized through prayer, I admit finding relief in reflecting upon a higher being through channels of prayer despite its alienating formulations. Interestingly enough, however, it was this initial sincere effort of wanting to change the world through the performance of the Teodori that altered my perception of it for, one day along the way, I found myself actually finding peace through the dance. I did not know why. Although I did not completely understand the liturgical language, the effects it had

anthropological makings that will appear in the following chapters and we believe that such constructs will be based primarily on a Geertzian approach. Yet what comes to mind is how can such a "native's point of view," an outlook which is vital to any type of work within the framework of an interpretive anthropology, be adequately rendered by an actual "native" yet in terms foreign to his own people? Throughout the making of what we consider to be as an anthropological bent analysis of a ritual dance, then, a further question indeed arises: how does the "experience-near" author settle within him the constant tension that may have come up while investigating a ritual dance that is considered to be so close?

We dedicate the next section to further methodological constructions which we presume to be featured as part of the overall Geertzian formulations in rendering alive the Teodori, not only in the formal description but also throughout the entire inquisitive.

A Methodological Consequence

The social sciences and the humanities have come to overlap one another in diverse ways and Geertz has referred to this intersection as "blurred genres" (Geertz 1983, 19–35). In this celebrated article, he differentiates the current trends in both "disciplines" and summarizes that there are three basic ways in which scholars dedicate much of their time analyzing their objects: the life as text approach, the life as game approach, and the life as drama approach. He notes that many scholars, including him, do not remain with only one approach but are free to use a variety of these approaches in the hopes of unpacking meaningful symbols within a particular society.

The general tendency in anthropological studies have also changed in the recent—especially with respect to the ethnographic descriptions made by the anthropologist on a different, and at times "exotic," culture. Many of Geertz's own disciples have taken on "experimental" directions towards creating different poetic trends in North American anthropology (Berreby

---

upon me gave proof that something transforms—whether the actual world or my perception of it—through a dance I initially disliked. I have often found myself asking, less antagonistically and more constructively, what that something is by trying to understand the interconnectedness between the performance of the Teodori and the changes in the world around me. Colleagues who ask about such dancing and its meanings have also amounted to many reflective moments. Nevertheless, an awareness of the corporal movements to particular verbal formulations became higher as I inquired deeper.

    This personal inquiry has eventually led to a systematic approach yet I regard the inner reflexive moment to be the impetus that will always be the enhancing precept of the Teodori. In the anthropological order, the Teodori has always been something to reflect about whether poignantly or submissively. In the recent, geared with anthropological tools for encoding it, I began to reflect back on such reflections only to understand that these were indeed stages that have contributed towards my personal reflexivity.

1995). What these scholars attempt to do is blend values found in literary theory, psychoanalysis, historical analysis, and postmodern criteria with the final product of an ethnographic text (Marcus and Fischer 1986). Further studies among the same breed of scholars relate the consequences of how cultures are written—at times even little distorted—to convey a particular theme of the "other" into question (Clifford and Marcus 1986).

The present study does not aim at amplifying such theories. Accounted for here, however, are a few points for which such writing took place. The most obvious confrontation that has occurred is the question of objectivity: how can the author be objective given that he himself is a qualified minister of the religious community where the ritual dance is situated? In rewording this question we have: does being a missionary of this particular religious community give the reader as clear a picture as possible, or does being part of the inside group create an obstacle that will naturally block the nature of this study from being objective?

We attempt to examine and pinpoint this strategic consequence in the section that follows. We argue from the onset that a "native's point of view" of a particular society—any kind of social group—is closer to the societal reality in question than, let's say, a "foreigner's point of view." This would be more so for a native anthropologist. There are many advantages of a native anthropologist doing research of his or her own culture. For example, s/he has intimate knowledge of everyday routines that an outsider may have difficulty in perceiving. Minor important details such as wearing certain clothes for particular occasions, what they eat daily and how it is cooked, or how they perceive the human body on a day to day basis are all quite evident to the insider yet less accessible for to the foreigner. Yet this self-knowledge—knowledge about the minute details of everyday life of the collective self—must be systematized in such a way that an "outsider" may also understand it.

Having said this, then, we encounter the objectifying process of a native anthropologist and we shall elaborate upon ways at striving for an objective perception so as to achieve a beneficial *reflexive* attitude in its stead. The aim of this section is to elaborate upon reflexivity—a highly utilizable tool—since we find this to be indispensable in our project to penetrate the ritual dance from an insider's experience-near point of view.

Detachment: Defamiliarizing the Familiar
The professional reputation of an anthropologist hinges on whether s/he has traveled to study a cultural other for a determined amount of time—engaging in fieldwork—which simply means another way of saying that a certain breach is made from one's own culture. Such severing, too, can

also occur in research done at the library.[6] Here lies one interface shared between the historian of religion and anthropologist in as much as a "break" must be coerced upon prior to experiencing any such enhancement of perception.[7]

Less and less fieldwork, however, by anthropologists in "exotic" cultures take place due in part by the cutting of funds and to the so-called "development" that has taken place in many of societies that once upon a time were untouched by ethnocentric Western standards. As recent events dictate, a contemporary trend among anthropologists has taken place where studies of one's own culture have become valid responses to such crisis.[8] The fruits of this new trend has also created further attractive pursuits in the academia and one is related to the defamiliarization process: the problem of how to become detached to one's native culture if one is going to begin to objectify it in the first place.

Detachment or distancing can be compared with the process of defamiliarization. It is one means of seeing the everyday world of one's life with unfamiliarity through distancing oneself from its collective whole. Detachment occurs, for example, when one is away from one's own web of relationship within a particular society and returning to it many years later perceiving it differently: a certain distancing has occurred. In being in another culture other than one's own, for instance, one naturally is foreign to the culture at first but gradually becomes a foreigner to one's own culture at the same time. In other words, encountering another culture is an unconstrained way of creating distance from one's own native culture. For the

---

[6] One author has noted the tension mounted in graduate level work in the American university (Spencer 1989, 161). He calls this phenomenon "yuppie anthropology" where, without leaving the boundaries of the college campus, a student is able to get away with fieldwork. Another author observe the same library approach (Rabinow 1986). And yet, another anthropologist interjects about the how one anthropologist literally got away with writing an ethnographic account without personal experience in the field (Pratt 1986, 29).

[7] Jonathan Z. Smith says: "[T]he historian of religion, like the anthropologist, will continue to gain insight from the study of materials and culture which, at first glance, appear uncommon or remote. For there is extraordinary cognitive power in what Victor Shklovsky termed "defamiliarization"—making the familiar seem strange in order to enhance our perception of the familiar. The success of any historian of religion's work depends upon a judgment as to whether this enhancement has take place (Smith J. 1982, xiii).

[8] Margret Mead is known for her studies in Somoan culture yet her basic assumptions there were addressing the problems of adolescents in North America. British anthropologists have used anthropological approaches to analyze the Old Testament (Douglas 1966; Leach and Aycock 1983). Roland Barthes, a French semiotician, has studied his native French culture in an anthropological fashion (Barthes 1957). In addition, there has been a sudden increase in the study of one's own culture, especially after spending many years studying another. One scholar has done expansive work for her own Japanese culture (Ohnuki-Tierney 1984; 1987; 1993). Of note, too, is one anthropologist who investigated a senior citizen's home of her own Jewish community (Myeroff 1980). This particular ethnographic text became the source of an academy award winning film.

anthropologist, then, this would imply that in order to study one's own culture one must first be detached, distanced, and defamiliarized to its respective native place in order to commence an objective examination of his or her own. Intellectual inquiries made into another culture prior to making such inquiries in one's own, then, are means towards objectivity. The overall problem, then, with studying one's own culture is a matter of first studying the "other," or through the encounter with the "other," so that one is able to distance oneself from the collective self.

A close parallel concerning the objectification of one's own culture has been noticed in the dynamic encounter found between anthropologist and informant during conventional ways of fieldwork. An anthropologist who does fieldwork in a totally different culture realizes that the assistance of an insider's emic point of view is an invaluable resource for the overall collection of data.[9] To this end, it is necessary to rely upon information produced by the person situated in the inside by an informant. Yet this process between anthropologist and informant leads to a very interesting dialectic.

Insights that are supplied by the informant may not always be true for, although they appear almost natural during fieldwork, the question remains whether such action continues even after the anthropologist has left the field. One anthropologist rightfully cautions us of such phenomena coining it "negotiated reality" in that the local community moderates a reality for the observing anthropologist and for themselves through questions posed by the anthropologist (Crapanzano 1980). It is as if an exaggerated version of the meanings and values of the host culture are being portrayed solely for the anthropologist. Yet this made up "reality" would not exist without the presence of the anthropologist in a host society. Crapanzano here is simply questioning the validity of experiencing reality of another culture when, in actuality, such encounter is simply one means for the host society to tell a "story they tell themselves about themselves" (Geertz, 1973, 448). At the root of this type of performative behavior lies the question of not only becoming objective about one's own society but becoming *reflexive* about it. In other words, where defamiliarization is necessary to enhance the perception towards becoming objective, acting upon such objectivity, then, invites an opportunity toward becoming reflexive.

---

[9] Kenneth Pike says: "Description of analyses from the etic standpoint are "alien," with criteria external to the system. Emic description provide an internal view … with criteria chosen from within the system. They represent to us the view of one familiar with this system and who knows how to function within it himself (Cited in Turner 1982, 65). Geertz, however, uses similar notions calling it "experience-near" and "experience-distant" (Geertz 1983, 56–59). Broader implications can be found elsewhere (Headland et al., eds. 1990).

Reflexivity: A Definition and Some Examples

Reflexivity is an important orientation for the native anthropologist in that it means to objectify the self—that the self is able "to become an object to itself" (Babcock 1980, 2). Put differently, it is the "capacity of a system of signification to turn back upon itself to make itself its own object by returning to itself: subject and object fuse" (Myerhoff and Ruby 1982, 5). Reflexivity often gets confused with reflectiveness although the latter is a requirement for the former. Reflection is thinking about ourselves, a "showing ourselves to ourselves" without which an awareness towards reflexivity does not take place. Where reflectiveness is attentiveness toward oneself, reflexivity pulls one toward the other (Ohnuki-Tierney 1984, 15). In reflexivity, then, not only does distancing and objectivity takes place but it further allows for a critique of the society in question to result.

Reflexivity in fieldwork takes place when informants are able to portray their culture in different ways imaginatively. In order for this imagination to occur, then, the informant of his own culture feels a certain distance—an objectification of the self is realized. At the root of this representation lies the notion of knowledge about the collective self. Paul Rabinow, who has done fieldwork in Morocco, suggests that neither patience nor intelligence of the informant were most beneficial in his fieldwork. Rather, it was "an imaginative ability to objectify one's own culture for a foreigner, so as to present it in a number of ways" (Rabinow 1977, 95). Although he does not use such reflexive terminology Rabinow notes that to objectify one's life-world is rare, even "unnatural," because not many can tolerate the ambiguities and strains that are described in the act of "self-conscious translation into an external medium" (Rabinow 1977, 119).

Reflexivity is not limited for the informant of the host society but should be equally applicable for the visiting anthropologist. As mentioned an anthropologist achieves distance from the self through study of the other. This leaves room for the objectification of the self and a reaching out for the other. We find that anthropologist in the field try to obtain social identities not their own since their success "is measured by how well they can become not themselves while at the same time retaining their own original identity" (Myerhoff and Ruby 1982, 30). In other words, the anthropologist remains in a reflexive stance in that a continuous check upon the self is being made while observing the other.

When we consider analogous perspectives of reflexivity we find that societies create occasions to reflect upon themselves and some eventually lead toward reflexivity. These occasions are usually in times of crisis, during collective ceremonies, through particular rites of passage, and thus not surprising to be found in religious rituals. During these occasions it is a time when members of a particular society is allowed to tell itself who it is or how it should be. As with the performance of the Teodori, or any other significant religious ritual, it is a *model of* and *model for* the participant in that it communicates the deepest value of the group regularly performing it. Through rituals, an individual or a community becomes self-aware and acts upon such an awareness.[10] Put differently, the collective self is constructed and reconstructed in ritual through the reflexive process and therefore assures for its continuity. Reflexivity during a cultural performance, as Turner puts it, goes as follows:

> Performative reflexivity is a condition in which a sociocultural group, or its most perceptive members acting representatively, turn, bend or reflect back upon themselves, upon the relations, actions, symbols, meanings, codes, roles, statuses, social structures, ethical and legal rules, and other sociocultural components which make up their public "selves" (Turner 1986, 24).

Examples from our own modern pluralistic setting may help to prove a point in order to highlight the notions of reflexivity.[11] Yet more obvious is the reflexive process that occurs at the level of individual beings. An anthropologist attributes a childhood illness that inspired certain reflexive moments to occur (Myerhoff and Ruby 1982, 32). She brings up the issue of finding herself in the midst of nature but could not differentiate between the actual and upside down reflection or the real and the pretend: image and reflection of an object were fused. Myerhoff gives credit to alienation as a "precondition for a reflexive attitude" but not reflexivity itself. This type of detachment transposed into insightful sensitivity when she began studying the social sciences (Myerhoff and Ruby 1982, 32). Extended period of travel also assisted her in the reflexive mode for something about the way people saw her transformed the way she saw herself.

---

[10] Gorman retains: "Ritual serves to make public the multiple and complex relationships embodied in society and to comment on the value, meaning, and condition of those relationships. Ritual is thus performed for the self and for society, but always with the understanding that both the self and society occupy the stage on which the performance takes place" (Gorman 1990, 21–22). Another ritual studies scholar offers a similar approach (Zeusse 1975).

[11] In music there is a genre of lyrics that describe convictions and experiences of the composer or performer. Lyrics as such are presented in a way that the composition is self-referential or autobiographical. Recordings that include the performer reminding the audience that it is simply a recording on a tape or CD—not a live performance—also aim at an opportunity for reflexiveness. Self-portraits are known to enhance reflective moments. Along this line we find many works where the artist himself is portrayed drawing the work of art *in* the work of art presented—an image of the broader image. In journalism, too, there is what critics have referred to as "new journalism," a type of journalism that reads like non-fiction and focuses on realistic descriptions of everyday life of ordinary people that aims for reflexivity when one thinks about the role and responsibility of the authors of such mediated message (Myerhoff and Ruby 1982, 10–17).

One Case in Point

Dorinne Kondo's insights of a small family business enterprise provide us with skillfully suggestive markers that concern how selves are crafted in a Japanese work place (Kondo 1990). One case in point that has been influential in the way she saw herself—therefore towards becoming reflexive—is attributed to her own ethnic identity.[12] At the onset of the book she reinstates her subjective frustrations originating from being looked upon as "an anomalous being" in the field (Kondo 1990, 11). This marginal state—not here nor there—is thus shaded with the notion of liminality since she was a person who appeared Japanese yet did not perform like one. Japan, she is to later find out, is a country where people focus more or less on formative attributes of the person rather than the qualitative—form over content. Thus the dilemma.[13] Although she may have looked completely Japanese—possessing a complete Japanese physiology—the language initially spoken when she first arrived as ethnographer was not enough to be considered "wholly" Japanese and therefore attributions of an "incomplete" personhood were a common remark by those around her. What made things worse was having several roles at one time: female, student, and young. All such standings were looked down upon by the gender-based patterns existing in contemporary Japanese culture, at least in the setting she temporarily found herself in.[14]

Her preference to become "Japanese" in its very context meant that she would have to "turn, bend, reflect back upon" a self she knew in another

---

[12] There are parallels between her work as a Japanese American in a Japanese setting and much of what the author of this study experienced in the "field." The accent on calling attention to being a "Japanese American" clearly demonstrates the ethnic question so much at an issue in current North American settings. Kondo's confessions support her American identity rather than a Japanese one. Another anthropological bent study on Japanese culture by a Japanese American speaks of this personal inquiry as one of "consciousness" (Hamabata 1990).

[13] This dilemma occurs often for people who do not fit in the scheme of classification in Japanese society. They are considered anomalous, marginal, and therefore to a certain extent, liminal. We find: "Besides "insiders" and "outsiders," there are various groups of people who are neither insiders nor outsiders in the Japanese scheme of classification. While the Chinese used to be the strangers/outsiders, they, together with other Asians, became marginals—neither insiders nor outsiders—when Westerners took over as the strangers/outsiders. The Japanese attitude toward marginals is at best ambivalent and usually downright negative. Included among the marginals are the Japanese who were born or raised in foreign countries, such as Japanese Americans. They are supposedly Japanese, and yet they are regarded as falling short of a full-fledged Japanese identity because their upbringing and behavior show departures from those of the "fully Japanese." . . . All people who lie "betwixt and between" in the conceptual scheme of the Japanese meet with prejudice and discrimination" (Ohnuki-Tierney 1987, 147–148).

[14] One anthropological study of contemporary Japanese corporate nightlife (Allison 1994) focuses on such male dominance in ritualized form.

context, namely a self in a North American setting. She had to objectify herself in order to reach out for the other—become reflexive by definition—and act upon that awareness. This option to do so made more sense than the "meaninglessness" which resulted from appearing Japanese yet not acting like one at face value. Furthermore, anthropological imperatives to totally immerse oneself in another culture intensified the desire to become accepted by her informants.

She moved in with a Japanese family to fulfill her reflexive awareness. Approximately nine months had passed since her initial surprise of being acknowledged by those around her as an anomalous being. By this time, however, her Japanese language skills had improved and she had mastered ways of conduct expected of young female students in the given context. She even recollects that her host family was very pleased to have her as the guest/daughter since she naturally seemed to conform to what was expected by one. In all, then, she admits at having to curb down action that is usually required by a researcher from a very prestigious American university in fulfilling to reach out towards the other.[15]

Yet conflict was present in many ways. On the one hand, she says, her intentions to be in Japan resulted from an intellectual curiosity to do fieldwork. As researcher, she was characterized by knowledge, decisive action, independence, and mastery. On the other hand, however, the obligations as a guest/daughter were characterized by duties, responsibilities, and interdependence (Kondo 1990, 15–16). Her foremost problem as an American woman, she interjects, was with serving meals the Japanese way to a gender opposite her own—something that simply did not blend well with her principles.

The decision to move out from the home of her host family was yet another reflexive moment. She happened to look up at the metallic area of a refrigerator within the supermarket and saw an image of what she thought was a young Japanese mother. The image—a true reflection in itself—was one of herself. It is as though she was surprised at what she had become through the process of being self-aware. It was again this moment of reflexivity that she once again found herself turning, bending, and reflecting back upon a self she had become even after she had reflexively done the same beforehand.

Two points need underling in Kondo's vignette. The first deals with the two-poled topic concerning inside/outside and front/back. Conceptual inconsistencies that do not fit in these categories are usually met with difficulty and hardship. When one is unable to place an object, as is common

---

[15] Kondo did fieldwork from 1978–1981 in Japan. This work was for a dissertation submitted to the department of anthropology at Harvard University.

in the above-mentioned setting, into a given arrangement such as inside/outside or front/back it is also a natural reaction that one is regarded anomalous. It follows, then, that a parallel exists between the anomalous and that which lies in the "not here nor there" but the liminal: bordering on a scheme of categories. It is conceivable that those standing on the edges of such a society as Japan are characterized as being "polluted" (Douglas 1966; Valentine 1990). Although they are looked down upon by those who conceptualize it as being so—polluted and mysterious—such is a fertile position towards becoming reflexive:

> The people, objects, or events that touch these margins may be taboo or polluted because they are out of place. They are sources of danger, a threat to our orderly conceptualization and desires for form and predictability, but also, as Turner shows, they are sources of renewal, possibility, innovation, and creativity (Myerhoff 1982, 117).

In this particular case, Kondo's appearance was completely Japanese yet her content did not concord with such form. Personhood in such a context results from not only a cognitive ability to speak Japanese but to appear as one. Kondo was regarded as mysterious since one scheme of classification did not match the other—an anomalous being "out of place." The opposite could also be mentioned. One may consider a white Anglo-Saxon who speaks perfect Japanese. In such a case, the Japanese themselves will commonly remark the strangeness of the form, the outside appearance of the white Anglo-Saxon person, is inconsistent with the inside grasp of one speaking the language perfectly. Although such people are regarded as abnormal by his or her social body it is at this intersect that opportune situations arise for them to turn themselves into their own object. In other words, people that stand on the perimeters and at the crossroads of a scheme of classification are bound to experience reflexivity in one way or another.

The second point in Kondo experience lies in the achievement "to grasp the other while seeing oneself sharply in terms of the other" (Peacock 1986, 87). The point here, however, is not only to simply grasp the other but to know oneself well enough to encourage the self to continue with the reflexive process. In other words, true reflexivity is continuous and characterized by a constant critique of the self. Yet such personally derived determination towards reflexivity is indeed difficult to arrive at (Ohnuki-Tierney 1993, 53). Kondo recalls the strain she experience when she had to also turn back upon a self she had known in another context—one which placed her far more independent than in her new setting. Some principles were beneficial in her work yet others created obstacles. She

28

became conscious of herself once again—bending back upon a self that she had bent in the first place—and reflexivity took place once again when she saw just how far she went at bending back and reaching out for the other as shown in her mirrored reflection. Acting upon the awareness of being considered an anomalous being made its way to become reflexive and yet this reflexive moment found leverage for further reflexivity.

The entire process, it is to be reminded, began with "distancing" and "detachment" from the collective self as key words. Knowing that reflexivity is indispensable—that such is a continuous objective critique of the collective self—proves to be a positive attribute when we think of anthropologists who have written accounts about societies from their very own subjective point of view. Here, we do not wish to argue against a complete subjective style in anthropological writings but we do acknowledge a subjective-objective approach to be one influential tool in the final analysis.[16] For us, then, it is important to simply remember that a reflexive process is continuous where one is able to draw attention to oneself and immediately act upon it.

Thus we contend that the native anthropologist's point of view, an insider's point of view, is a reasonable position, if not a favorable one, to describe and analyze a phenomenon found in one's own society. From a native anthropologists point of view, reflexive moments occur constantly since they are not bona fide members of their own society. They, by profession, almost always remain on the perimeters of well-categorized roles and they, above all, can turn back upon themselves to make themselves the object and fuse. They have also been exposed to diverse settings including a few years in a totally different environment regarded as the field. Further, native anthropologists will always need informants for the collection of certain data but the impact of participating in a "negotiated reality," a reality which occurs because of the presence of a guest in a host society, is perhaps less likely to occur.

---

[16] Colin Turnball accounts of this subjective-objective phase in his overall anthropological approach in working with a tribe of the Ituri forest. He refers to this encounter as the synthesis of a subjective and objective experience, and hence a liminal one. The first, he coins as "involuntary subjectivity" where he landed in the parameters of the tribe merely as an observers. The second trip was made specifically to make a documentation of the music through the means of film. He recalls this second trip to be more objective since he terms this as "voluntary objectivity" for things "seemed" quite different than his first time there now that he had a job to do and wanted to do it as best as he can. Finally, and for his doctoral thesis in social anthropology, he went for a third time to the field and to the same tribe. Armed with all the theoretical tools of his times he recalls this moment to be the "total field experience" and remarks that such analytical objectives were rooted in the previous subjective experience. He concludes: "It has been my experience that it was in those moments of abandon that the most significant discoveries were made which provided for the most fruitful subsequent investigation. After all, ethnographic description has to proceed analysis, and I am doing no more that suggesting the necessity for including description at another level, using all our faculties, not merely our minds" (Turnball 1990, 75).

This continuous reflexive approach, combined with the Geertzian formulations discussed in the first part of this chapter, will be the two most salient methodological drives throughout the study. With this in mind, we now turn to the actual study of the Teodori with the description of the text as our first step.

CHAPTER TWO

THE TEXT

The Author of the Text

Nakayama Miki was writer and choreographer of the Teodori. We begin our descriptive account by examining certain aspects of her earthly life in this section. In doing so, we hope to emphasize the historical person who mingled with others prior to her revelation in 1838, a *model of* compassion, and to underline the drastic changes in her life once she was settled as the representative of a new divine being called God the Parent, a *model for* single-hearted salvation. By taking these two considerations in mind, then, we shall construct a background of some of the major motifs that appear as possible strategies for writing the ritual dance. In other words, we contend that her religious yearnings during her historical life, as well as the occurrences that materialized around her, influenced the making of the Teodori.

Our purpose more specifically will be twofold. The first objective is to represent as best we can the life of the foundress of this newly arisen religion. It is important to know the historical traits of this woman with a special vision. To do so, then, many of the following accounts will be extracted from one authority in the field (Nakayama Y. 1986a, 1986b). We have added comments concerning the sociocultural tradition of the time when deemed necessary. The second objective in this section is to seek within her biography some of the major religious motifs—symbols—that may have influenced her writing of the religious dance. When we later categorize the Teodori into its verbal and nonverbal symbolic patterns, it will become evident that such patterns coincide with the religious yearnings of her life. Symbolic action and words of the ritual dance as performed by the members of the Tenrikyo community provide meaning when referring to the life of the foundress. That is, when the life of the foundress is made parallel with the Teodori, then, the understandings of both become all the more vivid and clear.

Nakayama Miki Prior to Her Revelation

The foundress of Tenrikyo, often referred to by followers as "Oyasama," translated as beloved parent, was born as Maegawa Miki on April 18, 1798 in a small village known as Sanmaiden, of Yamabe county, in the province of Yamato (presently Nara prefecture). Her father, Maegawa Masanobu, held a privileged social status and was, among other things, a *"musokunin,"* a samurai without the authorization to carry a sword. Her mother, Maegawa Kinu, was a housewife with a gift of creating fine needlework. Miki was one of four siblings in the family.

Tenrikyo followers believe in the stories concerning certain episodes of young Miki. There is an array of examples, but here, we mention just a few. Neighbors already spoke highly of her when she was only three years of age. It is of note that Miki was capable of imitating her mother's needlework just by sitting next to her at the age of six. She is said to have produced fine rice bran pouches and coin purses. It is at about this time that Miki is reported to have saved sweets given to her by others only to hand them out to other children younger than her. Miki's actions at a very young age were very special and followers of the Tenrikyo path take these episodes as the "really real" because of the divine nature attributed to her by members.

As Miki grew up, she is said to have had a very strong religious attraction for the Buddha, one the many characteristics of a very pious family. In particular, she was devoted to Pure Land Buddhism. She would accompany her mother to the temples and shrines and, as in the case of needlework, would imitate her mother in prayer. However, this imitation is said to have been merely temporary for Miki often found herself in self-tranquil introspection, or in the quest for truth. In fact, this spiritual yearning for the truth almost convinced her to enter a Buddhist convent to become a nun. But a different idea that came from members of the family nullified this aspiration: the wish for Miki to marry. Due to the special care and attention Miki had for others she became a model of a perfect housewife and thus, was proposed to marry Nakayama Zenbei. This offer came from the Zenbei's mother, and through the persuasion of Miki's parents who wanted her to deter from the spiritual life, Miki and Zenbei were wedded on September 15, 1810.

Miki had firmly stated that even after getting married she would continue her devotion and visit temples and shrines. With this in mind, Miki set forth to settle in with her new family at the age of thirteen in a village called Shoyashiki, just a few kilometers north of her native place of birth. On being a housewife, she did her best not only to please her husband but her in-laws as well. Taking up the responsibility as a wife of a well-respected family was certainly no easy task. She would rise early in the morning, participate in the farming activities, and further, was obliged to cook, wash, and sew whenever time allotted her to do so.

Although her marriage with Zenbei leads her astray from a complete and total devotion to a supreme being, she continued to visit temples and shrines during her free time. This gave her the greatest joy and tranquility and perhaps also the necessary strength to take up the many responsibilities endowed upon her. Parallel to her religious devotion was her initiation into the Jodo-sect ritual of "The Fivefold Transmission," usually a ritual carried out by elderly people yearning to arrive at the pure land after death.[1] After going through this consecrated act however, she is said to have never again recite the Buddhist chants or to listen to the sermons given at the Jodo centers. At this point in life, living humanly became the focal point of her attention.

> Oyasama did not distinguish between Amida, Kannon, or the Shinto gods.
> To Oyasama, actual human life was far more important. It was in this that
> Her faith was rooted deeply and began to develop as an independent faith
> (Nakayama Y. 1986a, 89).

A *Model of* Human Compassion

We are told of many episodes of charity that took place in her life. She gave to beggars that knocked at her doorsteps. There is one instance where she hired an indolent person in the neighborhood so that she could take care of him. The story goes that the worker was lazy by nature but she knew exactly how to transform his heart. Miki would daily repeat to him: "Thank you very much for your hard work," although he did not work as hard as the other dependents. Because of her compassion for this worker the person realized that he was not properly doing his work and slowly but surely, the story goes, he began to participate in the work that needed to be completed. In this way, despite the conforming rumors about a person's personal habits, Miki was able to transform a person out of the compassion she had demonstrated through words. This love, by the way, did not separate a lazy worker from an ardent one: distinctions for her did not seem to exist.

Also around the time of Miki's initiation into Pure Land Buddhism's mysteries, Okano, a maid, began to take advantage of her position in the household where she made personal advances at Miki's husband, Zenbei. Their relationship went to a point where Zenbei on occasions would take her

---

[1] As for the constituents of this particular ritual one reference says: "The *gojūsoden* (the Fivefold Transmission) consists of six days of lectures on the writings of the founder of the Jodo sect, Honen Shonin, and means of rebirth into the Pure Land of Amida through recitation of the Nembutsu, along with ritual exercises. On the fourth day a *teidoshiki*, a kind of Buddhist tenure, takes place, after which the initiate is considered a special disciple of Buddha. The initiates then receive lectures on Honen's successora, have their heads shaved, and promise to repeat the Nembutsu at least three hundred times a day and thus be assured of entrance into the Pure Land" (Stroupe 1983, 88). A Catholic scholar also describes the same ritual (van Straelen 1957, 34–36).

to Nara and other nearby villages for visits. On these occasions, however, it was Miki who prepared their lunch without a bit of grudge and even allowed Okano to wear Miki's own apparel: a maid to go out into public with a master was a disgrace to the master himself. Miki's generosity toward Okano became very special and enough to make Okano believe that she could become Zenbei's wife. It was in this state of mind that Okano mischievously placed poison in some soup that she had been prepared for Miki. Miki began to feel immediately ill and was in severe pain after drinking the soup. Others in the house noticed Okano's suspicious reaction and accused her of the mischief. Prior to having the local police intervene, however, Miki voiced concern that authorities were not necessary since her stomach was being simply being purified by the gods and Buddha. Okano was thus not successful in carrying out her intentions and Miki's reaction was simply too compassionate to bear. She left the household never to be seen again.

Another example worth mentioning, and perhaps the most well known among Miki's model of compassion, took place in 1828. At this point, Miki had already given birth to Shuji, her only son, and Omasa and Oyasu, her two daughters. It is in this context that she is reported to have put up the lives of both her daughters and her own life for the sake of saving an afflicted child of a nearby household. This family, known as the Adachi family, had lost all of their five previous children at an early age. Then, a sixth child was born, and like the pervious children, this child was also in danger from malnutrition. Miki decided to care for him since she was always plentiful with her own milk. With time, however, the child developed smallpox under her own care. Miki began to make prayers at various shrines and temples since she did not want the child to die. Under these circumstances Miki put up the lives of her two children in place of the life of the boy plagued with smallpox and, if this was not enough, her life could also be sacrificed to the gods, too. The child was miraculously saved yet her second daughter, Oyasu, passed away at the age of four and her fourth daughter, not yet born at the time of her resolute prayer, died at the age of three.

These experiences of compassion were filled with a model of selflessness. Miki always had in mind to put herself into the situation of others and would act accordingly to this principle. It seems that with time, however, she became even more benevolent and demonstrated a greater degree of charity.

The Shrine of God

October 1837 was a start of a very eventful period for the life of Shuji, heir of the Nakayama household. A sudden pain beset Shuji while working out in the fields. A doctor was consulted immediately for this problem but was of no use. The pain continued to persist. A local healing mountain ascetic,

Ichibei, was consulted. He was well known in the village surroundings for his efficacy in ritual healings. These religious procedures lasted for a year and a total of nine incantation rites were performed. Each time there was a performance, as was the custom of the time, Zenbei invited the neighbors of the village and served them with *sake*, Japanese white wine, and other foodstuff. Although the country was in a recession and social change was also evident, Zenbei spared no effort for his desire to see his only son get better, up on his two feet again.

The final incantation occurred in October of 1838. On this month, not only was the pain in Shuji's leg unbearable but Zenbei's eyes and Miki's back were also afflicted. This incantation was held on October 23 but the medium that played the role of intermediary for the gods during the rite was not available. Ichibei asked Miki to act as the mediator and agreed. Something suddenly happened, however, during this incantation. A divine voice augustly spoke: "I wish to receive Miki as the Shrine of God." Ichibei, asking for further figures concerning this message was told that the god was "Ten no Shogun, the ruling commander of heaven." It was later recorded as saying:

> I am God of Origin, God in Truth. There is causality in this Residence. At
> this time I have descended here to save all humankind. I wish to receive
> Miki as the Shrine of God (Tenrikyo Church Headquarters 1993a, 3).

Zenbei was shocked in the sudden change in Miki and immediately resorted to ask this god to go elsewhere since his family had its problems and that there were already more duties than one could perform. Zenbei, head of the household, was responsible to renounce or to accept the proposal. As was the custom of his day, he gathered together members of his family and consulted with them while Miki sat erect and upright on the *tatami* mat—the same stance as when commencing the ritual. The natural response from all family members was one of opposition. After all, they had never heard of this god before and even the invited ritual practitioner Ichibei was dumbfounded. Zenbei once again asked the deity to abandon the home but Miki's appearance took an adverse turn and a tone of command rang out:

> Whoever may come, God will not retire. It is natural that you are filled
> with anxieties at the present, but after twenty or thirty years have passed, a
> day is sure to come when all of you will admit the truth of My attention
> (Nakayama Y. 1986a, 181).

Again, rejecting the proposition to have Miki becoming a "Shrine of God," another revelation came through the mouth of Miki in the following manner:

You shall do as the God of Origin wills and comply with My demand. I shall save all humankind if you listen to Me; but if you should object to it, I shall destroy this house so completely that not a trace will remain! (Tenrikyo Church Headquarters 1996, 6).

A dialogue continued between God and relatives of the Nakayama family. Miki sat up straight with the *gohei*, paraphernalia used for inducing such trance state, throughout. At times, she is reported to have blood drip down her hands since she would rub her knuckles against the *tatami* mats. She did not have anything to eat nor drink: she either sat quietly or revealed the intentions of this unknown mysterious god.

Zenbei's choice was to accept or to decline the offer. He thought about what the new god had said about using Miki as a vehicle to save all humankind. Finally, after seeing that the health of Miki was out of the ordinary due to lack of sleep and food, Zenbei gave in to the demands of the divine. He said: "I offer Miki to You." (Tenrikyo Church Headquarters 1996, 7). That day was October 26, 1838 and is acknowledged as the day in which Tenrikyo was founded. Interestingly enough, the pains stopped from all three people, Shuji, Miki, and Zenbei. Yet these three, as well as those around them, were never to be the same.

From that day on, Miki became the Shrine of God and in becoming such, her behavior became totally different from that which was characteristic of her prior to this revelation. She was now indifferent to all those around her, especially to her own family members. For the following three years, from 1838 to 1841, she locked herself in the storehouse and all of her previous duties that were endowed upon her were simply left undone. People in the proximity of the storehouse would hear her talking with another despite her being alone. Dialogue between Miki and God took place during this period. God purportedly conveyed to Miki the essentials of the teachings and the purpose of God's manifestation at that particular time and at that particular place. She would come out of the storehouse on very rare occasions but was not the same altruistic person, a model of compassion, she was known to be prior to the revelation.

She had always been so devoted to her housework and had managed the Nakayama household so brilliantly. . . . Oyasama had been such a gentle and loving mother, but now, she would not even answer her children. In fact, she ignored them completely (Nakayama Y. 1986a, 142).

Poverty: Miki's First Mission

In April of the following year, God commanded Miki to plunge into poverty. This meant that Miki gave her belongings as well as the belongings of her family—husband and children included—to those in need. She began to give away cotton and grains that were put aside for their own use in the storehouse even when there were no other belongings left to give to the poor. Her husband was constantly taken up by Miki's complete change in behavior. Miki's encouragement, however, to those around her continued as the following demonstrates:

> Think in terms of water. Water that falls from the lofty heights will splash back up when it has struck bottom, no matter how others try to hold it down. Those who interfere with the path will provide you with the means to ascend, for they will become the rungs of a ladder that you will climb, one by one. Think in terms of a tree. If one cuts the tips of its branches, buds will sprout in all direction. If one begins to dig up the root, even it will sprout the buds. . . . Be as running water. Flow ever downward, ever downward. You cannot save others living in a mansion with a stately gate. Live in poverty, live in poverty! (Nakayama Y. 1986b, 2).

Rumors began to spread in the village that the Nakayama family was no longer the same family as before. Villagers commented on the drastic change in Miki and sought to make sense of the matter by saying that she became crazy. Friends of the family made attempts to prevent her from giving the family possessions haphazardly to others but were of no use. Nothing gave Miki more delight than giving away these materialistic conventions. One could imagine the rationale why the neighboring villagers believed she went out of her mind. People began to seriously wonder if a fox or a badger possessed her—a bad spirit that entered her—for it was the norm of the day, thus attributing a logical explanation to her uncommon practices. Part of village life held a view that those considered to be possessed by a fox or a badger was held in contempt of torture. There are no documents that state that Miki underwent forms of this type of cruelty but we find that "it is quite probable that Oyasama was also subjected to various forms of torture, such being the custom of the day" (Nakayama Y. 1986b, 7).

The epitome of her drive toward poverty occurred when God commanded her to dismantle the Nakayama mansion. This was far too much for Zenbei and, in protecting the interest of the family, he could not find himself in full agreement with the order. On previous attempts by Zenbei to stand firm on a position other than what was asked by God, Miki simply would become ill and her condition would became critical at times. In other words, Miki's husband had no choice but to comply with the will of God since the life of Miki was to be put on the line. We can clearly sense Zenbei's anguish and dilemma during these trying times. He had a dual position of kneeling down in front of God, which seemed to others as the "God of Poverty," and at the same time responsible for the state of affairs of the family with its possessions slowly disappearing. Certainly, Zenbei became the village's very own scapegoat.

The order to dismantle the home began by removing the roof tiles on the southwest corner and then proceeded towards the high walls demarcating the border around the house. The removal of the high walls eventually caused complete disharmony not only between Zenbei and his relatives but between him and his neighboring villagers as well. Relatives and friends no longer wanted to have any connections with the Nakayama family for the future of the household appeared very. On one occasion, Zenbei and Miki dressed themselves in white clothing. While sitting in front of the family altar, Zenbei pulled out a sword and asked if there was really a spirit in her. We find:

> Based on contemporary tradition that such spirits would flee when threatened with swords, her relatives and friends would brandish razor-sharp swords, waving them menacingly in Her face, or lay them beneath Her bedding when She would retire for the night. These people were convinced that Oyasama was possessed by such a spirit and they treated Her as such (Nakayama Y. 1986b, 8).

In 1848, at the age of 51 and ten years after the revelation, Miki began to teach young girls to sew and Shuji, her son, opened a private school for children to read and write. This was part of the divine intent in order to deter sentiments among the villagers about Miki and the family. Miki and Shuji both managed to have students of their own. Through these "cultural activities" they were able to regain some of the respect held in previously.

In 1853, however, her husband Zenbei passed away. Miki perceived the passing away of her husband with ease although it was simply common sense to sustain a period of mourning. It is at this time that she sent her youngest daughter, Kokan, to spread the name of God in the busy city of Osaka. More on this form of propagation when we map out the social reality of the Teodori. Here, it shall be enough to state that:

> Indeed Kokan undertook this mission without a thought for herself or for her own family, without a worry about venturing out into the unknown world, and without the slightest reservation despite the ridicule and the many hardships that were to be anticipated (Nakayama Y. 1986b, 37).

The Grant of Safe Childbirth

The year following Kokan's missionary activity in Osaka, Miki initiated a grant called the *Obiya yurushi*, literally, liberating oneself from a belt. This grant is the first of several healing rituals initiated by Miki to attract those around her. Later in her life she also developed other grants that included the Grant of Fertilizer (*Koe no Sazuke*), the Grant of Breath (*Iki no*

Sazuke), the Grant of Teodori (*Teodori no Sazuke*), and the Grant of Fan (*Ōgi no Sazuke*). She authorized the Grant of Water (*Mizu no Sazuke*) although she did not create it herself. Today, only the Grant of Teodori and the Grant of Safe Childbirth are distributed to members as means for helping others.

Many feared the pain and agony of giving birth to a child that subsequently led to certain beliefs before, during, and after giving birth to a child. In other words, we find a vast array of taboo concerning child bearing during this period. Some of the common folk beliefs concerning delivery and post-delivery processes during this period are as follows:

> For seventy-five days after the childbirth, a woman was submitted to the birth taboo. In this period her food was cooked in different pots and oven from those of the members of the family. She was confined indoors and . . . prohibited to enter the rooms with *tatami*. . . . Women gave birth to a child in a crouching attitude firmly holding a rope hanging from the ceiling, or restraint against a mill-stone. After the birth, she remained leaning against bundles of straw for twenty-one days. It was some time before the straw was withdrawn bundle by bundle until she would lie down completely on her back. This was meant to prevent the blood from going up to the brain (Matsuda 1986, 263–65).

In addition to these beliefs, there was a corset-like belt, called an *obiya*, worn by the mother around the waist, and thus, this particular grant was named *Obiya yurushi*. *Yurushi* means "to be liberated from," and thus it was a grant that liberates one from the corset-like belt. This custom has purportedly been used for centuries around the area of this particular village (Inoue and Eynon 1987, 415).

Miki is reported to have tested this grant on herself in 1841 but it was not until 1854 that she tried it out on her own daughter, Oharu, who easily gave birth to a son despite the advent of an earthquake during the delivery. Miki simply stroked the abdomen area three times, blew softly on it the same number of times, and conveyed the teachings of God. It was not until 1858 that others began to know Miki as "a living *kami*."[2] This began with a woman named Shimizu Yuki who heard about the miraculous workings through Oharu, up and around after the birth of her son. This marveled her. When Yuki was pregnant, then, she asked for this divine favor but remained ardent to the known traditions of her days in addition to adhering to what Miki asked of her. After giving birth, however, she came down with a fever and was ill for a month. Yuki found herself again pregnant and requested that a safe delivery be granted. This time, however, she promised Miki she would

---

[2] One writer proposes a general pattern of the "living *kami*" phenomenon in Japanese new religions by examining Tenrikyo and Konkokyo (Shimazono 1979).

not rely on the traditional modes. As a matter of fact, she was sound the day after giving birth since she remained steadfast to her resolution and diligently did what was asked of her. This experience became the basis for her to tell others and led to the propaganda that a peasant lady in a village called Shoyashiki assured pregnant women an easy delivery.

> Within the short span of one year, people throughout the neighboring countryside were saying, "There is a god of safe childbirth in Shoyashiki Village." The Grant of Safe Childbirth, as foretold by God, would be seen between the years 1861 and 1865 (Nakayama Y. 1986b, 42).

Thus, due to this breakthrough with the aim to save people, we see a step in which Miki construes a missionary pattern: first of utter poverty, giving away everything she owned to the poor and secondly, after a few decades in this state of affairs, she began to bless pregnant women with the tool of the *Obiya yurushi*, the Grant of Safe Childbirth.

It is not as if the Nakayama family, however, changed its course of life after the granting of this particular gift since they went ever more "downward" in poverty. This forced Shuji to sell vegetables and firewood within the area. Kokan and Miki, on the other hand, had to spin yarn throughout the night for some means of financial support. In 1855, Miki leased the remaining seven and a half acre field to the Adachi family, and the money was given once again to the poor (Nakayama Y. 1986b, 38).

As the months went by so did things to be consumed. Kokan, who prepared the meals for the family, said to her mother one day that there was no rice to be cooked once again. Upon hearing this, Miki replied in a joyous and very light-hearted manner:

> Kokan, there may be no rice, but surely we have some water. In this world, there are many people who are suffering, unable to eat, or even swallow water, despite food piled high at their bedsides. If we think of them, how blessed we are, for when we drink of water, it tastes of water. God the Parent has blessed us with exquisite gifts. We must be filled with joy (Nakayama Y. 1986b, 47).

Despite these conditions, however, Miki's teachings began to spread little by little in neighboring villages. Not only was Miki able to aid people with an easy delivery but there were also cases where physical afflictions were alleviated. Miki, already in her sixties, never hesitated once to assist those who came to her. They asked her to save someone from a particular illness and she would even personally go to the person's house on foot. Miki's early disciples came to her one by one and culminated between the years of 1859 to 1864 (Nakayama Y. 1986b, 53).

The Carpenter: Iburi Izo

The number of people saved from illness or other problems grew from one year to the next. One of the most influential disciples during this period is a man by the name of Iburi Izo, a carpenter from a village called Ichinomoto located a few kilometers from Shoyashiki village. The story goes that while people were already visiting the Residence asking for assistance, Miki is to have expected a carpenter from among such people:

> In the first year of Ganji (1864), when Izo was thirty-two, his wife Osato had a miscarriage resulting in complications. His workmate suggested, "The God at Shoyashiki is said to be very effective. Why don't you go to make a request for help?" So Izo went directly to see Oyasama. She was very happy to see him, and said, "Ah, the promised carpenter has arrived. God of the Eight Directions has been waiting (Takano 1985, 12).

We further find:

> The same year (1864), a very important addition was made to the new community from Ichinomoto village. After his wife was healed of childbirth fever by Miki with the assistance of Kokan, he became the most loyal and important of all believers outside the immediate family, first through the works of sacred carpentry which enhanced greatly the religion's concrete development, and then as *Honseki*, the faith's charismatic successor to the Foundress (Ellwood 1982, 43).

The notion of carpentry and constructing in general becomes quite persuasive in Miki's outlook. Her teachings consisted of building a joyous world and purposely made clear the importance of a carpenter—metaphorically and literally—to get the message across. In this case, however, Miki spoke of a particular person with a particular skill. The person's name happened to be Iburi Izo and the particular skill was carpentry. Through time, however, the provincial nature of it transformed into broader meanings since the connotations of it as a religious symbol becomes a powerful motif when it consistently interplays with paradigms such as "construction," "building," and "timber." All such expressions are at present very popular motifs in Tenrikyo. Yet such religious symbols can cross its borders and enter into the realm of its universality—namely, that the symbol of carpenter transcends provincial claims and enters into universal ones.

A carpenter, for one thing, can have a various number of meanings. In one sense, it can refer to a person endowed with a special skill for constructing. The carpenter is knowledgeable in his own right how certain materials are put together, what resources are needed, the importance of measurements, the general vision of the project, knowledge about the land in which it will be built, etc. In other words, it refers mainly to a special skill that not too many people are endowed with. This can implicitly concern the general notion of putting parts—whether things and even people—together to make a unifying whole.

Behind the denotative meaning of the carpenter we have notions that are connotatively drawn from it. Characteristics such as possessing the wisdom to put things together or knowing whether materials may withstand the heat of the summer and the chill of the winter are constituents of its meaning. Yet what best characterizes a carpenter—especially with respect to Tenrikyo meaning—is that s/he is sincere. This perception of the carpenter has been influenced by the life pattern of Tenrikyo's foremost carpenter, Iburi Izo. Upon reflecting on this idea, however, a carpenter must always be honest with material objects for s/he would not be able to unite one object with another if s/he were to be dishonest about the characteristics of two diverse objects. In other words, a carpenter must know, for example, that the foundation of a house will be sturdy enough to support a three-story building or, for that matter, that the walls s/he has constructed are straight and not bent out of proportion. This connotative meaning of molding pieces into unifying objects is indeed an important one since its symbolic meaning is vast. It can be applied, for examples, into other fields such as the ability to mold other people's perception of the world or the ability to bring people from varying world views together. In this way, then, the carpenter symbol possesses universal significance which, when examining it, began as a provincial one with Miki saying, "a carpenter will appear, will appear" (Tenrikyo Church Headquarters 1996, 40).

Since Iburi Izo was a carpenter, he wanted to repay Miki for saving his wife by demonstrating his gratitude through a building project. There were many followers by this time and were in need of a place to worship. Izo's project consisted in constructing a place where followers could pray together. Upon asking for instructions of what would be most appropriate, Miki simply replied to build something small. With the others of the newly founded group, Izo took down the cotton-storage building and the granary to make room for a worship hall. They were able to raise the roof on October 26, 1864 and held a celebration service for the occasion. They decided to continue their celebration on the following day at the home of another disciple located in a different village. Prior to leaving that day they were met by Miki in the following manner:

> So you are all going together? Well then, you had better be off. But listen,
> be sure to pay your respects when you pass before a shrine (Nakayama Y.
> 1986b, 66).

Yet the followers were carried away by their fervor when they came across the prestigious Oyamato Shrine. With their drums and wooden clappers pounding to a rhythmic beat they chanted: "Namu Tenri-O-no-Mikoto, Namu Tenri-O-no-Mikoto!!" [Hail the Divine King of Heavenly Wisdom, Hail the Divine King of Heavenly Wisdom!]. The priests at that moment were engaged in a solemn prayer and were not very enlightened to hear such peasant appraisal to a god unknown to them. The authorities were called to put things under control. As a result, the followers were arrested, questioned meticulously by the police, and were released only later. The aftermath, however, proved to be far more deafening to the special group of followers.

A majority of those who were retained no longer participated in Miki's activities. Yet this event scarred more than just the former members. This incident marked the beginning of what one scholar calls the "long-standing animosity between Tenrikyo—heretofore overlooked by officialdom—and the religious establishment" (Ellwood 1982, 43). Indeed, although considered a turning point in the history of the movement through an actual materialized construction, it also signified the beginning of pressure from Shinto priests, Buddhist monks, and local police. Kokan reportedly complained that most of the members who once had gathered abandoned the faith due to the incident. Miki reprimanded her: "Do not complain! This will be the basis of the teaching in the future" (Tenrikyo Church Headquarters 1996, 47). This message is interpreted by Tenrikyo followers as to how one can rely upon God despite the obstacles, antagonistic as they may be, that may confront a follower of the path. That is, this incident is recognized as the working of God the Parent putting members through a test—a test that separates silver from gold. Others, however, although not acknowledging the above-mentioned interpretations, recognize this historic event as employing useful tenets to promote interreligious dialogue.

Another outcome of the incident was that the completion of the worship hall, originally designed to illustrate the newly acquired membership, was delayed for only a few members remained. It was only during the following year that this hall was completed and the role Izo played within it cannot be underestimated. It is said that he was the single most active person in completing the building since it was his personal conviction to repay Miki for having his wife saved. These symbolic notions of building, as we shall see later, come into play within the Teodori text and can be used as one of its building tiers—literal and metaphorical—in decoding the dance.

Many sacrifices were thus made for the sake of Miki's teachings. Shuji, Miki's first and only son, went through much suffering. He was the heir of the Nakayama household with respect to the *ie* system (Bachnik 1983; Smith

R. 1985) but did not have a typical mother to look after. He did not even have an idiosyncratic God to believe in. We can say that he was caught up in a dual world where he had to conform to the traditional modes of upholding the family principle and, at the same time, turn against Buddhist and Shinto authorities. In 1867, then, we find him going to the Yoshida home in Kyoto for help, a long time friend of the Nakayama family with close contact with Shinto authorities.[3] He received authorization of the new movement with the Shinto order dedicated to Tenrin-O-Myojin. Yet recognition did not last. Crackdowns were made by State Shinto in order to preserve order and identity through means of imposing emperor rule. At other times, we find Shuji going to Buddhist temples in the hopes of attaining legal permission to do what the followers wanted most: openly practice the teachings of Nakayama Miki. Throughout is the struggle in Shuji's path to set up practical means to support the cause for the Tenrikyo movement. In later periods of Tenrikyo history, however, we find government pressures to stamp out these new currents that seemed to be problematic in the attempt to conform to a new ideology:

> Tenrikyo in the 1880's was promising "salvation of the myriads in the three thousand worlds" through its main deity Tenri-O-no-Mikoto and developed its propagation program to spread Tenri teachings to Japan and the world. The establishment of State Shinto meant a system of severe oppression of independent popular religious movements, and Tenrikyo came to be viewed as a heretical religion along with Maruyama-kyo and Remmon-kyo and suffered persistent persecution, threatened with the label of lèse majesté (Murakami 1980, 70).

Revealing the Teodori

In 1867, there were clusters of followers seeking to commit themselves to the path and the worship hall had been newly been built. It was perhaps from these incentives that Miki began to write the words to the dance from January to August 1867. She taught the movements to such songs for the following three years. She added the prelude, the *Yorozuyo*, in 1870, thus taking three years to write and teach her disciples what we categorize as the verbal and nonverbal symbolic patterns of the Teodori.

In the middle of this text-making, however, were the hard-line

---

[3] At the time there were two powerful Shinto branches that prevailed. One was the Yoshida house and the other, the Shirakawa. Both houses appeared to rule the entire country in terms Shinto that it became a matter of simply paying a fee in becoming affiliated with them. We find: "The Yoshida and Shirakawa sects, though they had arisen as a result of theological difference, had become financially and politically powerful, so powerful that they dominated most of Shinto" (Kishimoto 1956, 45). Another writer deals with the Shinto priesthood in the Meiji period and also touches upon ordaining priest in return for monetary payment (Hardacre 1988, 295).

thoughts of the Meiji Restoration. Many of the prevalent values were turned upside down during this period and "world renewal" seemed to be the catch phrase of the day.

> The word *yonaoshi*, if not its spirit, was incorporated into the messianic dreams of several of Japan's New Religions. Likewise, faith in Maitreya Buddha, associated throughout East Asia with popular rebellion, was taken over by the new sects and made part of their syncretistic smorgasbords. Under these new political circumstances, religious concepts like *yonaoshi* and Maitreya had to be used ambiguously if they were to be used at all. As symbols of otherworldly hope and salvation they could be counted on to attract the exploited masses. And finally, as expressions of the cosmic pretensions of the new Japanese messiahs, the same symbols could be used to advance the interests of the sects themselves (Davis 1992, 80).

This concept of "world renewal" is no new novelty since we find it in the teachings of Buddhism, in particular, with the idea of Maitreya, Miroku in Japanese, which consist of waiting for the world's end to begin paradise on earth (Kitagawa 1987, 233–249). One interesting book is done with respect to gender relations found in the interplay between social protest and a Japanese new religion (Ooms 1993). In it, the author claims these millennial beliefs and practices were most active in the nineteenth century, the century when social protests were also prevailing.[4] An analysis closer to our own concerns has been undertaken by a religious studies scholar (Shimazono 1986). In the article, he argues that both Tenrikyo and its offshoot, Honmichi, include millennialistic trends. His article provides a well-documented historical tracing of both new religions and uses, in the case of Tenrikyo, its normative texts as a chronological barometer for indicating millennial ideas of the movement.[5] In so doing, his emphasis is on a coherent group identity with respect to a millennial cosmology. Yet he concludes that the Mikagura-uta, the first of three normative canons, reflects an ideal world that is an "extension of the present village life" (Shimazono 1986, 69). He admits that a sense of "crisis" is lacking in the Mikagura-uta and therefore concludes that millennialism in this particular text is "very vague and amorphous" (Shimazono 1986, 71). The same could be equally said with his examination of the Ofudesaki in that:

---

[4] In perceiving the relationship between woman and social protest during the Meiji period, one social scientist says: "Although Japanese folklorists and historians of religions have found millenarian beliefs and practices throughout Japanese history, they all agree that such occurrences were most pervasive in the nineteenth century. During this period of rapid socioeconomic change and political upheaval, the utopian aspirations of the people were expressed in a number of religious movements and movements of social protest which employed millenarian symbols (Ooms 1993, 82).

[5] See chapter three for an explanation of the Tenrikyo scriptures.

In the Ofudesaki, we can observe millennialistic ideas which are somewhat clearer than those in the Mikagura-uta. . . . These ideas, however, were so heavily dependent on the perception of the situation that they could not be integrated into one system and so are expressed without a close, logical connection among them. Thus, this scripture does not form one organized millennialistic doctrine, but rather expresses in general nothing more than a millennialistic mood (Shimazono 1986, 75).

Finally, he does not venture deeply into the third set of normative scriptures since it is so voluminous and is difficult to analyze. Although he himself admits that this text demonstrates the most developed stage of the movement's group identity, he remarks that the millennial yearnings in the Osashizu are, as in the Ofudesaki, unsystematic and concludes that "millennialism in the Osashizu is no more refined than in the Ofudesaki" (Shimazono 1986, 76).

Certainly for Miki, drastic changes and the transformative social nature taking place was a sign that God was in haste to save people throughout the world. These social occurrences played a factor in influencing the way Miki constructed the Teodori yet were not the most important objectives in her mind. For Miki, the Teodori was a means to communicate the intention of God the Parent to the peasant population that did not include a dogmatic treatise of a millennial idea and crisis.

Returning to the Teodori, we have written account on how she taught her disciples the dance. There was no model to pattern after since the early disciples came to know of the dance only through Miki. Interestingly enough, however, Miki herself asked each disciple in attendance to create their own tune and to mend their own hand movements to it. None of them were satisfactory since the scope of dancing was "truth." The following is an excerpt:

When the sacred songs of the twelve chapters (songs) were completed, Oyasama told Her attendants: "These are the songs for the Service. Try singing them to the best tune you can find." Each of them sang to his own tune. After listening to it, Oyasama said: "Thank you for you singing, but none of them will do. You should sing them in this way." She sang loudly Herself. Then She told the attendants: "These are the songs of truth. So you must dance to the truth. Try dancing the best way you can." Each of them arranged the dance and showed it to Oyasama. Afterward, She said: "Thank you for your dancing, but no one danced to the truth. You should dance in this way. You should not just dance, you should dance the truth." So saying, She stood up and performed the dance movements Herself in order to teach the attendants (Tenrikyo Church Headquarters 1976, 12)

46

Miki instructed her disciples on the movements and the melody to the text, as well as giving special attention to the movement of the hands. In other words, her drive for an ordered form of nonverbal symbolic movements is of special interest. Further, one can notice where such orderliness comes from for we find:

> Hands that are limp in the performance of the Service betray a mind that is undisciplined. Also, it will not do to make even a single mistake in the manner of moving your hands. Through this Service, one's life can be renewed. So important is this Service (Tenrikyo Church Headquarters 1996, 71).

There is an account that when Miki was a child she was very timid and shy. And it was only when she became old—after the age of seventy—that she became spirited enough to dance in company of others.

> I had been reserved since My childhood, and it had always been difficult for Me to bring Myself to appear before company, but after I passed seventy I came to rise and dance in company (Tenrikyo Church Headquarters 1996, 72).

We end our biographical introduction of the writer of our text with this image of the seventy year-old writer dancing to the tunes of the Teodori. In the sections that follow we will focus on the text, the Teodori, by first illustrating its components and secondly, by portraying the performance of it in a monthly service setting. In describing such ritual behavior, it is salient that we arrange the text by outlining its two most basic and coherent textual categories. The first classification is the song-text itself. This classification is represented above all by the words to the dance movements. They accompany the dance movements throughout the performance of the Teodori. In our terminology we shall call these words the verbal symbolic patterns of the Teodori. The second classification will unveil the dance movements themselves. It consists of the hand gestures and the positioning of the body as it moves while performing the Teodori. For this aspect we will call these movements the nonverbal symbolic patterns of the Teodori.

The Teodori Text

The text's original has been put in a romanized form (Tenrikyo Church Headquarters 1985). On the one hand, we shall provide this version here with minor stylistic changes. On the other hand, however, Nakayama Miki adopted a special way to convey her religious message through a counting song. This type of song begins from number one and ends at ten. Yet it is quite difficult, if not impossible, to depict the same meaning in a different language, especially when dealing with such a two-lined counting song. The attempt has been to remain loyal to the original in reproducing it here. For this purpose, then, the edition put forth by one specialist was found most suitable for this study (Sasaki 1980b). We provide her version here with minor stylistic changes. Needless to mention, the overall intention of rendering the verbal symbolic patterns here is not for the purpose of replacing the official version but rather to make this study as "thick" as possible.

The Verbal Symbolic Pattern
Yorozuyo

Yorozuyo no sekai ichiretsu miharasedo, mune no wakarita mono wa nai.
Though I have searched through myriad generations of this world, there is no one who understands My heart.

Sonohazuya toite kikashita koto wa nai shiranu ga muri dewa nai waina.
It is natural, for it has not been explained. It is not unreasonable that you know nothing.

Kono tabi wa Kami ga omote e arawarete, nanika isai o toki kikasu.
This time, God has appeared in the open, and explains all things in detail.

Kono tokoro Yamato no Jiba no Kamigata to, yūte iredomo moto shiranu.
Although you call this place the Jiba in Yamato, God's Residence, you do not know its origin.

Kono moto o kuwashiku kiita koto naraba, ikana mono demo koishi naru.
If you hear of this origin in detail, everyone, no matter who, will yearn to come.

Kikitakuba tazune kuru nara yūte kikasu, yorozu isai no moto naru o.
If you come inquiring, wanting to listen, I shall explain the origin of myriad things.

Kami ga dete nanika isai o toku naraba, sekai ichiretsu isamu nari.
Since God has appeared, and explains all things in detail, one and all in the world will take heart.

Ichiretsuni hayaku tasuke o isogu kara, sekai no kokoro mo isame kake.
Because I am hurrying to save one and all quickly, all the hearts of the world will be cheered up.

Hito Kudari-me / Song One

Hitotsu,   *Shōgatsu koe no Sazuke wa yare mezurashii.*
One,   The New Year's Grant of Fertilizer; How remarkable!

Nii-ni,   *Nikkori Sazuke morotara yare tanomoshi ya.*
Two,   Receiving the Grant with a smile; How promising!

San-ni,   *Sanzai kokoro o sadame.*
Three,   Resolve to keep the mind of a three-year-old;

Yottsu,   *Yononaka.*
Four,   Then, a rich harvest.

Itsutsu,   *Ri o fuku.*
Five,   The Providences burst forth,

Muttsu,   *Mushō ni dekemawasu.*
Six,   And spread abundantly to all.

Nanatsu,   *Nanikani tsukuri toru nara,*
Seven,   When you cultivate anything,

Yattsu,   *Yamato wa hōnen ya.*
Eight,   It will be an abundant year in Yamato.

Kokonotsu, *Koko made tsuite koi.*
Nine,   Come and follow this far!

Tōdo,   *Torime ga sadamarita*
Ten,   The good harvest is fixed!

Futa Kudari-me / Song Two

Ton ton ton to shōgatsu odori hajime wa, yare omoshiroi.
Ton Ton Ton, The beginning of the New Year's dancing! How delightful! How lively it is!

Futatsu,   *Fushigina fushin kakareba, yare nigiwashi ya.*
Two,   When the marvelous construction is begun,

Mittsu,   *Mi ni tsuku.*
Three,   One is enhanced;

Yottsu,   *Yonaori.*
Four,   The world changes to prosperity.

Itsutsu,   *Izuremo tsuki kuru naraba,*
Five,   If everyone follows and comes,

Muttsu,   *Muhon no nē o kirō.*
Six,   I shall sever the root of rebellion.

Nanatsu,   *Nanjū o sukui agureba,*
Seven,   If you lift up and save the suffering,

Yattsu,   *Yamai no ne o kirō.*
Eight,   I shall sever the root of illness.

Kokonotsu,   *Kokoro o sadame iyō nara,*
Nine,   If you keep a determined heart,

Tōde,   *Tokoro no osamari ya.*
Ten,   Peace will reign everywhere.

Mi Kudari-me / Song Three

Hitotsu,   *Hinomoto Shoyashiki no, Tsutome no basho wa yonomoto ya.*
One,   The Service Place at Shoyashiki is the origin of this world.

Futatsu,   *Fushigina Tsutome basho wa, tare ni tanomi wa kakene domo,*
Two,   It is a miraculous Service Place although I make a request of no one.

Mittsu,   *Mina sekai ga yoriōte, deketachi kitaru ga, kore fushigi.*
Three,   Everyone of the world coming together; the construction comes to be—this is miraculous!

Yottsu,   *Yōyō koko made tsuite kita, jitsu no tasuke wa korekara ya.*
Four,   With effort you have followed and come this far; the true salvation begins from now.

Itsutsu,   *Itsumo waraware soshirarete, mezurashi tasuke o suru hodoni.*
Five,   Always laughed at and slandered still I shall work remarkable salvation.

Muttsu,   *Murina negai wa shite kurena, hitosuji gokoro ni narite koi.*
Six,   Do not make unreasonable requests; let your heart become single-purposed.

Nanatsu,   *Nandemo korekara hitosujini, Kami ni motarete yuki masuru.*
Seven,   No matter what, from now on go forth single-heartedly leaning on God.

Yattsu,   *Yamu hodo tsurai koto wa nai, washi mo korekara hinokishin.*
Eight,   There is nothing as bitter as illness; I, too, from now shall do hinokishin

Kokonotsu,   *Koko made shinjin shita keredo, Moto no Kami towa shirananda.*
Nine,   Although you have believed this far, you did not know the Original God.

Tōdo,   *Kono tabi arawareta, jitsu no Kami niwa sōinai.*
Ten,   This time, it has been revealed; this must surely be the True God.

52

Yo Kudari-me / Song Four

Hitotsu,   *Hito ga nanigoto iwō tomo, Kami ga miteiru ki o shizume.*
One,   No matter what people say, God is watching, so ease your mind.

Futatsu,   *Futari no kokoro o osame iyo. Nanika no koto o mo arawareru.*
Two,   Husband and wife together resolve your hearts; then everything will be
          realized.

Mittsu,   *Mina miteiyo sobana mono, Kami no suru koto nasu koto o.*
Three,   All you close to me, watch God's acts and accomplishments!

Yottsu,   *Yoru hiru don chan Tsutome suru, soba mo yakamashi utate
          karo.*
Four,   Night and day performing the service; to the neighbors it must be noisy and
          annoying.

Itsutsu,   *Itsumo tasuke ga seku karani, hayaku yōki ni narite koi.*
Five,   Since I am always hastening salvation, quickly become joyful!

Muttsu,   *Murakata hayakuni tasuke tai, naredo kokoro ga wakaraide.*
Six,   I wish to save the villagers quickly. But they do not understand My heart.

Nanatsu,   *Nanika yorozu no tasukeai, mune no uchi yori shian seyo.*
Seven,   Helping one another in all and myriad things; reflect on this in your own
          heart!

Yattsu,   *Yamai no sukkiri ne wa nukeru, kokoro wa dandan isami kuru.*
Eight,   I shall draw out the entire root of illness, and step by step your heart will be
          cheered up.

Kokonotsu, *Koko wa kono yo no gokuraku ya, washi mo hayabaya mairi tai.*
Nine,   This place is this world's paradise! I too want to go worship.

Tōdo,   *Kono tabi mune no uchi, sumikiri mashita ga arigatai.*
Ten,   This time the depths of our hearts are purified; how thankful!

Itsu Kudari-me / Song Five

Hitotsu,
One,
Hiroi sekai no uchi nareba, tasukeru tokoro ga mama arō.
Within this wide world, there must be many places which can save.

Futatsu,
Two,
Fushigina tasuke wa kono tokoro, Obiya hōso no yurushi dasu.
The miraculous salvation at this place! The Childbirth and Smallpox Grants are given out.

Mittsu,
Three,
Mizu to Kami towa onaji koto, kokoro no yogore o araikiru.
Water and God are the same, cleansing the muddiness of the heart.

Yottsu,
Four,
Yoku no nai mono nakeredomo, Kami no mae niwa yoku wa nai.
Although there is no one without greed, before God, there is no greed.

Itsutsu,
Five,
Itsumade shinjin shita totemo, yōkizukume de aru hodoni.
For however long you are faithful, you will be adorned with joy.

Muttsu,
Six,
Mugoi kokoro o uchiwasure, yasashiki kokoro ni narite koi.
Strike away a cruel heart! Become gentle-hearted.

Nanatsu,
Seven,
Nandemo nangi wa sasanu zoe, tasuke ichijo no kono tokoro.
No matter what, I shall banish suffering, for this place is the single-thread of salvation.

Yattsu,
Eight,
Yamato bakariya nai hodoni, kuniguni made e mo tasuke yuku.
Not only in Yamato, I shall go to other countries also to save.

Kokonotsu,
Nine,
Koko wa kono yo no Moto no Jiba, mezurashi tokoro ga arawareta.
This is this world's Original Jiba; a remarkable place has appeared.

Dōdemo shinjin suru naraba, kō o musubo ya naikaina.
If you will believe, let us bind together in a fellowship

Mu Kudari-Me / Song Six

Hitotsu,
One,

Hito no kokoro to yūmono wa, utagai bukai mono naru zo.
The human heart is a deeply doubting thing.

Futatsu,
Two,

Fushigina tasuke o suru kara ni, ikanaru koto mo misadameru.
As I work the miraculous salvation, I can ascertain every kind of thing.

Mittsu,
Three,

Mina sekai no mune no uchi, kagami no gotokuni utsuru nari.
All the world's deepest heart is reflected as in a mirror.

Yottsu,
Four,

Yōkoso Tsutome ni tsuite kita, kore ga tasuke no motodate ya.
With effort you have followed and come to this Service; this is salvation's foundation.

Itsutsu,
Five,

Itsumo Kagura ya Teodori ya, sue dewa mezurashi tasuke suru.
Always doing the Kagura and Teodori! In the future I shall effect remarkable salvation.

Muttsu,
Six,

Mushō yatara ni negai deru, uketoru suji mo sen suji ya.
Making requests thoughtlessly, without care–the threads of receiving are a thousand too!

Nanatsu,
Seven,

Nambo shinjin shita totemo, kokoroe chigai wa naran zoe.
No matter how many steps of faith you have taken, do not let your heart become mistaken

Yattsu,
Eight,

Yappari shinjin senya naran, kokoroe chigai wa denaoshi ya.
Yet still you must have faith; if your heart is wrong, start anew!

Kokonotsu,
Nine,

Koko made shinjin shite karawa, hitotsuno kō o mo minya naran.
Because you have come this far in your faith, you must see at least one good result.

Tōdo,
Ten,

Kono tabi mie mashita, ōgi no ukagai kore fushigi.
This time, it is seen; the invocation of the fan–this is miraculous!

Nana Kudari-me / Song Seven

Hitotsu,   *Hitokoto hanashi wa hinokishin, nioi bakari o kakete oku.*
One,   A single word is *hinokishin*, leaving behind only the fragrance.

Futatsu,   *Fukai kokoro ga aru nareba, tare mo tomeru de nai hodoni.*
Two,   Since My heart is so profound no one can hinder it.

Mittsu,   *Mina sekai no kokoro niwa, denji no iranu mono wa nai.*
Three,   In the heart of everyone of the world, there is no one who does not
          want a fertile field.

Yottsu,   *Yoki ji ga araba ichiretsuni, tare mo hoshii de arōgana.*
Four,   If there is a good field, each and everyone, no matter who, will surely
          desire it.

Itsutsu,   *Izureno kata mo onaji koto, washi mo ano ji o motome tai.*
Five,   For everyone it is the same; I, too, wish to have that field.

Muttsu,   *Murini dōse to iwan dena, soko wa meimei no mune shidai.*
Six,   I do not say forcibly, "do this or that"; it depends on each person's
          own heart.

Nanatsu,   *Nandemo denji ga hoshii kara, atae wa nanihodo iru totemo.*
Seven,   Since you desire the fertile field no matter what, it does not matter
          how much the price may be.

Yattsu,   *Yashiki wa Kami no denji yade, maitaru tane wa mina haeru.*
Eight,   This Residence is God's field; every seed sown here will sprout.

Kokonotsu, *Koko wa kono yo no denji nara, washi mo shikkari tane o mako.*
Nine,   Since this is this world's fertile field, I, too, shall sow seeds
          stronghearedly.

Tōdo,   *Kono tabi ichiretsuni, yōkoso tane o makini kita.*
           Tane o maitaru sono kata wa koe o okazuni tsukuri tori.
Ten,   This time, with effort, one and all have come to sow seeds;
          Those who sow seeds will reap a rich harvest without fertilizing.

Ya Kudari-me / Song Eight

Hitotsu,   *Hiroi sekai ya kuninaka ni, ishi mo tachiki mo naikai na.*
One,   Within the many countries of this wide world, surely there are both rocks and straight trees!

Futatsu,   *Fushigina fushin o suru naredo, tare ni tanomi wa kaken dena.*
Two,   Although I work the miraculous construction, I oblige no one.

Mittsu,   *Mina dandan to sekai kara, yorikita koto nara dekete kuru.*
Three,   If everyone from the world comes together step by step, it will be accomplished.

Yottsu,   *Yoku no kokoro o uchiwasure, tokuto kokoro o sadame kake.*
Four,   Strike away a greedy heart! Resolutely determine your heart!

Itsutsu,   *Itsumade miawase itaru tomo, uchi kara surunoya nai hodoni.*
Five,   No matter how long you continue to hesitate, it cannot be done by yourself.

Muttsu,   *Mushō yatara ni sekikomu na, mune no uchi yori shian seyo.*
Six,   Do not hasten so thoughtlessly, without care; you must reflect within yourself.

Nanatsu,   *Nanika kokoro ga sunda nara, hayaku fushin ni torikakare.*
Seven,   When your heart becomes a little clear, quickly set out to begin the construction.

Yattsu,   *Yama no naka eto irikonde, ishi mo tachiki mo mite oita.*
Eight,   I have penetrated into the mountain's depths, and have already seen both the rocks and straight trees.

Kokonotsu, *Kono ki kirōka ano ishi to, omoedo Kami no mune shidai.*
Nine,   You may wonder whether to cut this tree, or to take that stone; it depends on God's mind.

Tōdo,   *Kono tabi ichiretsuni, sumikiri mashita ga mune no uchi.*
Ten,   This time everyone's deepest heart has been purified.

Kokono Kudari-me / Song Nine

Hitotsu, *Hiroi sekai o uchi mawari, issen nisen de tasuke yuku.*
One,   Clapping our hands throughout this wide world, with a penny or two we
     go to save.

Futatsu, *Fujū nakiyo ni shite yarō, Kami no kokoro ni motare tsuke.*
Two,   I shall wipe out suffering; so lean wholly on the mind of God!

Mittsu, *Mireba sekai no kokoro niwa, yoku ga majirite aru hodoni.*
Three,   I see that in the world's heart greed is mixed throughout.

Yottsu, *Yoku ga aru nara yamate kure, Kami no uketori deken kara.*
Four,   If you have greed, please give it up, because God cannot accept it.

Itsutsu, *Izure no kata mo onaji koto, shian sadamete tsuite koi.*
Five,   For everyone it is the same; reflect, resolve, set out and come!

Muttsu, *Murini deyō to yūde nai, kokoro sadame no tsuku madewa.*
Six,   I do not say forcibly, "Go!" until you have reached the determination in
     your heart.

Nanatsu, *Nakanaka kono tabi ichiretsuni, shikkari shian o senya naran.*
Seven,   Indeed, this time one and all must thoroughly reflect.

Yattsu, *Yama no naka demo achi kochi to, Tenri–Ō–no Tsutome suru.*
Eight,   Even here and there in the mountain's depths the Service of Tenri–O is
     performed.

Kokonotsu, *Koko de Tsutome o shite iredo, mune no wakarita mono wa nai.*
Nine,   Although you are performing the Service here, there is no one who
     understands My heart.

Totemo Kamina o yobidaseba, hayaku komoto e tazune deyo.
Ten,   If you call out God's name, quickly come here to visit!

To Kudari-me / Song Ten

Hitotsu, *Hito no kokoro to yūmono wa, chotoni wakaran mono naru zo.*
One,   The human heart does not understand truth easily

Futatsu, *Fushigina tasuke o shite iredo, araware deru noga ima hajime.*
Two,   Although I have been working the miraculous salvation, now, for the
            first time, I appear in the open.

Mittsu,   *Mizu no naka naru kono dorō, hayaku idashite morai tai.*
Three,   This mud in the water—I wish you to take it out quickly!

Yottsu,   *Yoku ni kiri nai doromizu ya, kokoro sumikire gokuraku ya.*
Four,   Greed is bottomless like muddy water; when your heart is purified, then
            paradise!

Itsutsu, *Itsuitsu mademo kono koto wa, hanashi no tane ni naru hodoni.*
Five,   Forever these things will become the seed of stories.

Muttsu,   *Mugoi kotoba o dashitaru mo, hayaku tasuke o isogu kara.*
Six,   Although I speak severe words, it is because I am quickly hurrying
            salvation.

Nanatsu, *Nangi suru nomo kokoro kara, wagami urami de aru hodoni.*
Seven,   Even suffering hardships comes from the heart; you should blame
            yourself.

Yattsu,   *Yamai wa tsurai mono naredo, moto o shiritaru mono wa nai.*
Eight,   Although illness is a bitter thing, there is no one who knows its origin.

Kokonotsu, *Kono tabi made wa ichiretsuni, yamai no moto wa shirenanda.*
Nine,   Until this time, no one could know the origin of illness.

Tōdo,   *Kono tabi arawareta, yamai no moto wa kokoro kara.*
Ten,   This time it is revealed; illness originates in the heart.

Jūichi Kudari-me / Song Eleven

Hitotsu,
One,
Hinomoto Shoyashiki no, Kami no yakata no Jiba sadame.
The Jiba, God's Residence in Shoyashiki, has been determined.

Futatsu,
Two,
Fūfu sorōte hinokishin, kore ga daiichi monodane ya.
Husband and wife joining together in hinokishin; this is the first and basic seed.

Mittsu,
Three,
Mireba sekai ga dandan to, mokko ninōte hinokishin.
I see the world, step by step, bearing straw baskets in hinokishin.

Yottsu,
Four,
Yoku o wasurete hinokishin, kore ga daiichi koe to naru.
Forgetting greed and doing hinokishin; this becomes the first fertilizer.

Itsutsu,
Five,
Itsuitsu mademo tsuchimochi ya, mada aru naraba washi mo yuko.
Forever the carrying of earth; if it still continues, I, too, shall go!

Muttsu,
Six,
Murini tomeru ya nai hodoni, kokoro aru nara tare narito.
You should not forcibly prevent anyone, no matter who, if his heart is willing.

Nanatsu,
Seven,
Nanika mezurashi tsuchimochi ya, kore ga kishin to naru naraba.
How remarkable this carrying of earth is when it becomes an offering.

Yattsu,
Eight,
Yashiki no tsuchi o horitorite, tokoro kaeru bakari yade.
Simply digging up the earth of the Residence, and carrying it from one place to another.

Kokonotsu,
Nine,
Kono tabi made wa ichiretsuni, mune ga wakaran zannen na.
Until this time, of everyone, there is not one person who has understood My heart.

Tōdo,
Ten,
Kotoshi wa koe okazu, jūbun mono o tsukuri tori,
Yare tanomoshi ya arigata ya.
This year, without fertilizer you will reap an abundant harvest. How promising! How thankful it is!

60

Jūni Kudari-me / Song Twelve

Hitotsu,   *Ichini daiku no ukagai ni, nanika no koto mo makase oku.*
One,   First, everything is entrusted to the invocation of the carpenter.

Futatsu,   *Fushigina fushin o suru naraba, ukagai tatete iitsuke yo.*
Two,   If you will do the miraculous construction, invoke the oracle, then give
      instructions.

Mittsu,   *Mina sekai kara dandan to, kitaru daiku ni nioi kake.*
Three,   To all these carpenters coming step by step, from the world, spread the
      fragrance.

Yottsu,   *Yoki tōryō ga aru naraba, hayaku komoto e yosete oke.*
Four,   If there are good masters, quickly bring them here!

Itsutsu,   *Izure tōryō yonin iru, hayaku ukagai tatete miyo.*
Five,   Of all the masters, four persons are needed; quickly invoke the oracle!

Muttsu,   *Murini koi towa iwan dena, izure dandan tsuki kuru de.*
Six,   I do not say forcibly, "Come!" All, step by step, will follow and come.

Nanatsu,   *Nanika mezurashi kono fushin, shikaketa koto nara kiri wa nai.*
Seven,   How remarkable this construction is! If it is begun, it will never cease!

Yattsu,   *Yama no naka eto yuku naraba, araki tōryō tsurete yuke.*
Eight,   When you go into the mountain's depths, bring along the lumber
      master.

Kokonotsu, *Kore wa kozaiku tōryō ya, tatemae tōryō kore kanna.*
Nine,   Here is the fine-details master, the framework master, and the planer.

Tōdo,   *Kono tabi ichiretsuni, daiku no nin mo soroikita.*
Ten,   This time, one and all of the carpenters have gathered together.

The Nonverbal Symbolic Patterns

Photographs would have been more appropriate here but such a format in print does not exist. Authors of guides to the Teodori portray dancers that are sketched by artists or generically done with the help of a computer. For this study, the latter has been chosen.

The movements are first listed in alphabetical order. When Nakayama Miki instructed her disciples, however, she did not construe the names of the movements. She simply instructed them to "dance to the truth and sing to the truth." The names of these nonverbal symbolic patterns, then, are arbitrary in the sense that they have been classified for the purpose of teaching contemporary followers the dance patterns as found in *The Otefuri Guide* (Tenrikyo Overseas Mission Department 1992).

One will find numbers in the brief explanation. These numbers demonstrate the flow of the movement. One may read, for example, numbers in a sequential order under the heading of "parallel fans" with three differing movements. The numbers are linked to each diagram beginning from the left to the right. When there is no number, then, it simply means that there is only one motion or gesture for that particular movement. The representation of the dancer is a woman who, by the way, is wearing the gender apparel for the monthly service.

When examining the nonverbal symbolic patterns, the written explanation will say "right hand" when the graphic description of it appears to depict a left one. These representations have been set up in a mirror version—as if one is projecting the pattern onto a mirror. That is, all movements have been drawn out as if one is practicing the movements in front of a full-sized mirror. Through these textual devices, we hope to render the ritual dance more familiar to the reader. Needless to mention, the intention in providing the basic movements to the dance here is not to offer an authoritative guide to define each movement but rather to translate the text into something as "thick" as possible.

Activity

1. With both hands fisted right hand moves to right shoulder and the left hand simultaneously moves down to the left side; 2. Hands move up and down, changing position with steps.

Bind

1. Fingers of both hands are interlocked and pressed on right hip; 2. Then to the left hip.

Building

1. Finger tips of both hands touch just above eye level with palms facing down; 2. Hands open out and positioned vertically; 3. Hands move straight down to waist.

Carry baskets

Fisted right hand is placed near shoulder and fisted left hand is placed on its side. Hands remain in the same position while the body slightly sways from side to side with steps in forward motion.

Childbirth

1. With fingers slightly cupped in and palms up in front of the abdomen; 2. Hands open downward.

Chiseling

Fingers of left hand form a circle with thumb touching index finger. The right index finger traces three circles clockwise within the circle formed by left hand.

Circle in front

1. Hands placed just above eye level with palms facing down; 2. Circle is made with both hands positioned vertically; 3. Hands are then brought up to the chest level.

Circle in front with fans

Same motion as movement for "circle in front" with fans in hand.

  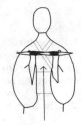

Circle with palms out

1. With palms facing out hands are positioned in front of face; 2. A circle is traced vertically with palms remaining open throughout the outlining of the circle; 3. Hands are brought to original position.

Circle from pray with fans

1. From pray position; 2. Open fans at a 45 degree angle; 3. Fans move in a scooping but circular movement to lower stomach level; 4. Fans are brought up to shoulder.

  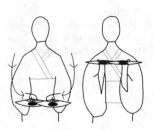

Circle with fans
1. With fans above eye level and palms facing down; 2. A circle is traced vertically with the lowest point of circle being the lower chest area; 3. Fans are then brought up to shoulder level.

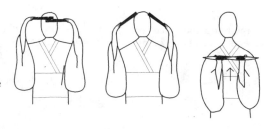

Circle on side
1. With body positioned at a right angle hands are placed just above eye level with palms facing down; 2. Circle is made and hands are brought up to chest level.

Clap hands
With body positioned slightly to left angle hands are brought together near left cheek. Hands are clapped twice with rhythm.

Come home
1. Right hand reaches to right side with palm facing down with left hand slightly holding right sleeve; 2. The right hand is brought to the center of chest.

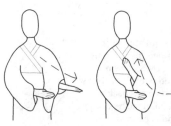

Come out
1. Hands are cupped below stomach; 2. Hands are diagonally lifted to the right in front of shoulder; 3. Hands are brought down to original position; 4. Movement is repeated to left side.

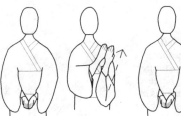
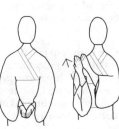

Come out with fans
Same gesture in movement for "come out" with fans in hands.

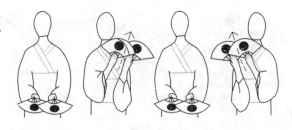

Come together
1. Hands are bent at wrist with fingers pointing up in front of hip area; 2. While stepping hands move to the right; 3. Then hands move to the left.

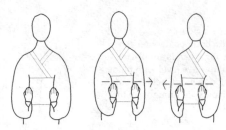

Consult divine will
1. Fan is taken from clothing area with right hand while left hand holds base of fan; 2. Fan is pointed forward with hands in same position; 3. Finger tips of right hand move to the base of fan; 4. Fan is errected in upright position.

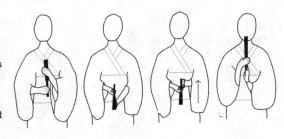

Converse
1. Palm faces out at mouth level with index finger pointing up. Right hand moves outward with left hand over right sleeve; 2. Right hand comes back to mouth with palm facing body; 3. Right hand is pushed forward once agiain and movement repeated.

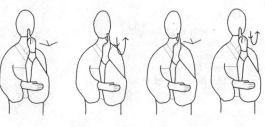

Cut: down and to left
1. With right index finger pointing up hand is brought vertically down to hip level; 2. A slashing movement is made across hip level from right to left.

Cut to right
1. Right index finger points left at lower chest level; 2. Right hand moves horizontally towards the right stopping when hand reaches slightly beyond shoulder width.

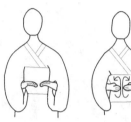

Draw out
1. Hands are placed side by side with palms facing down; 2. Both hands are drawn in and up making a turn over movement; 3. Palms are faced up at chest level.

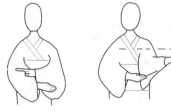

Drop (fan) edges
1. Fans are held in an upright position at wrists with left fan slightly over right fan; 2. Fans are brought straight down in front of hips.

Finger open out
1. Right index finger points left at lower chest level with left hand over right sleeve; 2. Finger then points toward right. The movement is repeated beginning with left index finger pointing left and right hand over left sleeve.

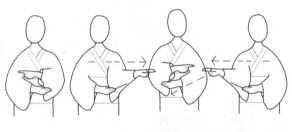

Folk dancing
1. Upper left sleeve is held with left hand while right hand taps left wrist; 2. Left hand moves to right side and right hand holds bottom end of left sleeve; 3. Left hand moves to chest area and right hand and moves slightly forward; 4. Same movement is repeated using right hand.

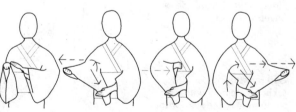

Frame
1. Hands open straight and positioned vertically just above eye level; 2. Hands move straight down to waist.

Gather to heart
1. Open right hand moves to heart; 2. Open left hand then moves to heart while the right hand goes down to side; 3. Repeated once again with right hand; 4. Movement ends with both hands on heart area.

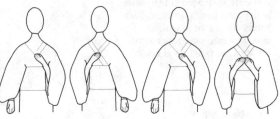

Gather to heart with fans
Same motion as without fans is executed.

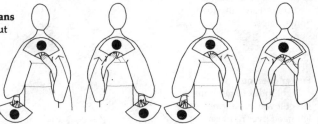

Give out
1. Right hand on left side with palm facing up with fingers touching thumb; 2. Right hand moves toward right side as fingers open up.

God looking
1. Hands are held with palms out in front of the eyes with torso moving to the right; 2. Movement switches to left side; 3. Then to the right side once again.

Grab to left

1. Right and left arms stretch out to the left at an angle; 2. With fingers curling in both hands move to waist. Variation: 1. Right and left arms stretch out in front of waist; 2. With fingers curling in, both hands move to waist.

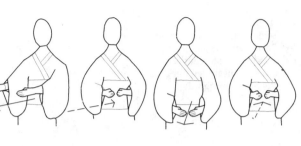

Half circle

1. With hands just above eye level; 2. A half circle is traced vertically with hands stopping just below shoulder level.

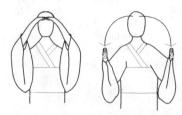

Hammering

Fingers of left hand form a circle with thumb touching the index finger. The right index finger taps two times on thumb of left hand.

Harvest

1. Hands are open faced down in front of hip; 2. Two half circles are made with both hands in front of waist on a horizontal plane; 3. Hands are brought back to hip area with palms positioned up.

Heart

1. Right hand moves to chest with hand open while left hand remains on the left side; 2. Left hand moves in the same manner to heart and left hand finger tips are placed slightly over right hand fingernails.

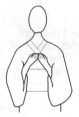

Heart with fans

The same motion as movement for "heart" with fans in both hands yet when both hands are placed on the heart, left fan goes directly on top of right fan.

Hesitate

1. Hands face down and slightly touch above eye level; 2. A circle is traced vertically; 3. Movement ends with left hand fingers in front of right a few inches from the face.

Hew wood

Right foot is placed diagonally in front of left so that torso naturally faces left. 1. With both hands fisted as if holding a pole over the shoulder; 2. Both hands move downward to the right side two times. The right foot taps floor with the two downward movement.

High throw

From "pray" movement, 1. Hands move diagonally to the left and slightly forward with left hand above the right; 2. Movement is repeated on the right side with right hand above left; 3. Left side is repeated once more.

Hoeing

1. Both hands are fisted with right hand over left and raised to head level; 2. Arms strike down directly in front of body.

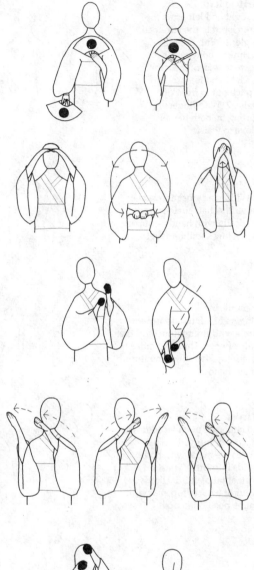
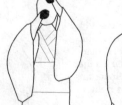

Illness

1. Right hand moves to right side with left hand slightly over right sleeve; 2. Right hand is raised to right shoulder just below the ear with head tilted slightly on back of hand.

Jiba

1. Hands are in front of waist with left index finger over right index finger with other fingers fisted; 2. Circle is made horizontally; 3. Hands are joined at waist area with both index fingers pointing forward.

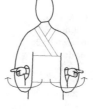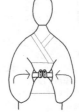

Lean back

Hands are fisted with sleeves slightly held by fingers. Hands are placed over the chest with left knuckle over the right and torso is arched back with each step.

Lift out

1. Hands are cupped at left hip; 2. Maintaining cupped positioned both hands are brought above right shoulder level.

Lift up

1. Both hands are at shoulder height with right palm facing down and left palm facing up; 2. Hands move down while inverting position of palms; 3. Hands return to shoulder height with reverse facing of palms.

Look
1. Palms face inward a few inches from face with hands touching; 2. Using wrists hands are turned inward and down; 3. Palms face outward at the same height.

Mark line
1. While squatting the left index finger draws a straight line from the right side to the left; 2. Right hand is brought down to floor level on right side; 3. Thumb and index finger of right hand touch and make as if plucking a string in front of right knee.

Master carpenter's scarf
1. Hands open with palms facing forehead; 2. Using wrists hands turn inward and down concluding with index finger pointing up in front of forehead; 3. Hands move to sides.

Mirror
1. Index fingers touch at forehead with palms facing outward; 2. Index fingers trace a circle and end tracing with palms facing inward.

Mix
1. Hands are cupped together with fingers pointing forward in a diagonal position to the right slightly lower than shoulder level; 2. In same position, hands move to the left.

Moon-sun
1. Index fingers touch above head with palms facing outward and head slightly tiltedup; 2. Index fingers trace a circle and end tracing with palms facing in.

Mountain
1. Standing diagonally to the left, index fingers are brought to forehead level; 2. A half circle is traced with index finger and ends when elbows touch side of the torso.

Negative
Open hands with palms facing each other are placed in front of waist at shoulder width; 1. Hands wave from one side to the other keeping elbows near the torso; 2. Hands are motioned to the other side in the same manner.

Night-day
1. Both fans are positioned at eye level with right palm facing out and left palm facing in. Right fan is pushed out and left fan is brought in; 2. Position and facings reverse.

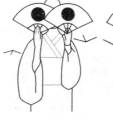

Open
Both hands open at chest level about shoulder width apart. Variation occurs with right palm facing up and left hand holding right sleeve.

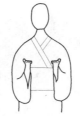

Open fan

1. Both index fingers touch in front of waist with palms facing in; 2. Index fingers move forward and out to sides; 3. Hands are drawn back to waist with index fingers pointing forward and end side by side - forming an outline of an open fan.

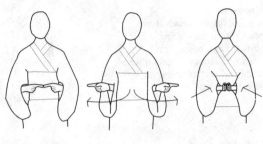

Open hands

1. Right hand opens to right side with palm up while left hand holds right sleeve; 2. Left hand opens to left side in the same manner; 3. Movement is repeated to right side.

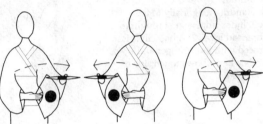

Open heart

1. With hands in movement for "heart"; 2. Both hands open slowly to shoulder width and palms face diagonally up.

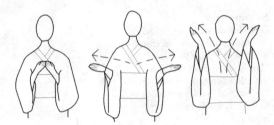

Parallel fans

1. Fans are held parallel on right side with shoulders situated between both fans; 2. Both fans are arched over to the left side in the same position as the right; 3. Movement is repeated to other side.

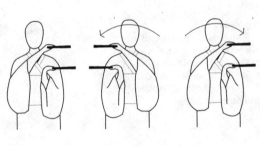

Pick up

1. Hands reach forward to the right; 2. Hands move slightly above the waist and fingers curled in a half-fisted manner.

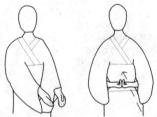

74

Place

1. Right palm down and left hand holding right sleeve; 2. Right hand moves from left to right; 3. In the same fashion, left hand moves from right side to left with right hand holding left sleeve.

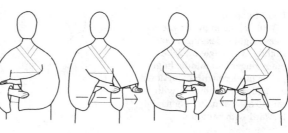

Place to place

1. Index fingers point forward and touch side to side at right waist level; 2. Hands move to the left; 3. Then hands return to right side always at waist level.

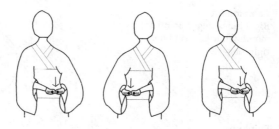

Planing

Left hand opens down on left side with right hand cupped in front of left hand as if holding a plane. Hands move backwards in three motions ending with hands slightly behind body.

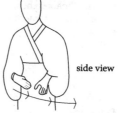

side view

Point chest

Right index finger points to center of chest while left hand holds right sleeve.

Point ear

Index finger of right hand points to right ear while left hand holds right sleeve. Right hand palm faces in.

75

Point forward

1. With left hand over right sleeve right index finger points slightly at an angle or; 2. Left index finger and middle finger points forward with palm down or; 3. Right four fingers, with thumb against palm, points forward with palm up.

hand variations

Point mouth

Right index finger points to mouth while left hand holds right sleeve.

Point up

1. Right index finger starts at middle of stomach level while left hand holds right sleeve; 2. A straight line is a traced with right index finger stopping just above the head.

Point side

Right index finger points forward to the ground area while left hand holds right sleeve.

Point right and left

Right index finger points forward to the ground area while left hand holds right sleeve. Right hand then points forward to left side while left hand continues to hold right sleeve.

Pray

Three types of movements for pray: 1. Hands are held in front of chest with palms held together; 2. Hands make a silent clap; 3. Hands go down to left diagonal side.

Pray with fans

Twp types of movements for pray with fans. 1. Fans are held in front of chest with palms facing one another; 2. Fans make a silent clap.

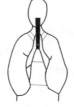 

Press

Hands facing down side by side in front of abdomen area are firmly pressed down and stopping at waist level. Same movement is executed with right fan slightly over left.

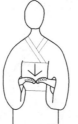 view from top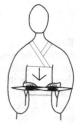

Press hip

Same movement for "press" except that hands are pressed alternately two to four times at each hip or only once at right hip or once at left hip.

Put on mask

1. Both hands simultaneously go behind the head with palms facing up; 2. Both hands motion from top of the head to front of face - ending with palms facing down.

view from side

77

Quickly
1. Hands side by side in front of abdomen area face down; 2. Hands move quickly toward the body and out to movement for "receive" with both hands touching and palms open.

Receive
1. Hands are cupped and held in front of chest area or slightly higher; 2. A variation is made with head slightly tilted forward and hands brought up near facial area.

Reflect
1. With head slightly tilted forward hands are brought to the center of the chest with left hand fingers over right hand fingers; 2. Same motion with fans.

Resolutely
Hands firmly on abdomen with left hand over right hand.

Rest
1. Hands move to right shoulder while cupped together and head leans toward hands; 2. A 180° left turn is made with body weight on heels in same position.

78

Rice bag on shoulder

1. Both hands are raised from waist area with palms up over right shoulder; 2. Hands return to original position in front of abdomen and then over to left shoulder; 3. Hands return once more to original position and over right shoulder.

Rotate fans

1. Fans held right over left with palms up and fingers pointing at each other; 2. Fans rotate outward in a circular motion and end with fingers pointing forward; 3. Fans then raised to shoulder level.

Scoop up

1. Hands are brought to a cupped position in front of abdomen and both knees bend simultaneously with the downward motion of hands; 2. Hands and body come up together.

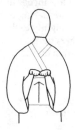

Search

Hands are positioned side by side with palms facing down; 1. Hands smoothly move horizontally to right hip; 2. Then to left hip; 3. Hands return once again to right hip.

Sever

1. Slightly cupped hands are placed side by side in front of abdomen with palms facing down; 2. Hands move horizontally apart to the side.

Shade eyes
Right hand with palm facing
down shades eyes as if looking
into the distant while left hand
holds right sleeve.

Shoulder
With hands fisted and torso
leaning forward, left and right
arm cross over at the abdominal
area with left arm over right.

Small circle
1. With tip of index fingers
touching a few inches in front of
face and palms facing outward,
torso faces slightly to the left; 2.
Index fingers trace a small circle
ending with palms facing in.

Smallpox mask
1. Hands near facial area with
palms open; 2. Hands curl over
behind ears using wrist to make
circular movement; 3. Hands
end on both sides of temples
with palms facing each another.

Sow
1. Left hand is positioned as
if holding a bucket at the
left side while right hand
moves under left hand with
fingers touching thumb; 2.
Right hand moves to right
side; 3. Right hand fingers
open and turn over so that
palm faces up.

Sprout up

1. Right hand moves to chest level and bends at wrists causing fingers to point up; 2. Left hand does the same motion and right hand simultaneously moves down to right side; 3. Right hand moves back up returning both hands to same position.

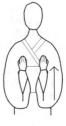

Standing fans left/right

Fans touch with left fan overlapping right fan. 1. Fans move from right hip; 2. To left hip with steps; 3. A variation occurs once with left fan in front of right fan without contact.

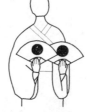

Stir heart

Right hand is cupped so that four fingers touch thumb and traces two or three small clockwise circles at the center of chest.

Stone

With both index fingers pointed and torso facing left; 2. Both hands trace a small circle with fingers ending at left hip.

Stop

1. Left hand near chest area and right hand holds left sleeve; 2. Left hand pushes out to the right side with palm facing out; 3. A variation occurs when same motion is done with pointing right index finger.

Straight tree
1. Right index finger points down to floor on left side with left hand holding right sleeve; 2. Right hand traces a line diagonally across the torso from the lower left side to upper right side.

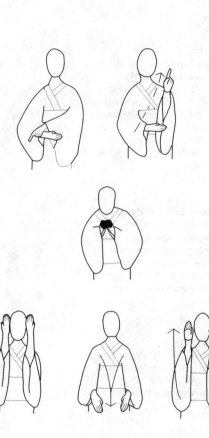

Suffer
Both hands are fisted with edges of sleeves in hands. Hands cross over chest with left knuckle over right. Torso leans slightly forward.

Sweep Body
1. Hands in front of face with palms toward body; 2. Hands motion a sweep down the body to full arm's length; 3. Hands continue upward to front of face with palms facing out.

Sweep heart
1. Both palms face body at shoulder level; 2. Hands motion down to waist level; 3. Palms face out at shoulder level with same motion.

Sweep up
Hands placed at lower left side of hip with palms facing body; 2. Hands sweep up to right with backs of hands leading and conclude with hands pointing straight up and palms facing out.

Take sword
1. Both hands positioned near left hip with all fingers pointing diagonally left; 2. Hands move to front of chest while forming a fist and stop when right hand is in front of left hand and palms face up. A small distance between the two hands is made in this final position.

Tap fans
1. Left fan is placed and tapped under right fan with right fan slightly forward; 2. Fans are brought to opposite side with right fan still on top of left.

Throw
1. Hands are placed diagonally forward to the right - more or less at a parallel; 2. Hands come up and the same gesture is repeated on left side.

Throw with fans
1. Same motions as "throw" with fans held in both hands.

Tie (head) scarf
1. From top of head hands go behind with palms facing inward; 2. Hands come back in front of forehead and are crossed while forming fists; 3. Fists are then spread to the sides.

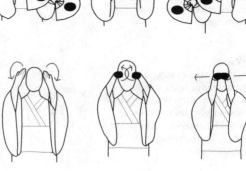

Tie thread
1. With palms up in front of waist; 2. Both hands are pushed upward toward body until hands have palms facing down with index fingers pointing forward; 3. Index fingers move simultaneously to the sides drawing a straight line.

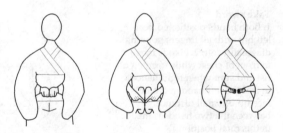

Turn around
1. Right hand with palm out is held in front of left shoulder and left hand holds right sleeve. A 360° turn is made with both hands in the same position; 2. The same gesture is done with fans.

Two hand circle
Hands are placed side by side with palms facing down. A clockwise circle is traced in front of waist horizontally with fingers remaining in same position.

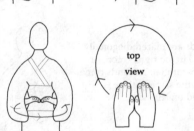

Use two mirrors
1. Left hand goes to left rear side of head with elbow bent and palm facing body. Right hand goes in front of right eye with elbow bent and palm facing head; 2. Position of hands are reversed; 3. Position of hands return to original movement.

Waves
1. With palms facing down, hands move horizontally at chest level from left to right; 2. When right hand reaches shoulder, movement switches to left; 3. Then once again to opposite side.

84

Wave to come

1. The right hand is positioned at shoulder level with hand open and palm facing out while left hand holds right sleeve: hand is bent forward at wrist so that hand flaps down; 2. Left hand is brought up to same height as right hand; 3. Same movement is done with left hand.

Weave

Both index fingers point up. Left hand in front of right with left palm out and right palm in. 1. Right hand pushes out and left moves simultaneously back; 2. Hands alternate back and forth.

Wonder

Right hand covers left hand on left hip and head tilted slightly to the left.

World

Left index finger points up and held in front of left shoulder with right hand holding left sleeve; 2. Torso and left foot pivot on heel moving to left side with arm moving simultaneously with torso.

Wrong

1. Left arm crosses right arm at wrist area near the waist; 2. Arms open up by moving to the sides; 3. Arms cross once again with right arm over left.

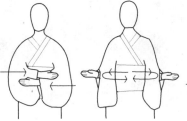

Wrong with fans
Same motion as "wrong" but
with fans in hands.

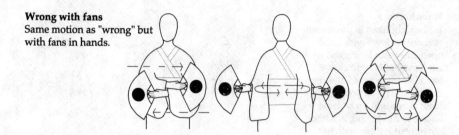

The Portrayal of the Text

This ritual dance constitutes a part of what is performed at a monthly service of Tenrikyo local churches and it would be most appropriate to describe such a background. The description in this section will therefore include action that occurs on a typical monthly service.[6] What is described in the following section is simply a generalized version of what one is able to find in any church setting during a monthly service. It is important to keep in mind that the performance of the dance, together with the playing of the musical instruments accompanying the dance, is the foremost religious act held at any Tenrikyo monthly service across the world in terms of its semiotic relevance.[7]

A typical monthly service at a church is executed on a set day once a month. In proximity to Tenrikyo Church Headquarters—churches located in Japan—local churches perform their monthly service on a specific day of the month. A monthly service can be performed on the eighth day of each month, for example, regardless of what day of the week it will fall. Most people agree that when this system is used for the monthly service, more followers assemble when the day falls on a weekend. On the other hand, most local churches outside the confines of Japan celebrate their monthly service with respect to a particular Saturday or Sunday, namely one day of a weekend. This means that a church, after being sanctioned by Church Headquarters, will establish a set day of the week, every second Sunday of the month for example, and establish this as its day to celebrate the monthly service.[8]

---

[6] The reason for underlying a general description of action that occurs at a monthly service is that the Teodori will be portrayed vividly to the reader as being performed the same everywhere despite the varying social and cultural realities. In other words, we are trying to systematize a basic pattern of what actually goes on during a monthly service. In this way—although stepping into the dangers of generalizations—the reader is given an opportunity to sense the uniformity of the ritual dance as well as the events which embody it.

[7] Without the execution of the Teodori a monthly service would not be called as such: one can take away the communal meal after the performance of the service, or the preparations for the cleaning for the service, or one may even take away some of the musical instruments used in the service. But one cannot take away the ritual dance. This is an important semiotic marker in any performance of the service.

[8] Many Catholic counterparts have asked the author on more than one occasion why the service is performed only once a month if it is so vital for the construction of the community of Tenrikyo believers. The answer perhaps lies in the fact that from the time of the foundress of Tenrikyo, Nakayama Miki, the performance of the service was executed once a month on the twenty-sixth day, and to this day Tenrikyo Church Headquarters continues to dedicate this day for its monthly service. The twenty-sixth day is also a salient marker with respect to the overall dogma of the Tenrikyo teachings: it was on October 26, 1838 when Nakayama Miki was settled as the Shrine of God; it was on January 26, 1887 when she "withdrew from physical life." This was the symbolic factor in determining the course for local churches to perform their monthly services.

Preparing for a Monthly Service

Depending on the hour for which the service commences, members of the church gather progressively with some followers assembling as early as two hours beforehand. The activities carried out prior to the service are divided into three: cleaning the church premise, setting up the space for the ritual dance, and preparing the communal meal to take place after the sermon. One or more of the male family members who live at the church usually does the cleaning.[9] This clean up consists of the sweeping and the mopping of the worship halls, the guest rooms, as well as sections which are usually used as bedrooms for family members. Some local churches outside of Japan sometimes house one or two live-in students ranging from junior high school to university undergraduates. They also form part of the family nucleus of the church. The church premise and grounds, such as the adjacent street and parking lot, are swept clean and afterward watered to give the entire area a fresh atmosphere prior to the service. Such exterior cleanliness becomes very apparent a few hours prior to the main performance of the service.[10]

A communal meal is prepared by the women membership and particularly led by the female members of the family who administer the church itself. Larger churches usually assign a rotation list so that duties can be assessed to members of the woman's association on a monthly basis. Despite the size of the church, however, this meal is to be shared by the community of believers after the service. Although the content of meals may differ from church to church two important attributes can be made. One lies in the fact that women followers are the ones responsible for the preparations. It would be difficult to perceive males at a local church who are willing to prepare a meal for the entire congregation. An exception is made when a male adherent is known to be particularly competent, such as being a chef at a restaurant. Another factor that characterizes this meal is that it is the same for everyone. Despite the differing age and varying social positions of the followers, members of the congregation sit down together to share a meal after the performance of the monthly service.

At one local church, the meal consists of a variety of foods yet modest in tone: potato salad, a simple green salad, pieces of chicken simmered in soy sauce, a traditionally made dish of rice, triangular shaped spring rolls, fish,

---

[9] It should be reminded that a family supervises all local churches, despite their shape, size, or location. The family household resides within the grounds of the local church and handles the performance of the daily service as well as keeping contact and guiding church followers.

[10] Such help in preparing for the monthly service is called *hinokishin*. The term means "daily contribution." This term appears frequently in the dance text and will be elaborated in chapter four.

and a cake with Japanese green tea to be enjoyed after the meal.[11] Beverages include a diversity of soft drinks and some beer. Both the cake and the fish are placed as offerings prior to the performance of the service. At this particular church, the menu remains quite the same throughout the year. What is noteworthy at any local church during the preparations is that the membership of women converse with one another about current events and voice their opinions to one another while they busily prepare for the meal. Characteristic of the kitchen during this preparatory period is one that is bright, cheerful, spirited, but nevertheless constantly moving about. The association of women gathered for the service demonstrates a strong bond of solidarity during this preliminary stage.

The Ritual Objects

Three or four males usually carry out preparations for the actual performance of the service. The number can increase or decrease depending once again on the size of the church. At larger churches, for example, there are as many as twelve to thirteen people responsible for this particular orchestration. At smaller churches, on the other hand, one person is capable of doing the entire chore. These people, however, do not necessarily belong to the immediate family for which the life of the church depends on but hold a relatively elevated position within the church hierarchy.

The most important aspect of this preliminary arrangement is the offerings placed on the altar in front of each shrine. At each Tenrikyo church, there are three altars that are dedicated to 1) God the Parent; 2) Nakayama Miki, the foundress of Tenrikyo; and 3) the defunct members pertaining to the church. All altars are lined next to one another with their backs directed toward the Jiba, Tenrikyo's focal point, so that when a follower faces the altars and prays, s/he also directs such prayer toward the Jiba. All local churches in the United States, for example, face west; all local churches in European countries face east. This would hold true for churches located in the western parts of Japan: their altars point toward the Jiba. Situated inside each altar is a wooden shrine with a mirror placed in front of it. The external areas of the altar—the top and two vertical sides—are decorated with bamboo screens appropriate to its size.

The largest altar located in the middle of the dais is dedicated to God the Parent; the next largest altar is to the right dedicated to the Nakayama Miki; the smallest altar located to the left is dedicated to the defunct. Depending once again on the magnitude of the altars, three to four wooden table-stands are placed in front of each shrine so that offerings to each shrine

---

[11] By "one local church" the author is describing the local church he is affiliated located on the west coast of the United States.

can be placed on top of these table-stands. Each offering tray, with the exception of a water container and *sake* (Japanese rice wine) container, supports a white dish on which the food offerings are placed. Once again, the number of offerings accords in direct proportion to the size of the altars themselves.

Offerings vary but there is a consistency of fruits and vegetables. Water, rice, fish, and *sake* are always offered. There is also room for dried foods such as dried seaweed and noodles. The largest fruit is perhaps a watermelon and the smallest being grapes, while a lettuce head or a cabbage appear to dominate the vegetables offered to the three altars. These offerings are prepared in a room set apart but within the proximity of the altars. The fruits and vegetables are rinsed with water prior to being placed on the dish. It is important to note that a mixture of foodstuffs, with the exception of dried food, cannot be placed on one tray. Each tray has one produce and not a combination of, for example, carrots and tomatoes or apples and onions.

When all offerings are ready to be placed in front of each shrine within the altar, the head minister appears before the shrine dedicated to God the Parent and the shrine dedicated to the defunct to open the portals.[12] Offerings are placed in its proper place by two persons after the opening the portals: one person carries one offering tray at a time and passes it to the other who proceeds to place it on the table-stand. Both wear an original Tenrikyo outfit called a *kyofuku* that is usually donned for the morning and evening daily services at the church. They also wear a white mask to cover their mouth made out of rice paper that is hinged behind the ears by a thread of the same material. Larger churches, on the other hand, utilize a special ritual for the food offerings that has been established by Church Headquarters. It usually takes place with the accompaniment of *gagaku*, Japanese court music, with the performance of the monthly service immediately following this particular food offering ritual.[13] This means that the ritual garb for the service is donned during the execution of this offering ceremony.

---

[12] The portals to the shrine dedicated to the Foundress, Nakayama Miki, always remains open. There is a particular reason for it. Prior to "withdrawing from physical life" she asked her disciples if she should "open the portals and level the ground or close the portals and level the ground." The disciples answered that she should "open the portals and level the ground." Thus her portals are open all the time for she taught that by "opening the portals" she will work for world salvation (Tenrikyo Church Headquarters 1996, 220–42).

[13] *Gagaku* is imperial court music that was first introduced into Japan in the Tang period from China through the regions of what is now Korea in the eighth century. During the Heian period (794–1185) *gagaku* stabilized in Japan and acquired its own identity. The Silk Roads, by the way, played an influential part in transporting *gagaku* from one region to another. In *gagaku* there is also dancing that accompanies the music in compositions that are intended for it (Togi 1971). Specifically designed music is played during Tenrikyo rituals of this sort.

The Ritual Space

Other preparations for the ritual dance consists of cleaning the ritual space, placing the musical instruments in their respective positions, and setting up the table-stands for the dancers and singers. We use the term "ritual space" to include the front area where the altars are situated. This area is also known as the upper dais since a wooden dais is raised a few inches from the ground floor of the church premise and differentiates the worship hall from the area where the ritual dance is performed. A lower dais, approximately half the height of the upper dais, is located on both the right and left sides of the upper dais.

Before any other preparation is carried out with concern to ritual space, both daises are dusted off with a dry cloth that is usually done by one or two males of the congregation. Musical instruments are also cleansed off with a cloth conserved particularly for the cleansing of these instruments. After they are dusted off, these instruments are placed in their respective positions. There are nine musical instruments used to accompany the Teodori. They are (one of each): wooden clappers, cymbals, large drum, small gong, flute, small drum, *koto* (zither), *shamisen* (lute), and *kokyu* (bowed lute). These instruments are approximately placed on the border of the upper and lower daises as follows:

Figure 2. Position of musical instruments on the upper dais

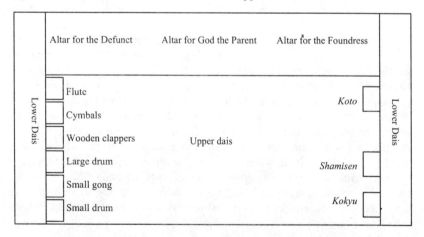

It is important to remember that the ritual space set-up is exclusively upheld at all Tenrikyo churches. The position of each instrument always remains the same although the distance between them may differ from church to church due to size. There are some churches, however, who have large altars and the altar dedicated to God the Parent alone may embody the span of the entire upper dais. In such a case the other altars are located on the upper end of the left and right lower daises, respectively. Also salient in point is that dancers perform on the upper dais, as we shall examine later, regardless of church size or location.

Table-stands for the dancers are prepared but placed on the upper dais only after the head minister reads the prayer on behalf of the followers. The table-stands are made ready by wiping each stand with a dry cloth and allotting two fans on top that are used for the dance. There are six table-stands for the six dancers. Although there are three male and three female dancers there are no variances in size or shape of the table-stand and fan. A table-stand is set up for the singer with a book containing the lyrics to the songs for the service. Placed along the side of the book is a wooden block that is hit against the table-stand to signal the beginning of each song. Placed along side this signal block is a counter enumerating the twenty-one times that the first section of the seated service is performed.

When the ritual space is set up, chairs or cushions for the worship hall, if not already set up as so, are brought in and lined up in horizontal rows. In the case of Japanese churches, however, chairs are not used. In such an instance, then, cushions are brought in and placed in the *tatami* matted worship halls. Needless to mention, it is in the worship hall that all followers assemble and remain during the performance of the monthly service. This is the location from where observation, an onlooker's point of view, of the dance occurs.

By the time the worship hall is arranged, then, followers can be seen talking to one another within the church premise. Prior to approaching one another, however, each follower enters the worship hall and makes a prayer to each shrine. Prayers of this sort are made from a seated position. It begins by clapping four times, inclining the head slightly forward with the eyes closed during the prayer, and finally, the prayer itself in silence. In the case where chairs are not used the follower kneels down on the *tatami* mats and makes the prayer in the same way as the seated position. The prayer ends with another clapping of the hands four times. The same prayer mode continues to the next shrine simply by changing the direction of the body while remaining seated. The same prayer style is adopted prior to leaving church grounds when the monthly service is over and followers are ready to return to their own homes.

The Ritual Wear

Followers are ready for the performance of the service when the three major phases of arrangements are completed. The final formation prior to the dance is changing into the ritual garb itself. This varies according to gender.

92

Both are called *otsutome gi* in Tenrikyo jargon, literally meaning, "apparel for the service." The female performer wears a black *kimono* with an *obi*, a special belt that is folded and rests against the lower back by being tied with another belt across the waist and hinged around the back region. The kimono itself consists of one piece with sleeves that extend down to about the thigh areas. The *tabi*, or footwear, are white in color and have clasps around the achilles tendons which, when fastened together, helps keeps the footwear tightly snuggled. The black kimono is vested with a crest at the upper back area, the upper left and right area of the chest, as well as both sides of each sleeve. This crest once represented the Nakayama family and has now been adopted as *the* symbol of the Tenrikyo religion.

For the male counterpart a *hakama* is worn. This apparel is also black in color and consists of two parts: the top and bottom. The top wear is somewhat like a very large shirt which, when not fastened by a belt, dangles to one's ankles. The bottom part, somewhat like a large skirt, overlaps the top wear from the bottom and held together with strings that extends from the waist area of this bottom half. The strings are tied in a knot in front of the waist area in such a way that a cross appears. The *hakama* also portrays the crests located in the same areas its the female counterpart, forming a very coherent and traditional look. As members begin to fill the worship hall in their respective ritual garbs the male followers sit on the left side with their female complement usually sitting down on the area to the right. For those who do not wear the formal ritual garb a black *happi* coat is most likely to be worn. These *happi* coats are exclusively a Tenrikyo wear with the name of the church written in the front with either the Chinese character for Tenrikyo or a romanized version of it. Such apparel also is usually worn during activities that concern *hinokishin*.

During a Monthly Service

When all assemble in the worship hall, the service is ready to begin. The head minister sits in the very front row with his two assistants sitting to the left and to the right of him, respectively. These assistants are appointed differently for each monthly service and assist with the ritual procedures for the reading of the prayer. *Gagaku* music is performed by a number of performers at intervals when the head minister and his assistants ceremonially move up and around the upper dais. The prayer is read in front of the altar dedicated to God the Parent in Japanese. In local churches located in areas other than the Japanese peninsula, a second reading of the same prayer is read out in its local language. The main contents of the prayer text are as follows: deep gratitude to God the Parent, stating the reason for the creation of humankind, activities held that month by the church, and a resolution spoken on behalf of all followers to strive for further spiritual maturity.

The assembled membership in the worship hall incline their heads, torso directed forward, and both hands on their thighs while in silence during the reading of the prayer. After the prayer is read all members of the congregation clap their hands four times to mark the closing of the prayer. The prayer ends with the ritual procedures of going off the upper dais and onto the worship hall with the accompaniment of the *gagaku* music.

At this point, the table-stands for the dancers are placed on the upper dais with the help of six members. They take hold of a table-stand and then line up in front of the upper dais. When all are ready they rise to the upper dais in unison and place the table-stands in a straight horizontal line that runs across the upper dais. A table-stand is also placed on the upper dais for the singer. Local churches that utilize wooden chairs make it a point to place these chairs in front of these table-stands.

Figure 3. Position of dancers on upper dais

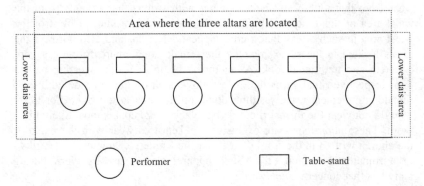

Performing the Seated Service

The actual Tenrikyo service structurally consists of two parts: the seated service, the performance to the songs for the Kagura and, the Teodori, the dance with the hand movements. The seated service is a service done according to its name, that is, it is not a dance but a ritual performed from a seated position. Hand movements and a specially made text to the movements accompany this primary section of the service. Performers of the hand movements sit on top of the upper dais in front of their table-stands. As for the song text, part one of this section is repeated twenty-one times, part two is performed once, and part three is done three times of a set of three. The text is provided below.

Each member of the congregation is assigned a particular part for the performance of the service. The head minister usually designates these roles and the roster is posted in the worship hall prior to commencing. In churches

94

that emphasize the perfection of the service, for example, a roster can be seen a week or two in advance so that a performer knows what part to play in its upcoming monthly celebration.

Regardless of church size, however, the six performers for the seated service represent vital figures for the life of the church. The three members seated on the left are male members and the other three consist of the opposite gender. Salient to mention is that this arrangement is sustained in all churches. The male performer closest to the shrine dedicated to God the Parent will always be the head minister. If the head minister is a woman, then, the same principle will hold true for she will perform closest to the shrine dedicated to God the Parent on her gender-based quadrant. Respectively next to them will be the second important figure in seniority, reaching finally to the third person and final person of each gender. On the other hand, if there are many members who prove to be vital to the community of the church they will alternate from month to month: the head minister always has the final say in who performs in what position. The musical instrumentalists, on the other hand, are people of the general congregation and are chosen at random. It is important here, however, to note that those who qualify to take part as performers for the seated service during a monthly service at a local church—the six members situated on the upper dais—remain for the most part unchanging throughout the year.

The song text for the seated service goes as follows. An English translation is provided by a dance specialist (Sasaki 1980b) and it goes as follows:

Part One:

Ashiki o harōte tasuke tamae,   Sweeping away evil, save us please,
Tenri-Ō-no-Mikoto.   Tenri-O-no-Mikoto.

Part Two:

Choto hanashi: Just a few words:
Kami no yū koto kiite kure,   Please listen to what God says.
Ashiki no koto wa iwan dena,   I shall not speak wrong things.
Kono yō no ji to ten to o katadorite   Taking this world's earth and sky as a model,
Fūfu o koshirae kitaru dena,   I created wife and husband.
Kore wa kono yo no hajime dashi.   This is this world's beginning.
Namu Tenri-Ō-no-Mikoto.   Hail Tenri-O-no-Mikoto!

Part Three:

Ashiki o harōte tasuke sekikomu,   Sweeping away evil, salvation hurrying,
Ichiretsu sumashite Kanrodai.   One and all purified, then the Kanrodai.

Performing the Teodori

After this first section of the service is completed all members get off the upper dais in a uniform manner and proceed onto the worship hall. Then the chairs, if any, are removed from the upper dais. A person usually then calls out the names of the people assigned to perform. The instrumentalists then proceed to their positions in front of the instruments they are assigned to play. The dancers, on the other hand, line up in a standing position in front of the upper dais with their feet positioned on the border between the worship hall and the upper dais. As the members are ready to commence the dancers bow once and move together on top of the upper dais, making their way toward the altars. When located in front of their respective table-stands the dancers kneel down in unison and make one more bow. While still in this position, the singer hits the table-stand with the wooden block. Everyone, including those in the worship hall, then clap their hands four times. From this kneeling position the dancers rise to a standing position, take two steps backwards, and put their hands in the position for "pray." The instrumentalists then take hold of their instruments. The singer looks to see that the other performers are ready and later hits the wooden block against the table-stand to signal the beginning of the Teodori.

The hand movements of the dance cannot be completely seen from the worship hall. What is observable is that the dancers move two steps towards the altars, and then move two steps backwards. From time to time their hands extend outside of their torso areas once to the left and another to the right. Some hand movements include reaching above the head while other gestures are made with a fisted hand. Other movements include a 360° degree turn. The torso remains erect for the most part of the dance yet at times the dancer makes a bow or extends the body weight backwards. All movements are ordered and synchronized by the six dancers. All dance movements continue from one form to the next as a stream of movements are composed. Songs Three and Four use open fans. Yet one striking aspect is that all six dancers move their hands and legs synchronically: there is no room for improvising.

Besides the dancing, however, the melody of the song text is maintained by those who sing it. The most noted singer is the singer himself who is sometimes supplied with a microphone, enabling him to be voiced on top of both daises as well as throughout the worship hall. Yet contrasting voices—both female and male, high and low—combine into one single tune that harmonizes with the melodic dancing of the Teodori. Behind such resounding harmony is the music provided by the musical instrument players. They, too, blend with the singing of the song text by the community of followers present. Yet the main visual attraction for the audience is the dancing of the six performers on the upper dais.

The Interval

When Song Six is over, the singer hits the wooden block against the table-stand once again. The dancers advance in front of the table-stands, kneel down on top of the upper dais, and they wait with their heads inclined forward for the musical instrument players to put their instruments on the table-stand. The singer slams the wooden block against the table-stand one final time to signal everyone, including the audience in the worship hall, to clap four times. Such clapping closes the first half of the Teodori. The dancers bow in unison in front of the altars, stand up, and finally, descend in unity from the upper dais onto the worship hall. The dancers, together with the instrumentalists and singer, bow a second time from the same stance in the worship hall. This bowing signals to the musical instrument players that they can proceed to the worship hall.

Once again, names are called out aloud into the worship hall and people for the second time flow into their designated areas. A different set of dancers line up once again in front of the upper dais as other performers sit in front of their respective musical instruments. The entire procedure of advancing on the upper dais is repeated and the dancing of the Teodori begins from Song Seven.

The Teodori is completed after performing Song Twelve. When this happens, the singer once again slams the wooden block against his table-stand. Just as what occurs prior to the interval described above, the dancers again advance in front of their respective table-stand and kneel down while the musical instrument players place the instruments on the table-stand. The performers remain with their heads slightly inclined forward until the singer hits the table-stand with a wooden block. This again signals the members of the congregation to clap four times. The dancers proceed off the upper dais first and bow with the other performers from the border of the worship hall. The others then advance off the lower dais and this marks an end to the performance of the Teodori within the setting of a monthly service.

The head minister makes a sermon to the congregation immediately after the performance of the Teodori. A large stand is placed on the upper dais where he faces the worship hall for his or her sermon. The time span of the sermon usually amounts to thirty minutes to an hour and the content of such talk usually evolves around a topic of Tenrikyo terms with reference to personal faith experience or events that the church will encounter. Hence it is a preacher type of discourse where the speaker communicates personal meaning to his or her audience while they listen. It should be noticed that the preacher in larger churches may change from month to month and are chosen from among the members of the board of directors of that particular church.

The Celebration
        Preparation for the communal meal, *naorai* in Japanese, closely

resembles arrangements made for a luncheon meal and a celebratory mood takes place.[14] Tables are brought in from the storage room and set up at the place where the communal meal takes place. At larger churches, however, the dining room is large enough to house all members present; yet one usually finds that the worship hall is transformed into a dining hall for the communal meal to take place. The female performers are the first to rush into the changing room to switch into normal clothing for the preparations. Male performers, on the other hand, continue to wear their ritual garbs with the task to transform the worship hall into an adequate dining hall. Some males, usually those who prepared the food offerings prior to the service, will assist in removing the offered food from the altar area into the room where they were first prepared. Others bring plates of foods and beverages that have been prepared prior to the service from the kitchen area.

Prior to the meal, however, everyone must sit in unity at the tables. Members pour beverages for one another and, when all cups are filled, the head minister presides with a cheer. Of note are those seated near the head minister. Usually senior members of the church sit near the head minister or, if there is a guest at the monthly service, he or she sits next to him. Though their husbands accompany many women members, the women followers usually sit with one another near the kitchen area. If the kitchen area, for example, is located to the right of the worship hall women members are most likely to cluster around that area there. In this case, then, the other members of the congregation take their meal on the other half of the worship hall.

If the monthly service began at 10:00 am, followers begin to leave one after the other upon finishing their meal at around 2:00 pm.[15] Members of the congregation make their final prayers to each respective altar from the worship hall prior to leaving the church. Some leave earlier than others if they have appointments to attend to later on in the afternoon. Others help with the clean-up efforts of re-transforming the worship hall, if it was used as the dining hall, into its original everyday set up. Before leaving, however, all members receive a portion of the comestibles that have been offered in front of each shrine. Such offered food are inserted in a bag to be taken home and shared with other family members. The quantity is small but followers accept

---

[14] The term *naorai* is apparently one that has been adopted by Shinto practice. On the meaning of the term one person concisely put it this way: ". . . a 'face to face encounter' when *kami* and parishioner share the joint food of 's offerings, offerings brought to maturity by the *kami's* beneficence" (Bownas 1963, 29). Literally, it means, "putting together" and current usage of the term does not necessarily deal with its religious import (Yoshida and Sesoko 1989).

[15] This is an arbitrary time. The time needed to perform an entire monthly service—from the reading of the prayer to the sermon—is approximately two hours. Followers will leave at a later time given that a monthly service can also commence in the late afternoon and may conclude with dinner.

these offerings by bowing their heads and using both hands in accepting them.

The Teodori is a ritual performed by followers of Tenrikyo in their churches, mission centers, and mission posts throughout the world for the monthly service. In the above section, we have described one typical setting in which the Teodori comes to be performed at a local church. There is the preparatory stage where cleaning takes place on the church premise through the active support given by followers who arrive at the church a few hours prior to its beginnings. Prior to the dancing of the monthly service, there are other constituents which have been underlined: the prayer, the *gagaku* music, the seated service, the manner in which one goes up and down the dais, and the engagement of the other musical instruments. After the Teodori is over, there are accouterments that render an actual monthly service complete: the sermon, the changing from ritual garb into everyday clothing, the celebration with the special meal, and finally, departing from church premise.

The Teodori, as we have seen, consists of the dance movements and the songs to such movements. The Teodori is performed collectively with others—usually in the setting of a monthly service—but in theory can be performed and is executed by anyone anywhere. It is now time to look further in what actually constitutes the Teodori so that it can be perceived as an object, a text, which can stand on its own.

CHAPTER THREE

FROM TEXT TO INTERTEXT

Conceptions of the World in the Text

An intertext in semiotic terms is when one text refers to other texts (Manning 1987). The common principle of an intertext is that, like a sign that may refer to another sign instead of an object, a text can also refer to other texts. Thus, constituents of the examined text can be traced in other texts. Consequently, an intertext is a hidden text within a text that informs the reader about the text itself with or without the knowledge of the author (Scholes 1982). This chapter focuses on the Teodori's intertextuality so as to unravel its world view, a *model of* cosmic reality. Prior to unfolding the intertextuality of the Teodori, however, a brief look at the notions of the world will be made. This will later direct the examination of the interexts that are relevant for this part of the study.

A start in unfolding the Teodori's world view includes aspects of time and space from our two main categories, namely the verbal and nonverbal symbolic patterns of the Teodori. The main question in this section will be the following: how are the symbolic patterns, both verbal and nonverbal, being used to convey cosmological meaning? The hope will be to describe the Teodori as "thick" as possible when viewing the text as such. Let us examine notions about the world in general that are constituent of the Teodori.

The Verbal Symbolic Patterns
World

The verbal symbolic patterns, *sekai*, and *yo*, both words translated as "world" in English, appear seventeen times in the Teodori. Appearing as many times as it does, however, not all nonverbal symbolic patterns that accompany them are the same. The nonverbal symbolic patterns that blend with the singing of the word, *sekai* and *yo* are synchronized with the following patterns: 1) lift up; 2) world; 3) turn around; and 4) standing fans.

The verbal symbolic patterns listed below affirm something about the world. The list below shows the song and verse number, the verbal symbolic pattern with the original in parenthesis, and finally, the nonverbal symbolic patterns that accompany the verbal ones. A general notion of the world will become more apparent through this type of elaboration. We have provided the basic verbal and nonverbal symbolic patterns of the Teodori from page 49 to page 86 in the previous chapter.

Song and verse	Verbal symbolic pattern	Nonverbal symbolic pattern
Yorozuyo, 1	world (yo)	world
Yorozuyo, 7	world (sekai)	world
Yorozuyo, 8	world (sekai)	world
Song II, 4	world (yo)	world
Song III, 1	world (yo)	standing fans
Song III, 3	world (sekai)	standing fans
Song IV, 9	world's (yo)	standing fans
Song V, 1	world (sekai)	lift up
Song V, 9	world (yo)	lift up
Song VI, 3	world (yo)	lift up
Song VII, 3	world (sekai)	lift up
Song VII, 9	world (yo)	lift up
Song VIII, 1	world (sekai)	lift up
Song VIII, 3	world (sekai)	turn around
Song IX, 1	world (sekai)	lift up
Song IX, 3	world (sekai)	lift up
Song XI, 3	world (sekai)	lift up

As demonstrated, a referent alone does not cover the entire meaning when the Teodori speaks of a "world." This term is thus polysemic in that it carries more than one meaning. In this case, world can be classified into four differentiating themes. The first concerns people of the world, that is, that the message speaks of people who live in and of this world. In particular, such concern people who do not understand the intention of God (*Yorozuyo*, 1); the hearts of the people of the world (*Yorozuyo*, 7; *Yorozuyo*, 8; Song VI, 3; Song VII, 3); the assembling of people of the world (Song III, 3; Song VIII, 3; Song XI, 3); and greed found among the people of the world (Song IX, 3).

At the same time, however, the assembling of people of the world also connotes a particular spatial set up which refers to the Jiba, the origin of the world, forming a second category. The Jiba, it is to be remembered, is the place of human conception. More will be mentioned on this theme when deepening an understanding of the cosmological notions of the Teodori. In connection to this constituent an explicit reference is made to the origin of the world (Song III, 1; Song V, 9).

Extended references to a specific geographical location constitute the third category. That is, mention is made concerning concrete places and their traits of this world. For example, reference to the area around the Jiba is being made (Song IV, 9; Song VII, 9). There is also notion of the world being vast with a multitude of places and objects in it (Song V, 1; Song VIII, 1). Finally, the last category speaks of the world as a transforming one that promises a brighter prodigality (Song II, 4).

Space

A symbol cannot stand on its own for it is always in reference with another object, act, event, quality or relation that serves as a vehicle of meaning. As Geertz argues, a symbol is something that stands for something else (Geertz 1973, 91). In this respect we attempt below to create a pattern of spatial features found in the Teodori that refer to concrete places. This classification at times will overlap with the one outlined above. This is only natural since we are attempting to depict a given concrete reality found from within a world the Teodori describes. In other words, the term "place" will symbolize some form of a given reality. Expressions such as mountains, a country, and names of known regions that carry meaning with respect to spatiality will be included. These dimensions make up the classification of space. We will first list the song and verse, the verbal symbolic pattern and the original term in parenthesis, and the nonverbal symbolic pattern that accompany the verbal one. This type of elaboration will generate a general notion of the spatial features coherent in the Teodori.

Song and verse	Verbal symbolic pattern	Nonverbal symbolic pattern
Yorozuyo, 4	place (*tokoro*)	press (open)
	Jiba (*jiba*)	jiba
	Yamato (*Yamato*)	mountain
	God's Residence (*kamigata*)	pray
Song I, 8	Yamato (*Yamato*)	mountain
Song II, 10	everywhere (*tokoro*)	pray
Song III, 1	Service Place (*Tsutome no basho*)	rotate fans
	Shoyashiki (*Shoyashiki*)	standing fans
Song III, 2	Service Place (*Tsutome basho*)	rotate fans
Song IV, 9	this place (*koko*)	press
	paradise (*gokuraku*)	pray
Song V, 1	places (*tokoro*)	throw
Song V, 2	this place (*kono tokoro*)	place
Song V, 7	this place (*kono tokoro*)	place
Song V, 8	Yamato (*yamato*)	mountain
	countries (*kuni guni*)	finger open out
Song V, 9	Original Jiba (*moto no Jiba*)	press—jiba
	place (*tokoro*)	throw
Song VII, 3	fertile field (*denji*)	hoeing
Song VII, 4	good field (*yoki ji*)	jiba
Song VII, 5	that field (*ano ji*)	point forward—jiba
Song VII, 7	fertile field (*denji*)	hoeing
Song VII, 8	Residence (*yashiki*)	turn around
	field (*denji*)	hoeing
Song VII, 9	fertile field (*denji*)	hoeing

Song and verse	Verbal symbolic pattern	Nonverbal symbolic pattern
Song VIII, 1	countries (*kuni*)	open
Song VIII, 8	mountain's (*yama*)	mountain
Song IX, 8	mountain (*yama*)	mountain
Song IX, 9	here (*koko de*)	press
Song IX, 10	here (*komoto*)	come home
Song XI, 1	Jiba (*jiba*)	press hip
	God's Residence (*kami no yakata*)	pray—building
	Shoyashiki (*Shoyashiki*)	lift up
Song XI, 8	Residence (*yashiki*)	turn around
Song XII, 8	mountain (*yama*)	mountain

These are the verses that portray a particular spatial construct and many of these verbal symbolic patterns are utilized in manifold ways to refer to one major symbol. The Jiba, the special sacred place in Tenrikyo, rises above all other symbols as the dominant symbol. The textual strategy applied in conveying the importance of such a concrete place is overwhelming. One finds it vigorously being repeated through the varying combinations of the verbal symbolic patterns and nonverbal symbolic pattern. Yet the message remains the same: the Jiba, the place where humankind was first conceived, has been settled and as such is the most important place for all human beings. It is referred to as paradise (Song IV, 9); a place where illnesses and sufferings are cured (Song V, 2; Song V, 7); a remarkable place (Song V, 9); and as the place where God resides (Song XI, 1).

In relation to the being the place where God resides, the text features words that explicitly makes use of such claims. Once again, the surrounding area of the Jiba is found to be the place where God resides—in particular—as God's Residence (*Yorozuyo*, 4; Song XI, 1; Song XI, 8) and as such, a place where one can call out God's name (Song IX, 10). If it is a place of where God resides, then, the text also speaks of two geographical localities known by those in the province where the teachings of Miki spread in the beginning, namely the name of the village where the Jiba was located and the name of the province where the village was located. The village was called Shoyashiki (Song III, 1; Song XI, 1) and the province was called Yamato (*Yorozuyo*, 4; Song I, 8; Song V, 8). Such geographical locations were used to help direct and pinpoint the exact spot of the Jiba to those familiar with such already existing places. Further, at this very important place there is an important religious ritual that takes place this refers to the Kagura Service (Song III, 1; Song III; 2; Song IX, 9). More on this aspect later.

Particularly in Song VII, however, we have a concrete place which metaphorically describes a dramatic life way. The symbol used here is the field—the working place for most of the peasant followers at the time of their conversion—and such a place carries deeper meaning when placed in a religious performance of a ritual dance. In particular, the text speaks of a good field (Song VII, 4); of one particular field (Song VII, 5); and of a fertile field (Song VII, 3; VII, 7; VII, 9). Yet, once again, the underlining meaning in using such a metaphor seems to point toward the importance of the Jiba and its confines being the field of God (Song VII, 8).

One final geographical category can be appropriated. This typology goes under the domain of mountains and refers for the most part to distance between the core of the world, the Jibà, and the rest of the world. In other words, the claim made in reference to mountains describes the fundamental need to tell others about a personal religious conversion and therefore concerns with going out to do missionary work in far away places (Song VIII, 8; Song IX, 8; Song XII, 8).

Time

In order to further develop a world view pattern, however, mere spatial categories will not suffice. Together with the symbolic notions of spatial amenities, temporal ones will cast on cosmological ones. In other words, by underpinning its temporal factors a deeper account of the world view in the Teodori will be portrayed.

As in the description of the spatial characteristics, we will first list the song and verse, the verbal symbolic pattern with the original in parenthesis, and the nonverbal symbolic pattern that accompany the verbal ones. Through this type of elaboration a general notion of its temporal features will become more apparent.

Song and verse	Verbal symbolic pattern	Nonverbal symbolic pattern
Yorozuyo, 3	this time (*kono tabi*)	press—throw
Song I, 8	abundant year (*honen*)	circle in front
Song II, 1	beginning (*hajime*)	lift up
Song III, 4	begins from now (*kore kara*)	standing fans
Song III, 7	from now (*kore kara*)	lift up
Song III, 10	this time (*kono tabi*)	lift up
Song IV, 4	night and day (*yoru hiru*)	night-day with fans
Song IV, 10	this time (*kono tabi*)	lift up
Song VI, 5	always (*itsumo*)	press
	future (*sue dewa*)	point left
Song VI, 10	this time (*kono tabi*)	lift up
Song VII, 10	this time (*kono tabi*)	lift up
Song VIII, 10	this time (*kono tabi*)	lift up
Song IX, 7	this time (*kono tabi*)	press at hip—lift out
Song X, 2	first time (*hajime*)	throw
Song X, 10	this time (*kono tabi*)	lift up
Song XI, 9	this time (*kono tabi*)	lift up
Song XI, 10	this year (*kotoshi*)	lift up
Song XII, 10	this time (*kono tabi*)	lift up

The following is a brief summary that can be extracted from the temporal aspects that are suggestive of a world view. There is reference being made to the day of origin when the teachings were founded. It should be recalled that it was on October 26, 1838 when Nakayama Miki was taken as the Shrine of God. Prior to that, however, Miki, nor the Nakayama family, did not understand God the Parent's will to save all of humanity. The first to come to terms with the will of God the Parent had to be the members of this family. It was from one particular revelation to one particular person at one particular time that the teachings of God could begin to spread. Therefore verses within the Teodori refers to temporal moments to compare the difference between the pre-revelatory situation and after (*Yorozuyo* 3; III, 10; Song X, 2; Song XI, 9). In retrospect, then, God appeared on a particular day and the people in the world will no longer be the same. It is taught that God will save all of humanity from this moment onwards through various forms: remarkable events and miraculous salvation will occur (Song III, 4; Song VI, 5; Song VI, 10; Song VII, 10). Yet these occurrences can only take place if the heart is purified. Such purification of the heart does not take place beyond this world nor in some future existence but can only take place at the present moment—here and now (Song IV, 10; Song VIII, 10).

For this purification to occur, however, God asks people of the world to respond. One such response arising from the importance of the 26th—the day of origin—is to perform the service (Song IV, 4; Song VI, 5). Another request that God asks timely of the people is to reflect as well as know the importance of the working of the heart and the consequences of such working (Song III, 7; Song IX, 7; Song X, 10). These commands are seemingly urgent in the eyes of God and therefore are intertwined and marked with temporal value.

Along with the temporal category of a divine fashion, reference is made to the already known temporal values that reflect life in a provincial agricultural setting. One category of agricultural life was its circular notion of time where the year was divided according to suitable parts for its work. Reference is therefore made to a chronology that borrows its meaning from the life of the people, namely one that is based on farming structures (Song I, 8; Song II, 1; Song XI, 10). Finally, carpenters assembling at one time in connection with the construction of the world of the Joyous Life are being referred to (Song XII, 10).

Such temporal components, as well as the spatial ones, lend meaning to the very notion of cosmology found in the Teodori. The possibility of deepening an understanding of how these two blend together had to be made by first dividing what the spatial and temporal patterns suggest. The spatial meaning embodied in the Jiba, in more than one occasion, has been referred to and timely conceptions have also expansively pointed to this place. An attempt will therefore be made to further penetrate into this construct for here lies the underlying governing symbol when speaking of the world view pattern. But first, let us take a look at the notions about the world in the nonverbal symbolic patterns of the text.

The Nonverbal Symbolic Patterns

The written textual aspect of the Teodori has been the primary source in the effort to delineate factors of the world view. This part has been referred to as the verbal symbolic patterns of the texts. In the following section, notions that may be drawn from the nonverbal symbolic patterns will be briefly examined. Although these movements are not constituents of a written text, such patterns can be read for their meaning—just as in a literary written one. It is a matter of how one goes about unpacking it in the hopes of demonstrating its meaning. For such purposes, then, reliance is made on a modest semiotic-bent explanation of the movements. This will hopefully provide for further information regarding the notion of a world view pattern.

The nonverbal symbolic patterns that accompany the verbal ones have already been delineated. For instance, when the word, "world" appears in Song XI, 3 the nonverbal symbolic pattern is "lift up;" when the word "countries" appears in Song V, 8, the nonverbal symbolic pattern is "finger open out," and so forth. Yet these nonverbal symbolic units that constitute a part of the text also carry a shared code of meaning in themselves. In so saying, then, the nonverbal symbolic movements will be categorized with respect to their directional qualities that will then be used to uncover a further orchestrated world view pattern.

A distinctive pattern can be framed through examining the seventy-six motions expressing notions of the world. These motions are closely linked with the directions that are found in the story of creation. This story will later be discussed at length. For now, it will suffice to remember that cardinal directions were pertinent markers for the creation of humankind in the Tenrikyo story of creation. It will be argued that the way in which the varying directions in the story how humankind was created—north, south, east, west, northwest, northeast, southwest and southeast—corresponds in motion with the nonverbal symbolic patterns of the Teodori. In other words, the movements of the hands during the dancing of the Teodori portray directional qualities and as such can be linked to other texts as well. To demonstrate such patterns, each movement has been classified according to its motioning characteristics.

Vertical Motions

A vertical motion of the hands semiotically indicates a north-south relationship. This up and down movement—with the dancer's own head representing north and his or her hip area representing south—is used throughout the ritual dance. Whether it be the nonverbal symbolic pattern for "building," "lift up," or "press" for example, the motioning of the hands depict one which moves from one horizontal position of the body (up/down) to another level of the body (north/south). That is, when extracting its semiotic value onto a two-fold dimensional plane, such movements themselves give a sense of direction and thus portray a north-south turn.

The following up-down/north-south movements play a quantitative role in portraying a world view characteristic. Figure 4 below portrays a list of nonverbal symbolic patterns that demonstrates this up-down/north-south attribute. The nonverbal symbolic pattern for "lift up," however, is one that is worth mentioning. The Japanese word for this nonverbal pattern is "*isamu*," meaning spirited, cheerful, or happy. This depicts the notion of an elevated or heightens sense of mood and motivation. One can nevertheless experience the expansive vertical spirit of the dance through this one particular pattern.

Figure 4. Vertical nonverbal symbolic patterns

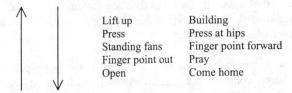

Lift up	Building
Press	Press at hips
Standing fans	Finger point forward
Finger point out	Pray
Open	Come home

Circular Motions

The motions of a circle are constituents of some of the nonverbal symbolic patterns. From the dancer's point of view, a circle is made with the motioning of the hand in front or to the side of him or her. At times, and this is more apparent for the audience, a circle is made when the entire body pivots on a heel or makes a circular movement with each step. This circular motion, although not conveyed in the story of creation, can symbolically signify "center." In this case, a circle refers in its most general sense to a particular spot on the ground, namely the Jiba.

Circular nonverbal symbolic movements also impose the tenet of circular time. For the agriculturally situated people of the era, time was indeed a circular entity with the changing seasons as the barometer. This, too, becomes a semiotic marker: its referents are brought into mind for meaning is created when executing circular motions. These circular nonverbal symbolic patterns also portray markers of wholeness—purity—of the symbolic instruments called forth by God in creating human beings, as we shall soon see, and this same attitude is what humankind ought to strive for. A circular notion of a "round" heart also connotes varying symbolic meaning. The following

108

movements listed in figure 5 below represent circular motions that suggest a world view meaning.

Figure 5. Circular nonverbal symbolic patterns

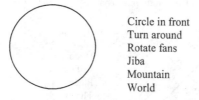

Circle in front
Turn around
Rotate fans
Jiba
Mountain
World

Horizontal Motions

There is one horizontally inclined movement with respect to a world view. This forms the notion of east-west when utilizing, for the sake of the argument, the head of the dancer representing itself as a marker for north. Although there is only one motion which crosses from left to right with respect to the world view, it is a salient one since it describes not only the east-west characteristic but the night and day attribute as is suggestive in the arbitrary title of the nonverbal symbolic pattern. Important to note is that fans were used in the early period of Tenrikyo's history which depicted a moon on one side and the sun on the other side of the fan. This clearly demonstrates the dimension of night and day. On a different level, we have both moon and the sun which moves across from east to west. Furthermore, the notion of the moon and the sun is a salient factor in the dogmatic representation of God the Parent. In so saying, then, it is also a relevant theme in the story of human creation.

Figure 6. Horizontal nonverbal symbolic pattern

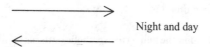

Night and day

Diagonal Motions

Finally there are the diagonal levels of the nonverbal symbolic patterns in construing a world view. The diagonal crossing motions of these nonverbal symbolic patterns semiotically mark notions of northeast–southwest and northwest–southeast points. Needless to say, once again, such genres are also found pertinent to the truth of creation. Of particular import, however, is the "hoeing" pattern. This pattern portrays in a very simple way the high value placed on working in the fields. This diagonal pounding of a tool provokes a nostalgic meaning since agricultural itself in our modern pluralistic setting has become evasive with respect to changing conditions.

Figure 7. Diagonal nonverbal symbolic patterns

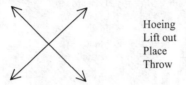

Hoeing
Lift out
Place
Throw

Order in the Nonverbal Symbolic Patterns

A multi-directional depiction of the nonverbal symbolic patterns is made when combining the patterns thus far mentioned into one diagram. Further, when perceiving this all-embracing signal in light of a different framework, it can be interpreted as a genre that portrays a formulation of orderly form. Simply put, the nonverbal symbolic patterns emphasize a world view which encompasses a model salient to the story of creation: the portrayal of the distinctive directions.

These patterns are illustrated here in order to demonstrate not only a particular course of direction but to delineate the import of order in what could be imagined as a formless state of being as well. Without enabling them to affirm something, as Geertz would say, the motions themselves would be meaningless. In other words, not only do the verbal symbolic patterns of the text imply a particular way in which order arises through spatial and temporal genres but that, even without the verbal symbolic patterns, the motions provide something similar to and compatible with Tenrikyo's most salient mythical representation, the story of creation. Figure 8 below encompasses what has been brought to the surface thus far.

Figure 8. The directions found in the nonverbal symbolic patterns

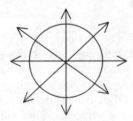

In his analysis of dance, one scholar offers the distinction between Appollonian and Dionysiac movements (van Der Leeuw 1963, 60–61). For him, the Dionysiac movement puts people into disorder. Through such ravaged confusion, however, humankind is able to continue life in an orderly fashion after the dance is over. A release, so to speak, is made in performing ecstatic, vivacious, and frenzy motions. The movements themselves are seen as actively powerful. On the other hand, the Appollonian movements are first and foremost a representation of order. Disorder seen and heard in life is thus complimented into an ordered configuration in a dance form: peace and calm fills the mind. He continues to say:

> The movement of the rhythm awakens awareness of a background to life, a cosmic order, which extends this life to its limits, where it has no purpose other than through and in that which is beyond, the holy (van Der Leeuw 1963, 61).

Taking into consideration this dichotomy, one notices almost instantaneously that the Teodori is strikingly Appollonian. The gestures and music are well ordered and serves as an impetus to fill the mind with quiet and thus settling it. Peace is one of the many outcomes that enter the dancer's mind after the performance. Needless to say, this dance extends into the realm of the sacred for the intention of the dance itself was one meant for God to rejoice in it.

In the story of creation, the world was once in chaos—a muddy ocean and formless—before any divine act took place. God, seeing this condition to be "unbearably tasteless," hit upon an idea to create humankind. In creating human beings, the first intention was to see humans live in joy—a condition that can be opposed with the chaotic state the world was in initially. In other words, an analogy of the term "joy" can be made with the term "order." This seems to be the foremost pattern of the dance itself. Things were formless at the beginning of time but both human beings and the world were created through God's intervention. This systematization of the world, with human beings playing a major role it, can be seen in connection with the nonverbal symbolic movements found in the world view: humanity is in chaos but order is made in the present through the performance of the dance.[1] More on this point as attention is directed to the intertext.

---

[1] By order, we refer to the conceptions of the general order of existence that Geertz speaks of in his work (Geertz 1973, 98–106). Order, of course, has also led other scholars to strive at approaching rituals singularly from this perspective. For instance, one view of this tendency can be outlined as follows: "Order, as used here, has three aspects. First, it suggests that ritual is a structured event that reflects a set of established relations between certain patterns of behavior and states or situations . . . . Second, order suggests predictability . . . . Finally, order suggests control and

Conceptions of the World in the Intertext

Truth of Origin as an Intertext

A few worthy observations can be made now that we have begun an analysis of the cosmological points found in the Teodori text. Our findings show that there is a pattern for which the symbols are being used, namely that they refer for the most part to the mythical portrayal of the teachings. The following verses refer specifically to what Tenrikyo associates as the "Truth of Origin" (*moto-no-ri*): *Yorozuyo*, 4; Song III, 1; Song III, 2; Song IV, 9; Song V, 2; Song V, 7; Song V, 9; Song VII, 8; Song VII, 9; Song IX, 9; Song IX, 10; Song XI, 1 and Song XI, 8.

A highly metaphorical construct of how this world and human beings came into existence, this story of creation is for many members the main thrust of the Tenrikyo teachings. In Geertzian terms, this story gives meaning to the paradox of how the world was created in the beginning and who created it. This story provides the key in figuring out the "problem of meaning" (Geertz 1973, 100) and therefore gives signification to those who believe in the aim of humankind's existence. In other words, the story of creation not only affirms something but holds the authority for believing it (Geertz 1973, 124).

Originally referred to as the *Doroumi Kōki* (Muddy Ocean Koki), or *Kōki Banashi* (Koki Stories), these stories were written by the early disciples out of their concern to remember the words conveyed to them by Nakayama Miki. These stories were written after Miki had already completed writing the Ofudesaki, one of Tenrikyo's normative scripture. The content and style of the Koki vary from author to author yet emphasis was placed on the event of what happened at the beginning of the world and how it was done. Because of its repudiating nature to the prevalent Shinto myths written in the *Kojiki* and *Nihonshoki*, copies of the Koki were confiscated several times as evidence against the early followers for "crimes of religious ideology" by the authorities (Niida 1986, 323).

From a historical point of view Miki did not write any of these scripts nor did she authorize any of them. These stories were written in the years 1881, and in each of the following years from 1883 to 1887. All together, various authors produced 40 versions by listening to the story narrated by Miki herself or by copying already existing ones (Iida 1986, 172). The two major writing styles used in these scribes were a narrative version and a 31 syllable Japanese poem style called *waka*. It was only when an official doctrine was compiled in 1949 by Tenrikyo Church Headquarters that the Koki Story, together with a thorough investigation of one of the normative scriptures written by Miki

---

manageability . . . . Ritual is, thus, a means of imposing order on the indeterminacy of the socio-cultural situation" (Gorman 1990, 26).

112

herself, the Ofudesaki, that the title "Truth of Creation" came to be (Iida 1986, 172).

Since this story is the crux of the cosmological meanings implied in the Teodori, we will insert the full English text of the story. This story can be found in chapter three of *The Doctrine of Tenrikyo*.

The Truth of Origin

In the beginning, the world was a muddy ocean. Tsukihi, God the Parent, finding this chaos unbearably tasteless, thought of creating human beings in order to see their joyous lives and thus share their joy.

Looking carefully through the muddy ocean, God saw a fish and a serpent amid many loaches. Planning to make them into models of husband and wife, God summoned them. Discerning their single-heartedness, God obtained their consent and received them, promising that when the years equal to the number of their first-born had elapsed, they would be returned to the Residence of Origin, the place of original conception, and would be adored by their posterity.

Continuing, God summoned an orc from the northwest and a turtle from the southeast. Again, after obtaining their consent, God received them and, after consuming them to test the flavor of their minds, determined their natures. Then God decided to use the orc as the instrument of the male organ, of bones, and of support; and the turtle as the instrument of the female organ, of skin, and of joining. Then God put the orc into the fish and the turtle into the serpent and established them as models of man and woman. God gave the sacred names of *Izanagi-no-Mikoto* to the model of man, the seed, and *Izanami-no-Mikoto* to the model of woman, the seedplot. To the divine principles of these instruments, God gave the names *Tsukiyomi-no-Mikoto* and *Kunisazuchi-no-Mikoto*, respectively.

Then God summoned an eel from the east, a flatfish from the southwest, a black snake from the west, and a globe-fish from the northeast, one after another. Again God first gained their consent, received them, and consumed them to test the nature of each.

God then decided to use the eel as the instrument for eating, drinking, and elimination, the flatfish for breathing and speaking, the black snake for pulling forth, and the globe-fish for cutting. To the divine principles of these instruments, God gave the sacred names of, respectively, *Kumoyomi-no-Mikoto*, *Kashikone-no-Mikoto*, *Otonobe-no-Mikoto*, and *Taishokuten-no-Mikoto*.

Thus, the models and instruments having been determined, the creation of human beings was begun. First God consumed all the loaches in the muddy ocean, tested the flavors of their nature, and made them the seeds for human beings. Then God the Parent, as *Tsuki-sama* (the Moon), entered the body of *Izanagi-no-Mikoto* and, as *Hi-sama* (the Sun), entered the body of *Izanami-no-Mikoto* and taught them the divine providence of creating human beings. Then nine hundred million, ninety-nine thousand, nine hundred and ninety-nine seeds were put into the body of *Izanami-no-Mikoto* in three days and three nights. *Izanami-no-Mikoto* remained there for three years and three months and gave birth in seventy-five days to as many children as there were seeds.

The first children thus born were all half an inch (5 *bu*) tall. Growing taller gradually, they reached a height of three inches (3 *sun*) in ninety-nine years. Then they all passed away for rebirth and their father, *Izanagi-no-Mikoto,* withdrew from physical life. However, *Izanami-no-Mikoto* again conceived the original number of children by the divine providence already taught her and, after ten months, gave birth to them again. The children, then too, were half an inch tall at birth and, after growing to three and a half inches (3 *sun* 5 *bu*) in ninety-nine years, all passed away for rebirth once more.

Then the children were conceived for the third time. They were again born half an inch tall and, this time, grew to four inches, (4 *sun*) in ninety-nine years. At that time, their mother, *Izanami-no-Mikoto*, said, "Now that they have grown so tall, in time they will reach the height of human beings five feet tall," and with a smile, withdrew from physical life. Then all her children, too, passed away for rebirth, deeply yearning for their mother.

After that, human beings were reborn eight thousand and eight times as worms, birds, beasts, and the like. Then they all passed away except a she-monkey. She conceived ten human beings at a time, five male and five female. They were born half an inch tall and grew taller gradually. When they grew to eight inches (8 *sun*), the bottom of the muddy ocean began to develop highs and lows by the providence of God the Parent. When they grew to one foot and eight inches (1 *shaku* 8 *sun*), land and sea, heaven and earth, and the sun and moon came to take form so as to be distinguishable. In the development of human beings from one foot and eight inches to three feet (3 *shaku*), twins were born from each conception, a male and a female. When humans reached three feet, one child was born from each conception and they began to speak. When they reached five feet (5 *shaku*), land and sea, heaven and earth, the whole universe, was completed, and human beings began to dwell on land.

God the Parent taught that human beings lived in water for nine hundred million and ninety thousand years, were trained for six thousand years in wisdom, and were instructed for three thousand nine hundred and ninety-nine years in letters.

(Tenrikyo Church Headquarters 1993a, 20–23)

Since there have been many interpretations of this story written elsewhere, (Hirano 1995; Iida 1986; Kurachi 1986; Matsumoto 1988; Morii 1990) the focus will be on the meanings of the story found implicitly with respect to the time and space dimensions of the Teodori. In order to do so, we will try to examine the basic symbolism in the story with reference to the original text, namely the Koki story. Prior to such dealings, an outline of the general meanings of the story by Tenrikyo members goes as follows: 1) human beings and this world were created by God and since all people are children of God; the relationship between human beings is that of brother and sister; 2) the purpose of humankind's creation is to live the Joyous Life; 3) the development of human beings is a result of God's workings; 4) the revelation by Nakayama Miki is in accordance with the promise made in the beginning; and 5) due to this creation a special service performance is made at the place of origin in accordance with the creation principle (Tenrikyo Overseas Mission Department 1986b, 33–34)

The Koki Texts

In a study of the providences of God the Parent (Sawai 1986, 79–110), the author outlines the special symbolic motifs used in the Koki story with reference to the Ofudesaki. He concludes that the four Koki Stories published elsewhere (Nakayama 1957) are coherent with the writings of the Ofudesaki. In so doing, and the point of our argument, the author affirms that there is an intrinsic relationship between the world and the human body and calls this correspondence *macrocosm* and *microcosm*, respectively (Sawai 1986, 97). This gives us the incentive to unfold such a world view which is related to the one found in the Teodori.

God the Parent's providence constitutes one of the major themes in the creation text. Using the imagery of different animals, giving them names of a mythical sort, and allowing them to move about according to these specific roles, it will be the task then to deconstruct a segment of it so that it can be applied to a world view that is coherent with the Teodori. It is important, nevertheless, to keep in mind that the people for whom this message was intended were people in the countryside of the early modern era in Japan for we find:

> They were not intellectuals but naive peasants, craftsmens, housewives, and the like, many of whom were illiterate. Their historical environment was one in which various traditional religio-cultural ideas and customs formed a melange. In order to understand the universal and eternal truth about the origin of mankind, Oyasama used many concrete symbols and metaphors which were familiar to them (Matsumoto 1988, 17).

Data collected by the writer mentioned above (Sawai 1986) will be made use of for the following description. The Koki materials used in his essay are four. The first set is titled "notes at hand" and were written in a narrative style in 1881. The disciple Yamazawa, in a poetic style called *waka*, wrote the second in 1881. The third text, written by another disciple named Kita, was written in a narrative style in 1881. Finally, the fourth Koki text examined in Sawai's article was written by a disciple named Masui in the year 1883 and is perhaps the most authoritative of the Koki Stories. As the historian Takano notes, however, Masui heard of Miki's talks longer than any other and as a result of this we find descriptive detail in his writings (Sawai 1986, 89).

It should be remembered that Miki did not authorize or approve any of the Koki texts that she read, despite their total number amounting to forty. These texts provide for this section the interpretations that were made by the disciples concerning a major tenet in the world view—the implicit meanings attached to various symbols. The written texts, either in narrative or poetic styles, reflect the writer's understanding of certain shared vehicles of meanings that affected the lives of the people. That is, the aim is to clarify the connotative meanings of the symbols that interrelate with the Teodori world view pattern through an observation of these Koki stories.

Animals That Carry Symbolic Meaning

First, an examination of the symbolic animals mentioned in the Koki texts is in need. All animals that were used in the beginning are said to have given their consent for the creational operation. These animals came from six directions to a single point in time and space known now as the Jiba, the place of creation. More importantly are the characteristics of these animals that consolidate worldly matters with the bodily physical ones. In other words, the characteristics of each animal demonstrate a telling story how the human body and the world around it came to be perceived as an embodiment of the divine.

The Yamazawa text notes the following: a *tortoise* has strong skin and does not fall down since it stands firm; a *grampus* which is powerful; a *fish* which has a human face and skin without any scales; and a *serpent* which is honest (Sawai 1986, 90–91). The Kita text, written in 1881, notes the following: a *tortoise* which does not fall down and has strong skin; a *grampus* good at propping up anything and has the spirit of propping; an *eel* which has a slimy skin and is slippery in spirit; a *flatfish*, one whose body is flat; a *globefish* which is good at cutting; *black serpent* with a long-range view; a *fish* that has a human face and smooth skin without scales; and a *serpent* which has a human body without any scales and a long body (Sawai 1986, 90–91).

The most authoritative of the Koki Stories, the one written by the disciple Masui in 1883, has the following to say: a *tortoise* whose skin is strong stands firm on the ground and does not fall on the ground; a fish called a *grampus* is powerful and props up very much; an *eel* which is powerful and so slippery one cannot take hold of it; a *flatfish* used like a fan in making a breeze since this one has a flat body; a *globefish* that when it is eaten very much one is made ill by it; a *black serpent* that is powerful but cannot be cut although one attempts to pull it apart; a *fish* that has a body like a human being and is honest; and a *white serpent* with a human body without any scales and since its heart is straightforward it is honest (Sawai 1986, 90–91).

It is obvious that these animals are not simply animals but are given special meaning since they signify to the authors of these texts more than what they actually are. They become the dominant symbols in the process for which

116

one is able to grasp the notion of the world: these animals carry deep meaning when viewed in light of the creation text. That is, they become important bridges for constructing a world view. Each of the above-mentioned animal was used in the creation of human beings and they were given the following divine names:

Kunisazuchi-no-Mikoto: tortoise   Tsukiyomi-no-Mikoto: grampus (orc)
Kumoyomi-no-Mikoto: eel   Otonobe-no-Mikoto: black snake
Taishokuten-no-Mikoto: globefish   Kashikone-no-Mikoto: flatfish
Izanami-no-Mikoto: serpent   Izanagi-no-Mikoto: fish

Divine Providences in the World

The above interrelationship between animal and its divine name becomes clear when attributes of their workings in the world are examined. Such workings in the world are known to be the providences of God the Parent and for this reason they are also considered to be instruments of God the Parent, not only at the time of human creation, but equally for the present. Each instrument, possessing an original animal-like character as underlined thus far, uses its trait to impart blessings in the world. That is, each *positive* animal trait corresponds to benefit the development of the world and its symbolic value becomes meaningful in protecting the present living world. This particular viewpoint, once again, can be traced in the Koki stories.

For this section, it would be important to keep the animals and their characteristics in mind. Once again, the Koki texts as examined by one author (Sawai 1986) will be drawn from and the providence given to each divine instrument in the world will be underlined. The text written by Masui reiterates that *Omotari* provides the providence of warmth; *Kunisazuchi* provides for the junction in the world; *Kashikone* fosters wind; *Taishokuten* is a divinity of the scissors in the world and provides the providence of cutting in general; *Otonobe* is the providence of pulling forth food, crops, and so on (Sawai 1986, 96). The Yamazawa text speaks of *Kashikone* as wind; *Taishokuten* as the providence of pulling forth food, crops, and so on; and together with the Masui text, the same writer speaks of *Taishokuten* as the divinity of crops and of pulling forth in general (Sawai 1986, 96).

Kunitokotachi, *Tsukiyomi*, *Kumoyomi*, *Izanami* and *Izanagi* were not mentioned to relate to the world in any way. Yet a clue to where they stand lies in the functions of the human body. Elsewhere, it is believed that the workings of God in the human body are the same as the workings of God in the world. The following is an excerpt in oral form of what Nakayama Miki said, "If you understand (the truth of God's providence in) the human body, you will recognize everything (of the divine providence) in the world" (Takano 1980,

76). We also find another event concerning the dichotomy between the human body and the world:

> One day when one of the followers asked Oyasama, "How far is it from east to west or from north to south?" She replied, "It is like when you lie down, stretching both of your arms." At that time Oyasama also said, "The earth is like the human body. Gold and other minerals correspond to nails in the human body. Hot springs are like the prime organs; trees and plants are like human hair; and rivers are like blood vessels. They have the same truth" (Moroi 1953).

In the Koki text there is reference being made to the interrelatedness of human body and the world. For example, in reference to *Kashikone*, the Yamazawa text marks it as the providence of speaking with breath and wind; in reference to *Taishokuten*, the same author adjoins that it is a divinity of cutting off the child from its mother at birth and cutting the breath of life when passing away—a divinity of the scissors of the world (Sawai 1986, 96). These suggest that the providences found in the human body should also connote the providences in the world.

All four Koki Stories further conveys something of the providences in the human body. The Masui text speaks of *Kunitokotachi* as a divinity who provides the providence of the eyes and the body fluids in the human body; *Omotari* as a divinity who provides the providence of warmth in the human body; *Kunisazuchi* represents the skin and joining and the female organ; *Tsukiyomi* represents bones and support and the male organ; *Kumoyomi* symbolizes eating, drinking, and elimination; *Kashikone* represents breathing and makes a human being speak with it; *Taishokuten* represents the function of cutting off a child at birth and of cutting off the breath of life when passing away; *Otonobe* is pulling forth in general; *Izanagi* is the seed of human beings; and finally, *Izanami* is the seedbed of human beings (Sawai 1986, 93–94).

The Yamazawa text, the Kita text, as well as the 1881 notes at hand, speak of *Kunitokotachi* as the function in the human body of the eyes and the body fluids; *Omotari* as representing the function of warmth; *Kunisazuchi* as representing skin and joining; *Tsukiyomi* as portraying bones and support; *Kumoyomi* symbolizing in the human body as eating, drinking, and elimination; *Kashikone* as representing breathing with the Yamazawa text emphasizing it as the divinity of breathing (Sawai 1986, 93). Furthermore, the three texts make reference to *Izanagi* as the seed of human beings and *Izanami* as the seedbed of human beings (Sawai 1986, 94).

For the Yamazawa text and 1881 notes at hand, *Taishokuten* symbolizes the function of cutting of the child from its mother at birth and cutting off the breath of life when passing away. The Yamazawa text, together with the Kita text, supplements the above suggestion of *Taishokuten* as a divinity who cuts off the child from its mother at birth. The writer of the Yamazawa text speaks of *Otonobe* as the providence of pulling out the child from its mother during birth. Supplementing this, the author of the Kita text speaks of *Otonobe* as the divinity of pulling forth in general (Sawai 1986, 93).

A few claims are made, then, by relating the providences in the human body and projecting them onto the world. That is to say, *Kunitokotachi* symbolizes water. *Tsukiyomi* symbolizes joining in general. *Kumoyomi* symbolizes the rise and fall of moisture. *Izanagi* symbolizes the seed and *Izanami* symbolizes the seedplot. Using the animals and the divine names given to each animal, figure 9 demonstrates the workings in the world found in the story of creation.

Figure 9. Divine names and their providences

Kunitokotachi
Moon
Water

Tsukiyomi		**Taishokuten**
Orc	**Izanami**	Globefish
Support in general	Serpent	Cutting in general
	Seedplot	

◯

Otonobe		**Kumoyomi**
Black snake	**Izanagi**	Eel
Pulling forth in general	Fish	Rise and fall of moisture
	Seed	

Kashikone		**Kunisazuchi**
Flatfish	**Omotari**	Turtle
Wind	Sun	Joining in general
	fire	

The Principle of the World: A Two-in-One Relation
There is much importance placed on this dichotomy found in doctrinal texts. In the above diagram the contrasting points of humankind and the world, as well as the oppositions that arise from within these pairs, are made clear. For example, the structure of severing/joining, fire/water, male/female, seed/seedplot, and pulling/pushing are notions which model pairs of opposites are placed together to form a somewhat harmonic unity at the same time.

Needless to say, the balance between these contrasting pairs is the foremost principle in the conceptualization of the world.

Contrasting elements of humankind and the world as perceived in the creation text are not the only two objects that serve as a world view pattern. These opposing and apparently conflicting factors give meaning to the disparities that can be thought of as a set of binary contrasts coming together. Such poles, however, are perceived not so much of their diverging degrees but for their harmonic unity. Members often speak of this dichotomy as the "truth of heaven," as the principle of "oneness-in-two," or the "truth of two-in-one." This consists of being one of the guiding world view markers in the Tenrikyo faith.

> This world, created by God the Parent, is based entirely on the law of the integration of two antitheses. This law is not restricted to integrating the individuality and sociality of man, or of the self and non-self. *Everything* from the order of the universe to the mental functions of man, including such antitheses as heaven and earth, water and fire, man and woman, the body and the mind, consciousness and unconsciousness, stand in this two-in-one relationship (Hashimoto 1979, 33–34; emphasis added).

There is reason to note that opposite pairs that formulate into a single unity are not limited to the realm of Tenrikyo's creation story. This world view character cannot be said to be a unique one. Yet highlighting such a character and dramatizing it—almost in an exaggerated style—gives deeper meaning for the adherents who profess it. Not only does this two-in-one principle lie within the realm of a mythical representation of when, where, and how humanity was created but becomes an important authoritative paradigm, a *model for* believing it. This underlying model is also one of the pillars for a world view found in the Teodori. It is a character of many religions of Asia and has its roots from the ideal known commonly as the yin-yang principle. Sasaki notes:

> Here in the Creation Story, the divine itself is shown to follow the same principle of two-in-one. And the ten providences or functions of the divine are also paired in this way, representing in the physical world and in the human body as well as social relations the delicate balance between opposite but necessarily complimentary parts. Harmony and unity is achieved in the proper balance (Sasaki 1980a, 52).

A summary of what has been mentioned so far can be stated from what Tenrikyo members refer to as the "complete providence of God the Parent." The providence is complete since it mirrors not only the workings of the world but the workings within the human body that reflect the world as well. Such macrocosm/microcosm entails the picture of what the world is constructed of.

Members of the Tenrikyo faith are known to recite this text in churches and some are required to recite this as part of a daily prayer. We read:

Kunitokotachi-no-Mikoto: in the human body, the providence of the eyes and fluids; in the world, the providence of water.

Omotari-no-Mikoto: in the human body, the providence of warmth, in the world, the providence of fire.

Kunisazuchi-no-Mikoto; in the human body, the providence of the female organ, of skin and joining; in the world, the providence of joining in general.

Tsukiyomi-no-Mikoto: in the human body, the providence of the male organ, of bones and support; in the world, the providence of support in general.

Kumoyomi-no-Mikoto: in the human body, the providence of eating, drinking, and elimination; in the world, the providence of the rise and fall of moisture.

Kashikone-no-Mikoto: in the human body, the providence of breathing and speaking; in the world, the providence of wind.

Taishokuten-no-Mikoto: the providence of cutting off the ties to its mother at birth, and also in cutting off the breath of life when one passes away for rebirth; in the world, the providence of cutting in general.

Otonobe-no-Mikoto: the providence of pulling out the child from its mother during birth; in the world, the providence of pulling forth in general.

Izanagi-no-Mikoto: the model of man, the seed.

Izanami-no-Mikoto: the model of woman, the seedplot.

(Tenrikyo Church Headquarters 1993a, 30–31)

The Kagura Service as an Intertext

Transcending the concept of the principle of the two-in-one dichotomy, however, is the Jiba, the name given to the spot of ground where all human beings is said to have been conceived in the creation story. Identified by Nakayama Miki herself in 1875 with the assistance of some of her closest disciples, this place is the center of the world for the Tenrikyo faithful. It is taught that this place is set apart from other places and the region which extends around the Jiba is referred to as "the Residence," a term that is repeatedly marked in the Teodori. The significance of the Jiba is threefold: it is the place where God the Parent and Oyasama reside, it is the place where humankind was first conceived, and it is the place around which the Kagura Service is performed.

Marking the exact location of the Jiba is a wooden pillar called the Kanrodai, literally "the sweet dew stand." The Kanrodai is a hexagonal structure consisting of thirteen tiered wooden blocks.[2] It is taught that when

---

[2] The first hexagonal tier, which lays flat on the ground, has a diameter of 90 centimeters and is 24 centimeters in height. The tier that is placed on top of the first one has a diameter of 73 centimeters and possesses the same height as the first. The next ten hexagonal tiers that are placed on top of one another have a diameter of 36 centimeters with the height measuring 18 centimeters. The

the Joyous Life takes concrete form "sweet dew" is to descend from heaven, vividly marking a reality of a new world order. This dew, as Tenrikyoists are taught, will only fall on apex of this stand when all human beings reach the desired level of spiritual maturity. It is around the Jiba that the central focus of Tenrikyo takes place for it is where the Kagura Service is performed. Needless to mention, this service constitutes one of the more important intertextual aspects of the Teodori.

The Significance of the Kagura Service
In the performance of the Salvation Service—another term for the Kagura Service in Tenrikyo—dancers representing the ten divine providences at the time of human creation perform a ritual that mirrors the creation story. These dancers, however, do not line side by side as done in the Teodori. On the contrary, however, eight of the dancers face the Kanrodai and encompass the center of the world. Two of the dancers, namely *Izanami* and *Izanagi*, wear hexagonal shaped headpieces to demonstrate their affinity to the Kanrodai. Although their true position should be on top of the Jiba, as foretold in the creation story, they stand face to face to the side. Through this ritual a reenactment of the creation is made in the present. The description of the other masks and the dancer's positions are as follows:

> *Kunitokotachi*: a male lion face with an open mouth and a long white hair. A tail hanging from the mask is fastened to the wrist of *Taishokuten*;
> *Omotari*: a female lion face with a closed mouth and black hair. Three tails hanging from the mask extend in three directions and fastened to the wrists of *Kumoyomi*, *Otonobe*, and *Kashikone*.
> *Tsukiyomi*: a male face representing a long-nosed goblin. A figure of an orc is strapped to the back of the dancer.
> *Kunisazuchi*: a female face. A figure of a turtle is strapped to the back of the dancer.
> *Otonobe*: a male face.The wrist of the dancer is fastened with a tail from the mask of *Omotari*.
> *Kumoyomi*: a female face. The wrist of the dancer is fastened with a tail from the mask of *Omotari*.
> *Kashikone*: a male face. The wrist of the dancer is fastened with a tail from the mask of *Omotari*.
> *Taishokuten*: a female face.
> *Izanami*: a female face with a hexagonal headpiece.
> *Izanagi*: a male face with hexagonal headpiece.

---

final tier, one that is placed on top of the stand, has the same measurement as the second tier from the bottom. The total height is approximately 249 centimeters.

This Service takes place on the twenty-sixth day of each month and celebrated only in the precincts of the main sanctuary around the Kanrodai. Worshippers are allowed to get only a glimpse of the dancer's movements since the architectural framework of the worship halls are constructed in such a manner that people sitting inside the sanctuaries are unable to see the Kanrodai which rises eight feet from the ground floor. Its enigmatic performance therefore remains in the hearts of the observers as a mystical source of energy for those attending and for the rest of the world.[3]

The performers of this sacred service are chosen from within the inner circle of the administrative staff at Church Headquarters. The ten performers and the musical instrument players alternate roles on a monthly basis. The role of the Shinbashira and his wife, however, remain the same throughout all performances and that is to dance in the position of *Kunitokotachi* and *Omotari*, representing the moon and the sun, water and fire, respectively. The song text for the Kagura Service is the same as that of the seated service mentioned above in the descriptive part of the monthly service. Part one is repeated twenty-one times and part two is performed only once. Part three, however, is performed seven times in a set of three, amounting to a total of twenty-one times.

In developing the structure and meaning of the Kagura Service one Tenrikyo scholar (Hashimoto 1981) illustrates that there are at least three meanings made explicit through the performance of this service. The first meaning is found in the construction of a prayer for which humankind ask for the blessings of God. It is taught that by this performance human beings pray to God the Parent so that His creative power at the time of creation and throughout the subsequent periods of development will continue in the present and far into the future. By this continuity, humankind is regenerated—capable of living anew—and hence, is able to lead a life full of joy. Salvation is manifested only through the workings of God and human beings must perform the service as a condition for invoking such blessings.

The second meaning is in the act of performance itself where humanity regains the relationship it has lost with God the Parent. In other words, aligning one's mind with the Jiba-Kanrodai—the source and origin—and taking part in the movements of the dancers that manifest God the Parent at the time of human creation, a relationship between human beings as children and God as parent is reconfirmed. This obviously points to the teaching that

---

[3] When an historian of religion paid a visit to an American Tenrikyo church setting a discussion on why the Kagura Service is hidden from the general public took place among those Japanese-American followers who gathered. Many voiced their opinion against having the most important Tenrikyo ritual hidden from them. The historian of religion attempted to resolve the question by speaking in terms of a scholar saying that things that are hidden represent most its sacred character (Ellwood 1974, 64–67).

humankind consists only of brothers and sisters of the world under one loving and caring God: there exists no stranger in the world.

Finally, the third meaning found in the Kagura Service concerns the import of living at the time of the beginning of the world. Following this assertion, then, humankind is able to live in accord with the will of God the Parent through the performance of the service. Humanity is reminded of what, where, and how God the Parent conceived human beings and how such order was created. More importantly, then, performing the Kagura Service signifies for Tenrikyo members a return to that pristine original state of being: the purified mind as recognized in the "minds" of the symbolic animals used. The performance becomes all that more appealing for the observers since a manifestation of this fresh state can be read in the story of creation. Hence the Jiba, with the Kanrodai representing this spot, is the focal point of Tenrikyo's cosmological project. It indicates to the Tenrikyo community the spatial and temporal dimensions of creation. The Kagura Service that intrinsically manifests this perspective is made clear via its performance.

The same dimensions, although not all that apparent to the performers, can also be seen through the Teodori. The Teodori, too, adheres the same qualitative factors of space and time found in the performance of the Kagura Service. It is argued here that the difference is a matter of degree and not one in point. That is, the Teodori world view cannot but be closely related to this ultimate particular ritual since similar inherent qualities are attributed to it. Such qualities as marking order and staging significance—making sense of something that would otherwise seem meaningless—is the scope of both world views.

In the next section we enter into a normative text, namely that of the Ofudesaki. The meanings of this text that are linked with the formation of the ritual dance are many so the citing of verses are limited to those which provide patterns of a world view coherent with the Teodori. This, for the most part, comprises of what has been said so far. Prior to concluding this section, however, we cite an interesting interpretation of the Jiba:

> The Jiba can be regarded as the center of the world, and the Kanrodai as the axis of the universe. This means the core of faith cannot be shifted and the direction man looks outward is one point, which is the source from which salvation starts. Furthermore, the Jiba is the place where the Parent of mankind resides. The centripetal faith that moves toward the one point, the Jiba, brings about in turn the centrifugal mission. The stronger the converging force toward the center becomes, the stronger the diffusing force becomes (Sato 1986, 163).

Scripture as an Intertext

A formulation of a world view pattern of the Teodori has begun to take shape. This section serves to unravel the claims made thus far by using intertextual material in the hopes of providing a "thick description." Prior to going into this, only a brief outline of the existing normative scriptures is called for since detailed information can be found elsewhere (Inoue and Eynon 1987; Tenrikyo Missionaries Association 1993; Tenrikyo Overseas Mission Department 1996).

Tenrikyo theology, as is any theology, is based on its normative scriptures. In the case of Tenrikyo, and unlike other religions that trace its theology to a single source, there are three separate scriptures that Tenrikyoists refer to as the inception for theology. They are the Mikagura-uta, the Ofudesaki, and the Osashizu—three distinct texts each designed with different titles.

The Mikagura-uta, as mentioned from the start, is the text utilized for the Kagura Service and the Teodori. Nakayama Miki wrote it with a specific purpose of accompanying it with the playing of musical instruments combined with dancing hand movements. In other words, the portrayal of the text is not only a form of Tenrikyo scripture but also a dance-song as some maintain (Sasaki 1980a, 64). Although the Mikagura-uta utilizes a different form of writing when compared with the Ofudesaki, one missionary has claimed that it can also be taken as another form of it (Fukaya 1962, 5). Repeated claims by Tenrikyo leaders are that the Ofudesaki and the Mikagura-uta are one and the same: both represent the model life of Nakayama Miki. As we have seen, the Mikagura-uta can be utilized as a scriptural source but many regard it as being complete only when the singing of the verbal symbolic patterns and the dancing of the nonverbal ones are synchronized and performed together with others. As Fukaya elicits:

> The Mikagura-uta is not intended merely for reading at a desk. It must be carried out into action (dance). It is not intended merely for me to read and to sing. It must also be read and sung by others (Fukaya 1962, 4).

The Ofudesaki, literally "the tip of the writing brush," is a poetic form of the Mikagura-uta. Nakayama Miki wrote this text from the years 1869 to 1882. This text consists of 1,711 verses divided in seventeen parts. To compile this text Miki used a traditional poetic style known as *waka*, a thirty-one syllable poem transcribed onto two lines. Noteworthy is the style of writing she imposed in the Ofudesaki which uses a minimum of difficult Chinese characters and a vast amount of Japanese phonetic syllabary. Throughout the entire 1,711 stanzas, only forty-nine diverse Chinese characters are used. This style was used so that people without literary knowledge of the language could easily memorize the verses (Inoue and Eynon 1987, xvii). An oral tradition handed down to members relates how Nakayama Miki composed the Ofudesaki:

> Concerning the Ofudesaki, Oyasama said: "You know there is the Fudesaki. What do you think of it? The seventeen parts were not completed in a short while. God spoke into my ears, saying, "Do not look at any writings, even the charge book from the bean curd shop." I wondered why. Then God said "Brush, brush, take up the brush." I took the brush up for the first time at New Year's when I became seventy-two years old. And when I took up the brush, My hand moved by itself. From heaven, God did it. After what was to be done was finished, My hand became numb and it could not be moved. God said, "Calm your mind, and read this. If you find something you cannot understand, ask Me." I added brush strokes when I found something that I could not understand. That is the Fudesaki" (Tenrikyo Church Headquarters 1976, 16).

Chronologically later in its compilation, the Osashizu, the Divine Directions, is the third set of normative scriptures in Tenrikyo. During the later period of Miki's life, she voiced concern to have a carpenter named Iburi Izo succeed her in spiritual matters. He would subsequently go into trance and speak the words of God. It was only after the passing of Nakayama Miki that he was completely settled as the *Honseki* or, the main seat, and a systematized version of his utterances became evident. For twenty years following Miki's withdrawal from physical life, disciples gathered around him and dictated his words onto paper and compared them. This comparison of notes eventually led to a compilation of the first Osashizu set published in its complete form in 1931 and then re-launched in the years of 1963 to 1966 for it to be distributed to churches. At present the Osashizu consists of seven volumes and only a fragment of these revelations are translated into other languages by Church Headquarters.

Two typologies can be made of the Osashizu. The first one concerns timely directions in the Osashizu. These instructions were given through the mouth of Iburi at any time of day. Many of these directions came during the middle of the night. The other type of writings in the Osashizu is called "questions in response to inquiries." These directions arose from petitions made to Iburi Izo by a follower concerning a disorder in the body, a problem, or future decisions that were to be made. Since the Osashizu consists of seven volumes the intertextual aspects of the Teodori's world view with respect to normative scriptures will be limited to the poetic verses of the Ofudesaki.

Ofudesaki as an Intertext

Many of the points—if not all—in question that concern the world view found in the Teodori pertain to the notion of creation and the mythical representation of it through the Truth of Origin. In the performance of the

Teodori, the creation of human beings and the exact place of that creation is exemplified. It has been argued that this, too, generates an expressive world view pattern. When the nonverbal symbolic pattern refer to "jiba," for example, a circle is made just in front of the dancer while the verbal symbol is that of singing, "jiba." Both body movements as well as the conceptualization of it become synchronized in a dance form.

To perceive a better understanding of the conceptualization of the term "jiba," however, it is important to look into other scriptural sources in refining its definition as well as broadening that meaning onto another level of understanding. In bringing this understanding to another level, then, an attempt to recreate an intertextual pattern that exists in the eyes of the performers themselves is being made. In other words, when a performer of the Teodori dances to the text of "jiba," it goes without saying that other objects enter his or her mind and are presumed to constitute the intertext.

By intertext, once again, it is assumed to be that which brings to mind other "texts" which assist in delineating or further embodying the main text. By doing so, a better perception is being provided—a thick description—of the original text, the Teodori under inquiry. As a rule, the more qualitative the intertext, the better the description of the text becomes. This develops and highlights other quadrants of the text that may not be all that apparent. The main question here is to unfold the Ofudesaki's intertextuality that implicitly generates back to the Teodori's world view. In doing so, the world view categories that have already been cited in the Teodori text are used.

The Origin

The story on how creation of the world took place is certainly a relevant intertext, as it has already been argued so far, and verses that explicate this point are repeatedly marked in scripture. This aspect has been emphasized in more than one occasion as supporting the Teodori with a world view. Finding it as a major motif for cosmological building in the Teodori, then, it is of no surprise to find the same theme running through other sorts of rituals whether tacitly or implicitly interacting with this world view. With this conceptualization of the world, other sources point to this significance of the creative action of God:

> The beginning of this world was a muddy ocean. Therein were only loaches. (IV, 122); I drew forth Izanagi and Izanami and taught them the providence of how to begin human beings (VI, 31); At the origin were a fish and a serpent in the muddy ocean. I drew them up and began the first couple. (VI, 32); In the beginning of origin, this world was a muddy ocean. Therein were only loaches. (VI, 33); Among them were a fish and a serpent. Looking closely, I saw that they had human faces. (VI, 34); These instruments being *Kunisazuchi* and *Tsukiyomi*, if I should put them into their bodies, (VI, 37);

And call together *Kumoyomi*, *Kashikone*, *Otonobe*, and *Taishokuten*. (VI, 38); I began human beings, taking a fish and a serpent as seed and seedbed. (VI, 44); Looking carefully within, I found loaches, a fish and a serpent, and other creatures, too. (VI, 83); I called them together and conferred with them to begin My providence for human beings. (VI, 84); In order to begin a world which did not exist, I, Tsukihi, devoted Myself at every step. (VI, 85); Even until now, everyone has known the moon and the sun, but there is no one who knows the true origin. (X, 14); The very beginning of this world was at Shoyashiki Village of Yamabe County in Yamato Province. (XI, 69); There, at the place known as the Nakayama Residence, appear instruments of human beginnings. (XI, 70); Among the instruments used in the beginning of human beings at this Residence, *Izanagi* and *Izanami*, (XII, 42); *Tsukiyomi*, *Kunisazuchi*, *Kumoyomi*, and *Kashikone* are the primary instruments. (XII, 43); Then the one called *Otonobe* is the primary instrument for the crops. (XII, 145); One is an instrument used to begin human beings. The other is for the providence for all crops. (XII, 149); Listen! This origin is the venerable *Kunitokotachi* and *Omotari*! (XVI, 12); After looking through the muddy waters, these personages drew a fish and a serpent to them (XVI, 13).

Mountains

After creating human beings and the world there is reference being made to people actually living in it. Among the many terms used when referring to the people in the world, the author uses the same symbol as in the Teodori, namely, mountains. When speaking of those on the mountains, however, there is reference being made to its antithesis, namely, the low valleys. This gives a hint at unfolding the meaning when the dance movement "mountain" is performed or when the verbal symbolic pattern "mountain" is sung during the ritual dance.

I can see fire and water in the high mountains. Can you not see this with you own eyes? (II, 40); Among the high mountains, the distinctions between those of *Nihon* and those of *Kara*[4] is also to be made by the pillar. (II, 46); The high mountains are doing as they please with the whole world, but they cannot see the future. (III, 48); The central pillar of the high mountains is that of *Kara*. This is the prime cause of the anger of God. (III, 57); After listening to the sermons of those on the high mountains, listen to the teachings of God in Truth and ponder. (III, 148); Until now, the high mountains have been boastful while the low valleys withered. (IV, 120); From now on I shall teach both the high mountains and the low valleys about the beginnings of origin. (IV, 121); Unaware of this, what is the thinking of the high mountains who are managing everything as they please?

---

4 Concerning *Nihon* and *Kara*, we find: "These terms are the components of a geographical metaphor that expresses the distance between the intention of God the Parent and a person's understanding of it. Consequently, these terms do not refer to any actual regions or to peoples inhabiting them" (Tenrikyo Church Headquarters 1993b, 266–267).

(VI, 66); Whatever the high mountains may say or think, it is all from their human thoughts. (VI, 69); Until now, the high mountains, boastful, have thrived and done as they please in every matter. (VI, 72); This is what My returns mean in truth. Beware, all of you on the high mountains! (VI, 79); Unaware of this, the high mountains at present are rampant and doing as they please. (VI, 89); Beware, you grand shrines and high mountains whoever! There is no knowing when Tsukihi will rush out. (VI, 92); In this return, I shall clear away the grand shrines and high mountains. Let all of you be aware! (VI, 115); Day by day and step by step, those on the high mountains will come to Me to request or inquire whatever things. (XII, 168); Tsukihi sincerely desires only to end the wars among those on the high mountains. (XIII, 50); It is difficult to do this Service because of the high mountains, but God gives you firm assurance. (XIII, 53); Listen! Though the high mountains, boastful, have done as they pleased to the low valleys, (XIII, 56); Whatever kind of people may be rampant on the high mountains, no one knows the truth. (XIII, 97); This talk is not for a particular place. It is for the high mountains as well as for the low valleys. (XIII, 109); Until today, though the grand shrines and high mountains have thrived and done as they pleased, (XIV, 30); Though until this time the high mountains have given directives on every matter, (XIV, 43); In this world, whether it be in the high mountains or the low valleys, everyone is a child of Mine, the Parent. (XIV, 53); Until now, the high mountains, boastful, have noisily done as they pleased. (XV, 57); On this matter, you on the high mountains as well as in the low valleys, set your mind so as not to be unaware (XV, 71).

As for a world view conception concerning mountains, then, we have already emphasized that the symbolic meaning of it in the Teodori places emphasis on a particular location—a geographical area that is far from the center. Such being the case, it takes on more meaning when perceived through a missionary paradigm, one in which a missionary must go into these areas in order to carry out his or her missionary work. The mountains represented regions where wilderness existed and such characteristics of unordered form were an attribute of the people who did not understand the teachings of Nakayama Miki. In other words, order was made present by a complete understanding of her teachings. In retrospect, then, going to the mountains to spread the teachings found in the Teodori is symbolically given new meaning. That is, mountains represent an unordered geographical location where order should be made as well as representing a given body of people who, because of this chaotic state of affairs, are far from understanding the teachings. The Ofudesaki, however, seems to go even more further as to explicitly concentrate on a particular shading of the mountain, that is, the high mountains.

In the verses of the Ofudesaki, we sense that the writer used the term "mountain" in particular reference to people outside and above—in the periphery—of her teachings. Nakayama Miki, in using mountain as a descriptive device also adds the quality, "high," to underline the distinctiveness of this particular usage. The high mountains for Miki were those people who lived far from the source but were known to rule others, for example, who lived in the bottom of the valleys. These people were considered in the eyes of the writer as an obstruction that interfered with the divine plan of God the Parent.

In perceiving the above motifs as such, then, we can see that there are more than one way to perceive such symbolically utilized tools in conveying meaning. In the Teodori the text speaks of mountains as areas of geographical import and therefore connotatively signifies a mind that is far from understanding the teachings. The Ofudesaki, on the other hand, makes a clear distinction that it is not only a geographical place at stake where one is able to engage in missionary work but reference is also being made to a minority who hold power and authority to impose political, economic, and religious ideals onto a larger body of people.

The World

Appearing twice in the Ofudesaki is a verse that can be said to provide a dominant world view. That is to say, the entire world is God and God the entire world.

> This universe is the body of God. Ponder this in all matters.
>
> III, 40 and 135

We can see that the entire universe is the body of God and the world is not an exception from this rule. It goes without saying that we are embodied in God's bosom and in likewise manner we are constantly under the protection of God. Such protection has begun from the time of our creation to the present and far into the future. In the verses that follow it is important to notice that God began the world: God is the originator of everything and God is the Origin. There are expressive commandments and likewise consequences upon voicing this claim:

> Among the words of God, who began this world, there is not even a single mistake in a thousand. (I, 43); I am God of Origin, who began the human beings of this world. Yet there may be no one who knows Me. (III, 15); God, who began this world, teaches the truth. Never take it to be false. (III, 68); To God, who began this world, all of you in the world are equally My beloved children. (IV, 62); I have not yet shown any of the free and unlimited workings of God, who began this world. (IV, 116); To God, who began this world, all things whatever are seen. (XII, 40).

A reflection on this world view portrays the world is given meaning as such in so far as there are lines which enable one to demarcate one place from the next. That is, because lines are drawn from one concrete reality to the next, a general order of existence is justly perceived. Harmony, which is an important outcome of the previously mentioned two-in-one principle, can only be achieved by first identifying such boundaries which will later enable the same factors to blend in unity. In other words, an identity must be revealed so that harmony among them can be realized. One is unable to know how to establish harmony if one is ignorant of the components that need to be mended together. Joy becomes manifest if harmony is realized between two diverging sources: order is acknowledged and meaning is found therein. Order can only come about in the world when disparities are combined into one.

Concrete Areas Encompassing the World View

In the attempt to map out the dominant world view pattern as traced in the Teodori text, its resources were unraveled from one intertext to the next. The springboard for such classification in the endeavor has been to utilize the verbal and nonverbal symbolic patterns of the text itself. It is from here that we have referred in most part to the other texts, namely our intertexts.

Concrete places, it seems, hold high antecedents that form part of an intimate world view category. In the aim to draw out a coherent depiction of a world view, particular places and explicit regions spoken in the Teodori become a powerful and meaningful pattern for the dancer. This significant pattern becomes part of a concrete reality in that, as Geertz would say, names and places are "really real" insofar as they convey a special symbolic conception. One way to illustrate this is that when the word "jiba" appears in the text and a dancer sings as well as draws out the nonverbal symbolic movement, s/he is also reminded of the really real concrete place known as Jiba. The aim here is to map out and demonstrate these concrete names and places. In doing so, an image of a really real world should become more visible from which the Teodori world view rests its very conceptions.

We begin by bringing to the surface an ordered, yet provincial, world view in the Teodori. The reason for referring to these regions with provincial meaning is that they expressively refer to a given space during the time in which the text was written. Such meanings can be recreated and carried onto a different level of meaning so that such symbols originally used in its provincial concrete sense is capable of becoming useful in its universal and dynamic sense. Thus, it will be argued that provincial world view claims are also capable of becoming universal ones since the celebration of the Teodori has spread and is being performed in diverse settings.

First, we have the Jiba. This Jiba is the place where God the Parent is said to have conceived human beings and can be traced both in myth and in ritual. This is the point in place to which the symbolic animals converged and assembled and where God's intervention took place. It is at this geographical point where the Kanrodai stands. This stand demonstrates the proof of where the Jiba is situated. Around this stand is where the Kagura Service is performed, a performance re-enacting the creation in the present. Needless to mention are the varying directions to which the Kanrodai symbolizes. As it has been maintained, these directions can also be portrayed through the use of nonverbal symbolic patterns in the Teodori.

From the Jiba, we find much reference being made to the Residence of God, that is, the area lying around the Jiba. Nakayama Miki foretold that the Residence of God is "eight-*cho* square." She also refers to this place a number of times in the Teodori text. Further from the Residence of God is what was once called the village of Shoyashiki. This becomes another manifest analogy to the world view scheme. Shoyashiki village is where the family of Nakayama Miki lived and the Jiba is also located on this soil. It is said that she had a deep affinity to this particular place as early as when she married at the age of thirteen. Within this village there are people, especially Nakayama Miki, who have a direct affiliation to the place. These people were taught to have a relationship to human being's creation—their souls were identical to the symbolic animals used in creation. A promise was made to these animals: "when the years equal to the number of their first-born had elapsed, they would be returned to the Residence of Origin, the place of original conception, and would be adored by their posterity" (Tenrikyo Church Headquarters 1993a, 20) Consequently each soul was brought back to Shoyashiki Village and played a detrimental role in Miki's mission.

Prior to Miki's divine revelation her family was considered one of the more respected families in the village. The family was wealthy and could afford to have servants for their daily necessities. After revealing the words of God the Parent, however, the family became the focus of ridicule by the villagers of Shoyashiki—some family members even loudly voiced opposition against them. It was not until Miki began to cure the sick that the term once again was utilized as a persuasive symbol. Here we see the spatial marker used to discern this village from the others since a special being dwells therein: "a living goddess in Shoyashiki village."

There exists the province of Yamato. This region is a basin where farm work is the main. We find Yamato a number of times in the Teodori text but reference is always made to agricultural activities. It speaks of a fertile field, especially in Song VII, representing to the reader that Nakayama Miki used these terms so that people in the entire region—and not only limited to her own provincial visions—would understand her message. The Teodori also speaks of Yamato as one of many countries in the world and that it is the will of God to go out to other countries to save. Since this becomes a very salient topic and references can also be as the starting point of Japan as a united country, we would like to dwell into this intertextual domain by briefly outlining its historical contrast in a section which follows.[5] In other words, the region of Yamato not only provides attributes of a world view but there are certain psychological and social emotions, an ethos, that lend authority to its existential meaning. This itself becomes an actual blend of world view and ethos which make up a system proper.

There is a conception of the world that embraces mountains. The Teodori claims once that the service is being performed in the mountains (Song IX, 8). There is another reference with God penetrating into the mountains to find rocks and tress—a symbolism of people or tools for the reconstruction of the joyous life (Song VIII, 8). Yet the general notion of mountains found in Japan has a long history of being permeated with sacred power. Shinto, from times immemorial, saw mountains as sites of the residence of the divine. Esoteric Buddhism, especially from the influence of Kukai, saw mountains as sites for the realization of Buddhahood and areas for protecting the state (Grapard 1982, 195–221). The notion in the Teodori concerning mountains makes a shift since it speaks of it as one place, among many, to save.

As we have seen in the Ofudesaki, however, mountains are referred more often in terms of the people who intervene the activities which Nakayama Miki. The writer of the text speaks of it in terms of a sociopolitical position where those on the "high mountains" are ruling those in the "bottom of the valleys" as they please and as such, the regret of God. In other words, when mountains are mentioned it is used metaphorically to refer to a particular social class—the ruling class—of the existing political body and to those people who upheld such a tradition at the time. Hence both Shinto and Buddhist authorities are mentioned—especially with reference to the system of administration related to the establishment. Miki simply wanted to convey to them the true sacrality of her teachings and by so doing was led to use the very analogies understood by them as well.

Finally, there is reference to the world. Notions of the world naturally concern the above-mentioned factors. The world is made of mountains, the province of Yamato, the village of Shoyashiki, and then, the center of these constituents: the Jiba. The Teodori text makes frequent references to the world being divided into different geographical places where a particular salvific plan is to be actualized (Song V, 1; Song VIII, 1; Song IX, 1).

When analyzing the world and the human body they become one and the same object. What we have attempted to demonstrate in this relationship is not that they are identical in quantity but that the workings of God are the same in both realities. Since the workings of God are the same in both realities we come to understand that the world, as the human body, is permeated with the

---

[5] See chapter four for a discussion on Yamato in light of a particular context.

divine. God the Parent is in control of all things in the world and this would include the body. Hence harmony, through the correct usage of the heart, with the divine is being asked of human beings in order for goals (joy and order) to be attained. A simple sketch of the concrete yet provincial world view is demonstrated as follows:

Figure 10. Spatial orientation with respect to the Jiba

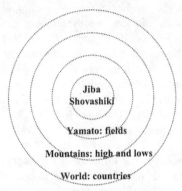

The *Teodori no Sazuke* as an Intertext

An appropriate way to end this chapter is to describe one of the most salient intertext of the Teodori. This particular intertext consists of the healing rite called the *Teodori no Sazuke*, which may be understood as the "divine grant of the hand dance." Besides possessing a name similar to the ritual dance, Tenrikyo members speak of the performance of the service and the administration of the *Teodori no Sazuke* constituting what comes to be called the "path of single-hearted salvation."[6] That is, performances of these two activities constitute the life of an ardent Tenrikyo missionary.

This healing ritual is referred often as the *Sazuke* by Tenrikyo followers [the honorific "O" is conventionally placed in front of the term, namely, "*Osazuke*"]. This grant is administered only to those with a physical disorder. It is taught that relief appears only as a result of the combined sincerity of the person administering the Sazuke and the person being administered. Ideally, then, God works miraculous salvation of curing an ailment by first accepting such sincerity. It is through this rite that many first time members are converted to Tenrikyo: illnesses and ailments miraculously disappear through

---

[6] When asked which of the two is more important one minister responded that both are vital to the life of a missionary. This particular minister likened the use of the performance of the service and the administration of the Sazuke to that of the left and right front tires of a car: both are necessary to go forward and both are necessary when turning either right or left. This analogy illustrates our point well. See (Tenrikyo Church Headquarters 1993a, 12–19) for further information.

the administration of the Sazuke. Performing the service, too, also plays an important role in relief. The Sazuke, it is to be remembered, can only be administered from one human being possessing the gift to another human being afflicted with an illness and therefore animals, crops, or objects cannot be considered prospects for healing.[7]

A brief overview of the various healing rituals found in Tenrikyo is called for. It was naturally during the lifetime of the foundress, Nakayama Miki, that these healing rites came into practice and all but one were incorporated by her personally.[8] The *Ōgi no Sazuke*, the divine grant of fan, was a rather simple divinitory technique where a follower would ask a particular question—most likely concerning an illness of a specific person—and the answer was given depending on the positioning of the fan.[9] This particular grant is mentioned in the dance text, in particular Song VI, 10. Another grant that is mentioned in the dance text is the *Koe no Sazuke*, the divine grant of fertilizer, appearing in Song I, 1. This grant, however, was not for the purpose of healing the physical body but used as special fertilizer for a good harvest that consisted of rice-bran, ash, and soil. It is also of note that the verbal symbolic pattern, *koe*, fertilizer, appears three times—Song VII, 10; Song XI, 4; and Song XI, 10—in the text.

The *Iki no Sazuke*, the divine grant of breath, was known to bestow the breath of life referred in the story of creation. It is said that this grant of breath was able to nourish children and heal the sick simply by breathing upon the child's body or on the afflicted area. Rice paper was breathed upon and was later utilized to cure afflictions of the skin area by placing the paper directly on top of the wound. The *Jikimotsu no Sazuke*, the divine grant of heavenly food, was a grant that distributed sanctified rice called "*goku*" to the sick. This was known to have "remarkable strength" if it were dipped into warm water three times. This type of healing through a sacred product is commonly found in Shinto shrines throughout Japan. Furthermore, there was a *Kanrodai no Sazuke*, the divine grant of the Kanrodai, that consisted of an elaborate ritual involving dancing around the Kanrodai while the afflicted person remained nearby. Finally, there was the *Mizu no Sazuke*, the divine grant of water, the only grant that was not commenced by Miki. Instead, the carpenter and first disciple, Iburi Izo, initiated this particular grant. This consisted simply of offering a cup

---

[7] One scholar offers a comprehensive treatment on healing in one of the new religions of Japan (Davis 1980). Another author describes particular healing rites found in present day Japan and traces their origins to Buddhist healing rituals (Hardacre 1982). In a different volume, the same author demonstrates the dual use of healing and preaching through her fieldwork involvement with one Japanese new religion (Hardacre 1986, 88–98).

[8] See (Offner and van Straelen 1963, 211–214). Two other sources also provide accounts of Tenrikyo healing (van Straelen 1957, 115–117; Stroupe 1983).

[9] One folklorist explains the meaning of the fan in Japanese culture (Casal 1960).

of water to the afflicted person. Prior to giving the water to the afflicted person, however, the administrator sipped the cup three times in commemoration of the symbolic notion of the first conception of human beings found in the story of human creation.

Needless to say, these healing rituals model the symbolism of life within the framework of Miki's teachings. It does not take much to recognize the meaning of water, breath, and rice to demonstrate that the manifest conception behind these symbolic elements is life itself. So saying, then, there is peculiar resemblance in the way the human body is given its renewed power when unable to function: association of other life-like materials onto the human body replaces the malfunctioning parts and makes them renewed. That is, the dominant symbol is that the perfectly functioning human body becomes simply a synonym for the bestowal and creation of life itself. This is an important point to remember especially in reference to the social body. More on this correlation as we dwell on the contextual framework of the Teodori.

The Besseki Lectures

At present the only grant that is being bestowed is the *Teodori no Sazuke*. To receive the *Teodori no Sazuke*, or simply Divine Grant, one must "return" to the Jiba to listen to a series of lectures called the Besseki, literally "separate seat" lectures. The content of each lecture is the same and one must listen to the lectures nine times in order to receive the Sazuke. The lecture talks about the basic tenets of Tenrikyo: the Truth of Creation, Miki's historical sufferings and compassion, the mind-body relation, the dusts of the mind, true sincerity, the importance of the service and the administration of the Sazuke, and ethical manners in social relations.

These lectures are held in an insulated place in one of the wings of the Oyasato-yakata complex.[10] The potential follower must first take an exam that consists of pledging in front of an official member of Church Headquarters prior to listening to the first lecture. This is to affirm that the candidate is spiritually open to accommodate the teachings into heart.[11] The pledge, which

---

[10] The Oyasato-yakata complex is a building project that began in 1954 by the Second Shinbashira, Nakayama Shozen, to realize the claim of the "Residence of God" being eight-*cho* square (945 square yards) with the Jiba as its center. The Foundress, Nakayama Miki, revealed that the Residence of God is eight-*cho*, and in order to visualize it in concrete terms a project to mark its boundaries was made. Presently, the series of buildings are used to house dormitories, offices, various schools, and a hospital. The Besseki Lecture Office is located in one of its wings. At present, the Oyasato-yakata project has twenty-four completed wings.

[11] As part of the services offered by the Overseas Mission Department the author of this study has worked as interpreter for such pledges during the years 1990 to 1993. Many would agree that this is simply a formal procedure and no one actually "fails the exam" (Ellwood 1982, 77).

should be memorized and recited word for word in front of the official, contains the basic creed in summarized form.[12]

After a series of questions and answers between minister and perspective faithful, s/he is taken to a room for the actual hearing. The lecture hall is filled with rows of benches that can accommodate as many as one-hundred people and, the lecturer comes in to commence the unchanging talk when the room is filled. For the most part, the lecture is in Japanese and a tape recording of the lecture is provided for "simultaneous" interpretations for listeners that do not understand the local language.[13] On special occasions, however, the Besseki lecture office provides for lectures in the language closest to the audience as possible—especially during periods when a flow of pilgrims have made the journey from a different country.

Despite being taught in different languages, however, the length of the lecture is established at ninety minutes and construed specifically for listening nine times prior to obtaining the right to receive the Sazuke. Ideally, the candidate listens to one lecture a month so that by the ninth month s/he is qualified to receive the grant. This idea behind enabling one to receive the Sazuke on the ninth month—symbolizing that a new life is conferred upon during this time—once again demonstrates the parallel with respect to the symbolic thrust of life itself. Yet this procedure is often difficult to maintain since many candidates are unable to "return" to the Home of the Parent once a month for nine consecutive months. In order to adjust to the modern condition, rules according to one's proximity to Jiba have been made and many overseas potentials are bestowed the Sazuke within the span of their visit.

The Bestowal of the Sazuke

One receives the grant directly from the Shinbashira, the leader of Tenrikyo, from inside a room adjacent the sanctuary dedicated to Nakayama Miki at Church Headquarters. The emphasis in this particular instance is not on

---

[12] The pledge goes as follows: "We call God the Parent, Tenri-O-no-Mikoto. God the Parent is God of Origin, God in Truth, who created human beings and the world where there was no form. God the Parent revealed the divine will to humankind through Oyasama as Shrine. It is due to Oyasama that we learned of the will of God the Parent for the first time. Oyasama is Miki Nakayama. God the Parent created human beings to see their Joyous Life and share in it. Thus the Joyous Life is the goal of our existence. I have come to know of God the Parent through the guidance of _____ and have learned of the divine will. And because I desire to understand it more clearly and to fix it in my mind, I have returned to Jiba at this time. We are taught that the Jiba is the place where God the Parent resides and where the Service for universal salvation is performed. I desire to learn the teachings of God the Parent thoroughly at Jiba, to follow the Divine Model of Oyasama with adoration, and to bring satisfaction to God the Parent and happiness to others" (Tenrikyo Missionaries Association 1993, 37).

[13] Since the lecture is a fixed text it has been translated and recorded into thirty different languages. The candidate, then, is obliged to listen to the lectures with a headphone for the entire ninety-minute recording.

the Jiba—where creation of mankind took place—but on the significance of becoming the "hands and feet" of the everliving Oyasama (Tenrikyo Church Headquarters 1993a, 66–72; Tenrikyo Missionaries Association 1993, 31–36). In other words, followers become Yoboku—useful timber—for building a world of the Joyous Life because such is consented by Oyasama, Nakayama Miki, through the Shinbashira. Needless to say, it is here where the symbol of carpentry interplays with the notion of building the world of the Joyous Life.

For this rite, all candidates are obliged to wear the ritual garb that is donned for the performance of the Teodori at a monthly service. The new Yoboku becomes a member of believers by kneeling in front of the Shinbashira. Both arms are extended out in front of the Shinbashira with hands that are cupped. After a church official has read out basic information about the candidate, the Shinbashira utters words of sanction, exclaiming, "*Sah, sah, ashiki harai, tasuke no kouno no ri o shikkari to Sazuke okou.*" An English translation states this as: "Now come, and I will bestow firmly on you a redeeming power which can be exercised through the performance of the *ashiki* ceremony" (Offner and van Straelen 1963, 212). It is only in this way that a person becomes an official member of the Tenrikyo community: appearing in person in front of the Shinbashira at the Foundress' Sanctuary.[14]

The bestowal of the grant is called the *honseki*, literally, the "true seat." It is interesting to note that the candidate attended "separate seat" lectures, the Besseki lectures prior to receiving the Sazuke. It would not be all that contemptuous to say that a semiotic value lies in experiencing "detachment" only to be renewed at the place of "attachment." In other words, a modest attempt is being made at disciplinary practices in an isolated place prior to coming to the real site where the gift signifying membership and its special meaning are consolidated in ritual form.

The Yoboku: Timber

On a crowded day more than two hundred people can receive the Sazuke. On such a day the candidate is no longer a mere candidate that attended lectures in isolation; contrarily s/he has achieved a new status by going through this ritual passage (van Gennep 1970). S/he is considered a Yoboku, a useful timber, and is reasonably translated as missionary. Yet the day in which the person receives the Sazuke is a special one for no longer is s/he mixed up "aimlessly in a mundane world" but now a special task—a

---

[14] The nonverbal symbolic pattern here is equivalent to a kneeling version of "receive." From a structural point of view, only the Shinbashira has the authority to bestow the truth of the Sazuke. When he is on a pastoral visit, for example, the Sazuke is not bestowed. It follows that when he is not physically well candidates cannot receive the Sazuke. This occurred after the third Shinbashira, Nakayama Zenye, underwent his second heart surgery in November 1995, where there was no increase in the number of Sazuke recipients for a few months.

particular mission—is endowed upon the person to build a new world within the old. We read:

> The truth of the Sazuke, bestowed on the sincere mind one has on the very day one pledges oneself to single-hearted salvation, is a treasure for a lifetime and for eternity. As Oyasama's instruments, Yoboku should embody the intention of Oyasama, who is hastening single-hearted salvation, and administer the Sazuke at every opportunity for a lifetime (Tenrikyo Missionaries Association 1993, 60–61).

Administering the Sazuke

If we utilize the analogy noted earlier, a missionary attempts to "move forward" by utilizing both tires of his car in a forward parallel position. Performing the service is not a difficult task since it takes place everyday at the local church and it can also be done alone almost anywhere and at anytime. The difficulty in moving forward, to continue with the analogy, is in the attempt to find one who is willing to have the Sazuke administered upon. Missionary work in a door-to-door fashion—the most frequent and traditional method of propagating the teachings—does allow for opportunities for the Sazuke to be administered. At the same time, however, visiting a friend who is hospitalized is also considered an occasion for the Sazuke to be administered, not only to that particular friend, but to others in the same room as well. Recent visits by Japanese missionaries to the United States, for example, have been quite successful in the attempt to experience an encounter with the sick. The technique used in such a case is that the missionary will advertise in a newspaper or a magazine that a particular healing ritual will take place for those needing it. In such a way, the missionary is able to confront the sick, convey the teachings to him or her, and administer the Sazuke.

The Sazuke is administered in the following way. First, the missionary who performs the rite claps his/her hand twice while facing the afflicted patient. Silently, the one administering the Sazuke relates to God the afflicted person's name, address, age, physical ailment, when the ailment began, and the prayer itself, namely the prayer to cure the person's affliction. After a minute or two in silence the actual administering begins. The missionary chants: "*Ashiki harai, tasuke tamae, Tenri-O-no-Mikoto*" while performing the same nonverbal symbolic patterns to the seated service. A literal English translation signifies: "Sweeping away evils, save us please, Tenri-O-no-Mikoto." This is repeated three times. After the third time, the afflicted part is lightly stroked upon three times with both hands while chanting "*Namu, tasuke tamae, Tenri-O-no-Mikoto*" with each stroke. Once again, the literal English translation signifies: "Hail, save us please, Tenri-O-no-Mikoto." After the third stroking of the hands on the afflicted part, the practitioner begins with the verbal symbolic patterns and accompanying nonverbal symbolic patterns for another two sets. In all, then, the chanting, together with the stroking of the hands, is repeated three times in a set of three. When the entire set is over the performer is once again silent for a minute or two and claps the hands twice. This ends an administration of the Sazuke.

Missionaries spend much of their time administering the Sazuke to people—the majority of which are non-church members—in the hope of spreading the teachings of God the Parent. The primary activity, then, of an ideal missionary is to administer the Sazuke to as many people possible who suffer from an illness or other physical affliction. When blessings become proof for conversion, the new believer may resolve to go on a pilgrimage to Jiba and attend the three-month course called Shuyoka, a spiritual retreat where the basic teachings are taught and put into practice.[15]

A Few Testimonies

Many miracles are reported through the combination of this particular healing rite, the Sazuke, and prayers that are synchronically transmitted through the performance of the service. It is without doubt, moreover, that the use of the Sazuke is the major mode of introducing the teachings of Tenrikyo to a newcomer on an individual level. Yet this alone does not suffice. As we have already once mentioned the "path of single-hearted salvation" in Tenrikyo terminology consists of a twofold project: the administration of the Sazuke and the performance of the service (Tenrikyo Church Headquarters 1993a, 12–19).

In one publication (Tenrikyo Overseas Mission Department 1987), a series of faith experience testimonies translated into English from articles that originally appeared in the Tenrikyo newspaper, Tenri Jiho, stirring titles as "TENRI JUNIOR SEMINARY STUDENT RECEIVES BLESSINGS THROUGH THE SERVICE AND SAZUKE," "THE CANCER CELLS HAVE DIED...," "I WAS SAVED BY SAVING OTHERS," and "SAZUKE RESTORES STRENGTH TO LEGS," to name only a few, are found. In the same volume, we find the following religious experience narratives.

The first brief extract concerns a missionary who utilizes the Sazuke for the first time to an ailing person. The result of the prayer was positive which accordingly brings about the daily visit of the missionary:

---

[15] Shuyoka is the spiritual development course offered by Tenrikyo Church Headquarters. It is a three-month course where people reflect, resolve, and practice the teachings of Tenrikyo at Jiba. The students commute to school from their respective church dormitories located in Tenri city. The morning hours are dedicated to lectures on the doctrine, the life of Oyasama, mastering the hand movements to the dance, and learning the musical instruments for the performance of the service. The afternoon hours are in large part dedicated to *hinokishin*. The same course is offered at mission headquarters such as the one in the United States and Hawaii but the period is restrained to one month (Tenrikyo Overseas Mission Department 1993b, 8–11).

[A]nd she administered the Sazuke, the Divine Grant, to me. She also administered the Sazuke to my child, who was then suffering from the inflammation of the tonsils. After Mrs. Okuno [the missionary] was gone, I was surprised to find that my temperature was back to normal, though I had been running an extremely high temperature just a while before. After that, Mrs. Okuno visited me each day to administer the Sazuke and convey the teachings to me (Tenrikyo Overseas Mission Department 1987, 26–27).

A missionary makes a resolve to God the Parent in the hopes that it will demonstrate sufficient sincerity to alleviate the pain from the afflicted person. Then, she administers the Sazuke:

Immediately after the first administration of the Sazuke by Yukiko [missionary], Utako [paralyzed from waist down] started to feel "something" around the lower half of her body, which had, for two months, been absolutely numb. She rejoiced at feeling the "something" and stayed up all night to ensure it would not go away while she was asleep (Tenrikyo Overseas Mission Department 1987, 35).

Finally, we have an account of an American who had been suffering from skin cancer and other related sicknesses for years. Through the daily realization of the Sazuke, however, she finds sudden alterations taking place upon the physical body:

Mr. Hirai [former head minister of Tenrikyo High Seattle Church] continued to administer the Sazuke every morning, and each day contained new, even more marvelous revelations. I couldn't get enough. . . . By the fourth morning, there was a visible difference in my hands. In a few places, scabs were actually starting to form. Even more impressive, no new lesions had appeared any further up my arms. . . . After one week, Mr. Hirai returned to Seattle, and Head Minster Kojima of Sacramento Church took over administering the Sazuke each morning. When I looked at my hands that Sunday, I really saw what was happening. Almost half the sores were reduced in size and many had completely disappeared (Tenrikyo Overseas Mission Department 1987, 47–48).

A transformation of the human body, one that is cured of a particular illness, also connotes some type of alteration in social relations. Our position, as we shall later argue, is that the human body can be seen as the natural symbol in which structures the patterning of how one relates to others: the way one perceives the human body will also influence the way social relations are construed. In this sense, with the use of a particular healing rite, not only physical changes occur but modifications in social encounters are created as well. As these few episodes underline, the person who experiences evidence of divine intervention in the human body through the administration of the Sazuke also goes through a sudden transformation in how s/he relates to the social world. In other words, the Sazuke not only holds such ontological assertions in the form of physical salvation but sociological ones in the form of the new relationship a person has with the religious community. One scholar writes:

> In so far as he is being brought into [in the case of a non-member] the structure of the religious community, the transformation implicates and involves both its participating structures and members, for if the performance were to 'fail' it would indicate a lack of the purity or harmony [of the members] which are thought to be capable of invoking God's restorative powers and upon which the religious community, at least in principle, is founded (Stroupe 1983, 126).

A brief summary is in order prior to launching into the final chapter. The Teodori, together with the verbal and nonverbal symbolic movements, construe a world view. The constituents of this particular world view are notions embedded within the symbolic economy of the Jiba, the place of human creation. Since this particular spot is the source of everything in this world for the Tenrikyo faithful it cannot be simply regarded as an ordinary place. In other words, humankind is able to place things in order in light of the Jiba since, by definition, the world and human beings originated at this place from a formless chaotic condition. This formulation of affirming how humanity was created is a world view concept and occurs primarily through combining two oppositions into one. This is one major constituent giving rise to a world view pattern.

To further elaborate this point, tenets such as the microcosm and macrocosm dichotomy between the human body and the world play their role in constructing a world view. What one sees in the world is a reflection of the body, and the body is a reflection of the world. God the Parent, being the provider of the universe, is the key to understand this claim. God protects the body as equally as it does in the world. In reference to the Teodori, then, specific geographical places within such a universe are mentioned with reference to a specific time. These spatial realities existed in the writer's region yet allow room for carrying broader meanings—of demarcating symbolic boundaries of a universal sort.

An indispensable intertext in arguing for the dichotomy of macrocosm and microcosm is the Tenrikyo story of humankind's origins. This has special meaning since it is implicitly interconnected with the Jiba. In Tenrikyo jargon it is called the Truth of Creation (*moto no ri*). The imagery portrayed in this story is a highly dramatic one using a variety of symbols and metaphors. From this story, as it has been suggested, the foundation of the principle of two-in-one is found. These binary oppositions are not dualistic features of different objects but concern themselves more with the functional categories of

142

two aspects working in complimentary modes. An example can demonstrate this point. We have the providence of fire and the providence of water represented by the workings of *Omotari-no-Mikoto* and *Kunisazuchi-no-Mikoto*, respectively. In the body, they function as warmth and the fluids. The perfect balance between the two, as commonly pointed out by Tenrikyo adherents, is proof of the workings of God in the human body. The body will malfunction without the warmth of the body temperature or the fluids that circulates within it. In other words, it is the complimentary modes of such unity that help both sides function in the just manner. Alongside this particular functioning of the human body, once again, is the same workings found in the world—the providence of fire and the providence of water. The world and the body are seen to function according to the same principle through such imagery.

The world view in dance form in light of this intertextual pattern is the basic transformation from chaos to order. The nonverbal symbolic movements themselves are well structured and patterned as opposed to frenzied and ecstatic ones. With this basic structure of meaning—closely related with the basic structure of meaning in the creation of the world from a formless chaotic state to an ordered meaningful one—humanity is able to transform formlessness into meaningful patterns through the performance of the Teodori. It follows, then, that the importance of the dance for Tenrikyo members lies in reaffirming a world view. By way of the body, the dance movements structurally interlink with a chaos/order dichotomy.

In this way, the dancing of the Teodori is a cosmological building, the building of a world view. Tenrikyo followers refresh themselves of this particular world view by way of the body—the dancing body—and carry this sentiment into their daily lives. By doing so the authority vested in the action of this ritual dance becomes very important for the community of believers since it renews the awareness of such a world view and furthermore affirms it as well.

143

CHAPTER FOUR

FROM INTERTEXT TO CONTEXT

Dispositional Components Through Context

In alignment with the method we have brought upon ourselves, namely one relying on Clifford Geertz, we must still uncover the underlying ethos of the ritual dance. To reiterate, the ethos is the moral, aesthetic, and evaluative aspects of a cultural system. An ethos consists of dispositions provided by the people proper of the given culture believing in it. Dispositions, says Geertz, are moods and motivations that are induced by religious symbols. The ethos lends authority to the world view and vice versa so that the believing of it continues in its tradition. It is important, however, to remember that these dispositions are not actions in themselves but are highly probable of being carried out by a social actor whose view of the world coincides with a particular ethos. In this way, we endeavor how the Teodori not only is a form of cosmological building but a way of edifying a common ethos as well.

The heart of the matter of such an inquiry can be answered by asking where these dispositions arise. These dispositions spring from a context of a particular place and time. The Teodori, seen from a sociocultural context, will provide important information concerning these dispositions that in turn will make the analysis closer to the Geertzian approach. The main question for this section goes as follows: how does the Teodori make its participants interact to express a common ethos for themselves? Such a context-centered approach to the Teodori must be assumed. That is, although we cannot look into a complete diachronic investigation into all corners of context, we will attempt to look into some of the major motifs so as to extract some of its more obvious dispositional components.

The endeavor will begin with two general descriptions on dance and pilgrimage found in the context of where the Teodori was articulated. Since there appears to be a moral, aesthetic, and evaluative attitude in dance and in pilgrimage, both should play their own roles in inducing certain moods and motivations when one dances the Teodori. In other words, the aim here is to indicate similarities and differences by comparing the Teodori with these two important religious motifs. A third yet minor motif concerns an inquiry into

important religious motifs. A third yet minor motif concerns an inquiry into the meaning of the term "Yamato." Although this spatially crafted geographical area was part of the world view makings, a subtle symbolic meaning lies in the word itself that has its consequences in molding an ethos all of its own. In all three areas, however, an attempt is made to add some examples of how the Tenrikyo community of believers interacts to express a common ethos.

The second part of this chapter will concern itself with a general principle found in areas of self, social order, and language. The principle is called the *uchi/soto* axiom, or, inside/outside dichotomy. Recent studies have shown that social interaction in Japanese culture rests on such an axiom. Since a form of social reality is found in the ritual dance, this principle will be helpful in highlighting it. We contend here that this principle is vividly portrayed in and during the performance of the ritual dance, demarcating and restricting the social reality of its performers in everyday life. After discussing key elements of this issue, we embark upon an elaboration concerning the patterns found in a more "inside" setting. That is, an effort to correlate the social body with the physical body briefly accounted for in the previous chapter will be made in hopes of narrowing the context of the Teodori. The major proponent of this theory is anthropologist Mary Douglas. In so doing, we argue that the attitude one has of the physical body will also influence relations with the social body. Such a course will also help to extract a cohesive ethos.

Dance in Context

Dance, per se, within the setting of the Japanese context has played an important role. From times immemorial, the notion of dance in Japanese culture has been attractive to its people (Kitagawa 1987, 23). We find in mythologies, for example, of how Amaterasu, the Sun Goddess, hid herself in a cave to escape from her brother's violent acts. To lure her out, Ame-no-Uzume, a female *kami*, is reported to have danced.

> During some considerable turmoil which endued in the heavens caused particularly by Susano-O, her younger brother, Amaterasu is said at one point to have hidden herself in a cave, thus plunging heaven and earth into darkness. In their efforts to lure her out, the other deities used a bronze mirror again, and another goddess performed a comical dance with the aid of a spear, so that the ensuing laughter aroused Amaterasu's curiosity and she peeped out (Hendry 1987, 9).

The dance was comical which helped lure Amaterasu out of darkness and the world was granted sunlight once again. Along the same vein, an empress in the middle of the fifth century danced to celebrate the completion of a new imperial palace. *Asobi*, literally play, is also an important motif with connotations of dance and the imperial court (Kitagawa 1987, 23). It is suggestive, then, to think of dance closely connected to the imperial court and thereby making the notion of dance a very royal and sacred act. Further, one source hints that the narrator of the Kojiki, Hieda-no-Are, is said to be a descendant of Ame-no-Uzume-no-Mikoto, the dancer who lured out the Sun Goddess.

> It is relevant to note here that Hieda-no-Are, the narrator of the Kojiki, is also said to be a descendant of Ame-no-Uzume-no-Mikoto. In short, both the court narrator-historian and the court dancers were women who descended from Ame-no-Uzume-no-Mikoto, who represents the shaman-dancers of ancient Japan. (Ohnuki-Tierney 1987, 111–12)

Since times prehistoric, beginning with Amaterasu, the Sun Goddess, and the logical handing down of its tradition to the imperial court, dance has, as we have seen, played an integral role in pacifying and arousing the gods. Perhaps ritual as a whole, then, is one of the appropriate ways to replace chaos with order. The underlying theme in Japanese culture has valued ritual and ceremony to a point where the notion enables itself to pass down from generation to generation, solidifying it. If this were true, then, the ritualistic attitude itself should have taken firm root in the minds of the people during the feudal period when peace and order was the predominant characteristic and where ceremonies gave meaning to such attitudes. Anthropologist Robert Smith explicates:

> Masao Miyoshi has observed that ritual and ceremony are expressions of the most essential values of the Japanese, and that throughout the Tokugawa period they provided the framework of unity of the society: "In the great chain of being that—theoretically—connects the Emperor to the humblest laborers via the Shogun, lords, and myriad ranks of samurai, farmers, artisans, and merchants, all must perform ceremony so that *order* may be maintained throughout" (Smith 1983, 37; emphasis added).

Dance was a devise used in placating the gods. Furthermore, rituals and ceremonies themselves were modes of appeasing the general public by means of imposing order through formalized actions. Rituals were a mode of maintaining and establishing order in society at large—encompassing all classes of society. Yet the general mood in the latter half of the nineteenth century was characterized by social unrest. This, as we shall see, also influenced the way dances were construed. The important question is how did an orderly ritual dance as the Teodori originate in the same society where ecstatic and frenzied character dances were predominant?

147

It has been argued that the way rituals take form reflects the very society it is born in—as the notion of world view and ethos would imply. When rituals change, then, this simply implies that the attitude among the people in society has also changed. This point can be illustrated through considering a different type of dancing that took place at about the same time Miki began to teach her disciples in the late nineteenth century. But first a few words should be made concerning a basic dichotomy for which dance is perceived by dance scholars themselves.

An Approach to Japanese Dance

Dance anthropologist Judith Lynne Hanna offers some interesting insights on the relationship between dance and religion through very descriptive data (Hanna 1989). Her article explores the relationship of dance with the divine and offers an analytic typology of some of the ways in which dancers and spectators draw the power of the supernatural to the human world. She mentions in one of her examples how male and female shamans in Japan danced to induce divine possession, categorizing it under the realm of "inner transformation" (Hanna 1989, 286).

These conscious transforming rituals were called, according to her, Japanese *kami-gakari* rituals of possession. Within these particular types of rituals, she makes a distinction between the circular movement called the *mai*, which invited possession, and the *odori*, where the dancer became possessed. In the case of the *odori*, the dancer moved in vertical and ecstatic patterns and accompanied the dance with some sort of musical instrument or another sort of inner impulse (Hanna 1989, 290). That is, she makes a distinction in the nonverbal symbolic movement of the ritual dances while maintaining that the subjective consciousness remains the same in that they both induce possession.[1] Yet when looking at the broader aspects of this distinction we find categories of *odori* and *mai* are important in general dance terminology of Japan.

One Japanese dance scholar (Valentine 1986) notes similar attributes of this distinction. Yet he does not limit a basic dichotomy to the shamanistic tendencies of the Japanese populace but imposes a category onto the whole of Japanese dance. He does not assume the same position as Hanna but takes the view of what the constituents of dance are as identified by the Japanese themselves. He says:

---

[1] It should be remembered that Hanna's typology is concerned with divine possession and trance. It is naturally quite different from the underlying meaning of the Teodori under question, despite the fact that the Japanese word *odori* is used. We have brought this theme up since it is part of the procedure for analysis of Japanese dance.

148

The two basic terms used for dance in Japan are *mai* and *odori*, with an apparent distinction between the two along the lines of classical versus folk, and a freer versus more rigid rhythmic structure (Valentine 1986, 112).

The disparity of folk/classic and rigid/free rhythmic movements of Japanese dance become for him the main categories to which dance can be perceived. That is, the nonverbal symbolic patterns to which all dances have are the main thrust for this typology. Keeping this in mind, then, we will attempt to describe in brief the nature of a particular dance that was quite popular during the time of Nakayama Miki—the *eejanaika* dancing.

Eejanaika Dancing

Dancing continued to be a prime means of expression even in the latter part of the Tokugawa period yet with a meaning quite different to the one found in the myths and ceremonial processions. Instead of finding dance to provide a means of transforming chaos into order, as in the examples above, forms of dance are discovered to be an expression of chaos and meaninglessness with respect to the social crisis from which it was produced. It is therefore this sort of aimless dancing that is found during Miki's lifetime. We read:

> In addition to the *namazu-e*, the 1850s and 1860s witnessed several other popular religious movements which expressed millennial yearnings. These included mass pilgrimages to temples and shrines (*okage mairi*) and mass outbursts of frenzied dancing and singing (*eejanaika*). In 1867, reports that talismans believed to be omens of divine favor were raining down over Kyoto, Osaka, and Edo (Tokyo) triggered a number of the latter events. Poor peasants and townspeople wandered through the countryside in large groups, begging for alms and engaging in wild and licentious behavior. Convinced that a new world was about to be established on earth, the participants proclaimed the advent of Miroku and rejoiced in their good fortune (Ooms 1993, 83).

This *eejanaika* dancing, as well as the use of procession, portrayed an expression of disenchantment of the general populace. Religious symbols such as that of world renewal and the coming of Maitreya aided the people into an almost revolutionary spirit. Violent revolts are reported to have taken place, especially during times of socio-political instability, yet the authorities suppressed all of these insurrections. Coincidentally, however, it is during periods of social crisis that have resulted in the uprising of new religious movements and Miki's movement seems to be an example of this. During the nineteenth century in Osaka and Kyoto—two major cities relatively close to the village of Shoyashiki—some interesting dances occurred as a means to vent out feelings and discontent.

The Sand-Hauling Festivals (*suna-mochi*) popular in Osaka around 1800 often resulted in a refusal to settle year-end accounts. During a harvest dance called Butterfly (*chocho odori*) held in Kyoto in 1839, rich and poor alike dressed up in lavish costumes and frolicked about. Forming groups of as many as two hundred people, dancers broke into the homes of strangers and brazenly pranced around on the tatami mats with their shoes still on. Such dances, called *odori-komi* or "dance-ins" became common in later *okage-mairi* and were raised to the level of an art in the *ee-ja-nai-ka* of 1867 (Davis 1992, 61).

More can be said about the *eejanaika* dancing. Literally it means, "anything goes." This type of dancing grew out of an 1867 pilgrimage to Ise during the *okage mairi* of that year. The *okage mairi* were mass pilgrimages to Ise Shrine taken by people of all classes. Although the great *okage mairi* took place in 1705, 1771, and 1830—taking place every sixty-one years—there were smaller pilgrimages on a nation wide scale every twelve years for over 200 years (Davis 1992, 48–49). The *eejanaika* dancing coincided with the *okage mairi* but some scholars do not consider the frenzied dancing to be part of the major pilgrimage of the era since *eejanaika* did not consist of a real sacred visit to the famous shrine. If anything, the *okage mairi* demonstrated two things that influenced politics and religion at the time. One was that the *okage mairi* demonstrated an attitude toward the Ise Shrine and the other was that it possessed an embryonic theory of social reform (Oguchi and Takagi 1956, 320). Although scholars generally point out that *all* founders of new religions during this period were part of pilgrimages and dances, there is no reasonable evidence that Nakayama Miki went on one herself.[2]

Other reports convey that *eejanaika* dancing was performed almost instantaneously, regardless of the surrounding situation. The hungry and dispossessed people began with a drumbeat and a few dancers but soon many were on their feet. In the same province in which Nakayama Miki was born, raised, and later preached her teachings, namely Yamato, we find the following experience of an Osaka merchant in the 1830s.

Another merchant, a wholesaler dealing in fertilizers, went from Osaka to Yamato to collect some debts. When he came to the shop of one of his customers he learned that the man's brother had recently died and that the

---

[2] The founder of Kurozumikyo, Kurozumi Munetada (1780–1850), was quite impressed by the Ise Pilgrimage becoming a pilgrim himself. The founder of Konkokyo, Kawate Bunjiro (1814–1883), made the pilgrimage to the 88 temples in Shikoku at the age of thirty-three as well as taking part in the Ise Pilgrimage (Hori 1968). There is no proof, however, which shows that Miki participated in the pilgrimage despite a major route which passed near her home.

family was in mourning. Not wanting to bring up business matters abruptly, the merchant politely extended his condolences to the family and then asked whether it was true that the Ise dance had become popular in Yamato. "It certainly has," said the bereaved brother, "we'll show you." With this, he jumped to his feet and started to dance, accompanied by his wife and child on the *shamisen* and drums. Soon the neighbors heard the music and joined in, and before long there were thirty people dancing. The merchant, unable to say anything about his bills, went back to Osaka with nothing to show for his trip (Davis 1992, 57).

Using Valentine's notion of *mai* and *odori* as a key to unfold what the *eejanaika* movement constituted, it would not be unreasonable to say that this *eejanaika* dance was a form of folk dance not only because it was an expression of the ordinary people demonstrating their revolutionary desire to the authorities but because the nonverbal symbolic patterns characterized such dance form as well. Further, the *eejanaika* during 1867 was a form of releasing unfavorable feelings towards the social qualities of the day but arising from an expression of an inner transformation brought about by the external factors of human life, namely that of social change and crisis.

At the same time, however, it is most likely that Miki witnessed in person the *okage mairi* passing through her village. Although she herself did not make the trip to Ise she must have been quite impressed by the flocks of people with banners, drums, and hoisters.[3] This must have influenced her way of constructing a type of worship that would later be known as the Teodori. Yet, contrary to a frenzied type of dancing, the Teodori portrays a soothing and ordered nonverbal symbolic pattern, a form that does not characterize the predominant ecstatic and spontaneous movements found in the then predominant *eejanaika* dancing at the time. In other words, there is a transformation in the symbolic economy of dance. Mary Douglas speaks of such symbol reversals in the following way:

If a people takes a symbol that originally meant one thing and twisting it to mean something else, energetically holds on to that subverted symbol, its meaning for their personal life must be very profound (Douglas 1970, 60).

Nakayama Miki, in drawing out a ritual dance, could have chosen from a vast array of symbolic forms and decided, above all, to invert the prevalent attitudes of dance at the time. Surely, the people who came to her for help knew the transformative nature of such *eejanaika* dances and profound interconnectedness with the Ise Pilgrimage symbolism. In opposition to what

---

[3] We read in one account concerning the nature of the festive nature of the *okage mairi*: "Men and women, old and young, all enjoy Okage dancing with golden *gohei* and banners hoisted" (Marukawa 1986, 286–287).

was maintained and valued by the people of her time, Miki pushed for a dance that reflected more an aspect of "maintenance," "control," and "order." To do so, however, she must have felt a deep kind of religious experience as Douglas points out.

Pilgrimage in Context

In connection to what has been mentioned concerning dance in Japanese history, pilgrimage, too, plays the same important role in context. A few things have been mentioned on the Ise pilgrimage which was, although not altogether connected with the *eejanaika* dancing, an important event which influenced the minds of the people during that particular historical period. Yet since the world view of the Tenrikyo community of believers hinges on a pilgrimage theme, then, a history of pilgrimage in Japan becomes pertinent for its contextual dispositions. Furthermore, both dance and pilgrimage use the human body as the fundamental instrument for each activity to occur. It follows that the two will be naturally intertwined with one another with respect to bodily activities in Tenrikyo.

The development of pilgrimage in the Japanese context has been greatly conditioned by topographical, geographical as well as cultural and religious factors. A summary presented by the historian of religions Kitagawa will assist us in identifying what Tenrikyo pilgrimage signifies within the modalities of these pilgrimages (Kitagawa 1987, 127–136). The three pilgrimage types, Kitagawa notes, are the following: 1) pilgrimages to sacred mountains; 2) pilgrimages to temples and shrines based on divinities that are enshrined; 3) pilgrimages to sacred places based on the special powers of a charismatic person.

Pilgrimages to sacred mountains were based on the Buddhist notion of self power—*jiriki*—an idea which made the self strong through ascetic practices (Kitagawa 1987, 135). It was believed that training was needed in order to achieve power, and the place where one went for such training to obtain that special power was through frequenting particular mountains. It was natural for a person to be respected by the people if he went through such rigorous training. Non-Buddhist specialists such as shamans, healers, and ascetics, as well as the general public acquired special powers. Furthermore, the order of mountain ascetics turns out, in fact, to be a combination of these specialists who practiced in those high regions.

It was in the mountain regions where the sacred resided and by analogy a person was able to penetrate into the mysteries of the sacred by going through austere practices at these places. Victor Turner's (1977; 1979) notion of "betwixt and between" is not difficult to sense when discovering what meaning mountains had for the populace:

152

[W]e see that the mountain is believed to be the world of the dead; the meeting place of the living and the dead; or a passageway from this world to the next—from the profane to the sacred and from earth to heaven. The mountain is also believed to be the world of the spirits and of the deities, buddhas, or bodhisattvas, where shamans and ascetics must undergo the austerities of hell to receive the powers and blessing of paradise and where souls of the dead also must undergo initiation in order to enter paradise or Buddha's Pure Land (Hori 1968, 177).

During the middle ages (eleventh and twelfth century) aristocrats believed that pilgrimage to sacred mountains would enable them to experience the Pure Land while still living (Kitagawa 1987, 129). Further, it was believed that the *kami* of these mountains were in reality manifestations of Buddhist divinities and only special ascetics were capable of guiding such aristocrats to these places. In the latter half of the nineteenth century, in fact, there were as many as seventeen thousand senior guides to known sacred mountains. As the courtship and aristocracy declines—during the early Tokugawa period—we see a new phenomenon arise within the already existing belief of mountain pilgrimage. This was the devotional confraternities, *kō*, belonging to either Shinto/Buddhist or both groups, that found its stimulus in pilgrimages to sacred mountains located far away from their homes (Ito 1952). Special devotion to mountains such as Kumano or Koya in the present can lead to a formation of a *kō* with pilgrimages as one among the many duties to be fulfilled by the group (Agency for Cultural Affairs 1972, 139–140).

Kitagawa's second typology concerns going to places such as temples and shrines. At its source is the Buddhist notion that relies on the power of the other—*tariki*—as contrasted with the former ascetic-bent practice that is designed for obtaining self power (Kitagawa 1987, 135). Its soteriological meaning is futuristic when compared with the second type of pilgrimage for there stands a belief of salvation that can only be realized after the present life. The purpose behind taking part in a pilgrimage to a particular temple or shrine is that the gods enshrined within the premise will become pleased at "seeing" such devotion. It is believed, therefore, that the gods will return the favor of granting salvation to those making the pilgrimage. Temples and shrines, then, are considered places to be visited since the divine dwells within and such gods impart salvation for those demonstrating the physical effort to devote their time to do so.

Popular images for this typology include Kannon, the goddess of mercy; Amida, savior of all creatures; Jizo, the protector of souls in hell; Yakushi, the healing Buddha; and Miroku, the Buddha of the future (Kitagawa 1987, 130). A major pilgrimage of this type which dates back to the tenth century and continues even today is the Saigoku Kannon Pilgrimage which consists of circuiting thirty-three temples dedicated to the goddess Kannon in central Japan. Accordingly, this pilgrimage is the oldest recorded pilgrimage in the country (Mori 1986). The most notable Shinto pilgrimage of this typology is the pilgrimage to the Grand Shrine of Ise that houses the Sun Goddess, Amaterasu-O-Kami (Miller 1987a, 543).

The third type of pilgrimage is based on faith in certain charismatic holy men and may simply be characterized—using the two previous analogies—as an intersection between the power of the self, *jiriki*, and the power of the other, *tariki*. Such a crossover brings into mind the overlapping image of an attempt to reinforce the self yet mediated through the power of the other. The saving power is actualized in this life with the self as guide while relying on the benefits of the deity for the future.

Kitagawa notes that the Japanese were very well disposed to people with charisma prior to its contact with Buddhism (Kitagawa 1987, 132). This pattern of thought did not change with the arrival of Buddhism. Prince Shotoku (573–621), who played the major role for the diffusion of Buddhism in Japan, became a figure of adoration by ardent Buddhist. This would go the same for the popular Buddhist healer Gyogi (670–749) of the eighth century. People made pilgrimages to places that were related in some way or another with these charismatic men so that salvation would be guaranteed. It is believed that making pilgrimages to these places in relation to, and dealing with, these men is a type of discipline for the betterment of the self. Parallel figures in this typology would include men who have established schools of Buddhism in Japan such as Shinran (1173–1262) for the True Pure Land School and Nichiren (1222–1282) for the Nichiren School. Yet the most famous among these founders is the systematizer of the esoteric Buddhism in Japan, Kobo Daishi (773–835).

The Tenrikyo Pilgrimage

Using the same typologies as indicated by Kitagawa, namely those themes that are quite predominant in the history of Japanese pilgrimage, we shall now analyze the Tenrikyo pilgrimage. By so doing, contextual issues regarding pilgrimage can be traced. Examples will be illustrated so that a setting will be portrayed while analogies will focus on the areas outlined above.

The *jiriki* aspect concerns the Buddhist notion of self-power through ascetic bent practices. Contrarily, *tariki* is the power that is to be granted from the other, namely from a divinity known for its particular power and popular favor. Although of Buddhist origins, both ideas have to a certain extent permeated into Tenrikyo with regard to the perceptions of its pilgrimage. In other words, notions of *jiriki* and *tariki* are found very much alive within pilgrimage practice although it may not necessarily be described with such phrases.

Empowering the Self: *Jiriki*

One reason for returning to Jiba—namely to go on a pilgrimage to Jiba—is to build inner strength for the self. This personal strength, of course, cannot be as significant elsewhere since the Jiba is *the* special place set apart of the ordinary. Certainly, followers are known to cultivate themselves at local churches yet local churches, as Tenrikyo theology puts it, would not exist without the Jiba. In other words, the Jiba is the root and local churches are its branches: branches grow only by attending to its roots (Tenrikyo Missionaries Association 1993). Furthermore, special insight into "tapping the power of the divine" can be obtained by receiving the truth of the Sazuke. This would mean that a person must make a pilgrimage to Jiba for it is only there that one can obtain it. The Besseki lectures, the lectures that are required for receiving the Sazuke, are also given at Jiba and would otherwise lose total relevance if it were held anywhere else.

Undergoing special training, too, is a means of disciplining the self at Jiba. Again, there are special courses that one may attend to discipline the self in order to cultivate the mind. Shuyoka, the three-month spiritual development course, is designed for those who wish to learn about the will of God the Parent as well as practice them in daily life. Moreover, each association sponsors annual events designed in having the participant increase their own "strength" needed in facing the ever-changing world. In other words, they organize retreats at Jiba so that they can refresh themselves and then return to missionary work.

There are more than a dozen educational institutions in Tenri designed not only to educate people in their basic intellectual requirements but also to base such learning on the teachings of Tenrikyo. Staff members of Church Headquarters, too, speak of accumulating "merit" for the self while stationed at the Home of the Parent since each person has been endowed to be responsible for taking care of pilgrims that arrive. A person, then, can receive an education in Tenri city and later become a staff member at Church Headquarters. Both instances would of course speak of the experience as a "means of cultivating the mind" for the self. The idea of residing for a period of time gives the habitant a sense of "planting seeds of sincerity" at the "Residence of God" that will ultimately sprout for missionary work in the future. Here is where we find—although not in the same wording—the structure of *jiriki*. These examples emphasize a particular place. Where "mountains" are known to be special places in the history of Japanese religiosity, the Jiba, too, has taken on a similar meaning for certain spiritual practices.[4]

Another case in point from the general idea of going through spiritual practices for obtaining self power can be perceived in the conception of making a pilgrimage on foot to Jiba from a respective pilgrim's hometown. Although the means of transportation for most pilgrimage to Jiba is by modern means of transportations, there are those who make the journey by foot in order for them to obtain special merit that can later be applied to their work in the mission. We live in the modern predicament yet Tenrikyo believers make a pilgrimage to Jiba by foot from, lets say, the capital city of Tokyo. This endeavor will take the pilgrim a few weeks to complete and the human body is surely put to a test. Yet a pilgrim goes through the physical training necessary in order to overcome concrete problems that may stand in his or her way at a later time and place. In other words, the spiritual aspects are strengthened through a pilgrimage, testing the physical aspects of the pilgrim. Once again, the symbolism of the human body is at work.

Other pilgrimages by foot are from the traditional Kyoto province, where, because of the proximity of the province to Jiba, many churches have been established despite the strong historical roots of Buddhism. The distance is approximately twenty-six to thirty kilometers, depending on where the pilgrim begins. Seminarians of the junior seminary are obliged to complete the walk, a pattern that has continued as a model for other members of the church.[5] The on-foot pilgrimage is not restrained for the Kyoto area only, contrarily, believers make a pilgrimage on foot to Jiba from wherever they wish and this connotatively represents in some ways part of the *jiriki* suggested above.

Power from the Other: *Tariki*

One goes on a pilgrimage to Jiba to "return" home. The Jiba is the place where mankind was conceived but it is also the place where God the Parent resides. The foundress, Nakayama Miki, is taught to be always present in the sanctuary dedicated to her. Members of Church Headquarters prepare meals and a bath for her on a daily basis, as if she was indeed still physically alive. Such notions of dwelling can affect the pilgrim's motive for making the

---

[4] Grapard also notions that people would attempt to touch those who went on a pilgrimage during the medieval period in the hopes of receiving the same sacred power themselves. In other words, here lies the notion of bringing elements of sacred into profane areas (Grapard 1982, 207). Blacker also mentions a similar structure (Blacker 1975, 100).

[5] A program established in 1984 by the Tenrikyo Overseas Mission Department for high school students in English speaking countries called the Oyasato Seminar. Among the various activities of the month long course is a pilgrimage on foot to Jiba from Kyoto, the same one which is carried out by seminary students. The author has been on this trip four times.

journey in the first place. Since it is at the Jiba where both God the Parent and Oyasama reside it is also there that blessings are purely and unobstructively shown. Contrary to the notions of *tariki* in its original Buddhist sense, blessings from God the Parent manifests in form of salvation in this life. Taking part in a pilgrimage saves a person who is suffering from an unknown disease. A person having problems makes a pilgrimage to Jiba to invoke a response from God the Parent despite the fact that a local church is located just a few blocks down the street.

Pilgrimages by foot, of course, are contrary to modern means of transportation. In one respect, then, making a pilgrimage by foot is to refine and discipline the self in contrast with the modern condition. A certain character is required prior to the journey but one's character is built by experiencing it. At the same time, however, a pilgrimage by foot can be a form of resolution in order to receive a certain type of blessing. That is, missionaries are known to recourse themselves to this form of resolution in order to demonstrate the necessary sincerity to help assist another in receiving a blessing from God. In other words, sacrificing one's transportation fee of going to the sacred place in the hopes of receiving a blessing in return can be taken as a form of *tariki*. On a different level, however, followers on a pilgrimage on foot to Jiba make use of the meaning contained in the teaching of "a thing lent, a thing borrowed." The human body is a thing lent by God and it is because of God that the body works as such. In so saying, then, the pilgrim is able to complete the pilgrimage by foot because protection and blessings from God of a healthy body has been endowed upon. Seen from this perspective it is because of the power from the other—*tariki*—that members take part in Tenrikyo's pilgrimage to Jiba.

Holy People in Tenrikyo

The junior seminarians mentioned earlier make a triangular pilgrimage of approximately one hundred kilometers. This particular pilgrimage is one that begins from Jiba en route to an important historical site only to return back to the Jiba. When the entire journey is completed the trek forms a triangular pattern. This is the same path that Miki's son, Nakayama Shuji, made when he made contacts with Buddhist priests at Jifuku Temple at the foot of Mt. Kongo to obtain legal recognition of the religion.[6] This journey was made in order to obtain affiliation with this temple so that the early

---

[6] Miki reprimanded her son Shuji on this idea: "If you do such a thing, God the Parent will withdraw." Yet despite the objection, her son set forth with another person named Okada. Affiliation eventually was granted and the movement was named "Tenrin-O-Kosha." Buddhist rites were executed for the inauguration. It is of interest to note, however, that the crossing of the pass caused Shuji considerable difficulty and several months later, Shuji passed away (Tenrikyo Church Headquarters 1996, 110–112).

disciples could perform the service without interventions from the local authorities. Miki, however, never consented to such ties (Tenrikyo Church Headquarters 1996, 110–112).

A walking pilgrimage, one that is more popular than any of the others listed thus far, is frequently made from Osaka, a trek consisting of more than twenty kilometers.[7] This particular pilgrimage by foot has a particular residual from the past, namely, a mountain pass which still carries its original name: *jūsan toge*, literally, "pass number thirteen." This mountain road connects the two provinces. This pass is the same one taken from Nakayama Miki's time to enter the bustling city of Osaka from Shoyashiki Village. Miki's daughter, Kokan, trekked this road with three others at the age of seventeen to spread the name of God in Osaka following the death of her father in 1853. Presently at the peak of this mountain stands a monument dedicated to Kokan. Pilgrims who make the journey by foot definitely stop at this monument to make a prayer.

In line with pilgrimage routes of charismatic "holy people," there are many members who make a walking pilgrimage to Jiba as made by their predecessors. Notably in this field are people who have established churches that can be traced back to the life and times of Nakayama Miki. For the follower pertaining to such a church, however, predecessors are not looked upon simply as ordinary people but truly special people who were in close proximity with Nakayama Miki. These predecessors have gone through many hardships and are looked upon as being special people by their affiliates with distinct powers. Seen in this way, there is a notion of the intersection between *jiriki-tariki* .

An Anthropological Approach

The meaning of the Tenrikyo pilgrimage has been inquired into by describing what a pilgrimage may signify according to the typology put forth by a historian of religion. By borrowing some of the motifs that prevail in a historically transmitted system of meanings, then, the same motifs were pointed out in Tenrikyo with a different tag to it. That is to say, the objective was to underline how contextual features assist in tracing the meanings of the pilgrimage aspect that is in some respect interrelated to the Teodori. In continuing the discussion, however, there are other approaches one may take in analyzing the vast phenomenon. Here, a few words concerning an anthropological approach to the Tenrikyo pilgrimage is befitting.

One anthropologist mentioned earlier perceives pilgrimages as a means of venturing into religious experience through use of the physical body

---

[7] The author has taken part in this pilgrimage several times. There are members, however, who make it a point to venture on the walking trek pilgrimage on a monthly basis.

(Turner 1973). His work on liminality during rituals that involve transformation from one social status to another (Turner 1969) has been applied in the general field of pilgrimage, especially that of popular Christian pilgrimages (Turner and Turner 1978). What they note, however, is that the process of the pilgrimage itself can be divided into three phases: the separation (start of journey), the liminal (the journey itself), and the reaggregation (the homecoming). The emphasis in all such analysis is in the journey itself where the notion of *communitas* prevails: once it has started it is rich in symbolism, unstructured, and outside the bounds of religious orthodoxy. Another scholar (Ellwood 1982) has dedicated an entire volume on the idea of pilgrimage as being the basic metaphor for Tenrikyo. His subtitle for his book is appropriately "a pilgrimage faith" and it aims to demonstrate the structure and meaning of Tenrikyo through the use of pilgrimage as metaphor.[8] He draws from a variety of perspectives and suggests, among many things, the above mentioned Turnerian perspective:

> It is a moving away from the ordinary and familiar with its structures through a process of crossing the borders—entering liminality—on many levels. As one bids farewell to the sights of home, the hierarchies of home also tend to fall away, and persons usually separated by class and caste fall in together (Ellwood 1982, 18).

And further, underlining the central meaning of pilgrimage in dialectic between the world at large with the Jiba, combined with the building of the various edifices that Tenrikyo builds in maintaining the hospitality which it needs in response to such pilgrimage, Ellwood continues:

> The ambitious temples and Oyasato-yakata at Tenri externalize the immense importance of that place and the requirements of huge throngs of pilgrims; the imposing buildings Tenrikyo erects everywhere when it can are but reflections of this perpetuation of the work of the "master carpenter" so important to the first generation of the faith. A religion centered on travel affirms the value of the world yet sits loose to most of it; the world's true value is encapsulated in the one special place set apart upon which eschatological hope rests— "the center out there." The world is good insofar as the center is accessible in it, yet one must move to taste its full goodness (Ellwood 1982, 114).

A perspective of the Tenrikyo pilgrimage can be seen other than through the dichotomy of *tariki-jiriki*. It can be perceived through the Turnerian concept of *communitas* at certain levels of the pilgrimage. From this perspective, the Tenrikyo pilgrimage is perceived first as bringing

---

[8] His interdisciplinary method can be found in (Ellwood 1982, 9–23).

together people from different pathways into one general scope—an anti-structuring of ordinary experience and into a peculiar religious experience. The beauty of it lies in the fact that this is possible despite the differences that are constructed during the ordinary routines of everyday life between one person and another.

An example of this can be illustrated once a person has commenced the trip, let say, by bus or train, with others of the same pilgrimage. S/he is recognized as a coexisting family member of the pilgrimage group, despite the fact that s/he meets others for the first time. First time pilgrims comment on how borders and constraints of ordinary life are not sensed during the trip. Regular pilgrims of the church community treat the others as simply part of the same brotherhood of members. The ordinary structures of life do not separate members of the group from one another but a special bond among them is made: traveling to a special place outside the structures of their normal life assure this. Needless to mention, such a place is a center—the center "out there"—and leaving one's familiar settings assist in the manner of which the entire journey is to be perceived.

One embodying symbol during this liminal period is perhaps the *happi* jacket being worn, if not during the pilgrimage to Jiba, then definitely seen dressed in the proximity of its destination.[9] There is little doubt that a sense of unity among the members of the group is alive—together with the people who are already there—as they see approach the sanctuary premise for they see others everywhere with their *happi* jackets on. Bryan Wilson, upon experiencing a journey himself to Jiba, has this to say:

> ["Happi" jackets] serve as the symbol through which people show their unity, by placing themselves on the equal level in order to throw away their individual differences or self-centered thoughts and to devote themselves to God. It also means to deeply settle their own missions in their minds. They are serious, but at the same time, humorous, cheerful, and joyful regardless of what actions mean to be (cited in Mori 1986, 112).

A second significant marker that strikes a chord in a pilgrim is when those awaiting his or her return to Jiba utter: "welcome home." This means that those who make the trip to Jiba automatically have a homecoming reception ready for them at the destination. Needless to mention, it is at home where people break down their customary barriers since it is antithetical to

---

[9] *Happi* jackets are a piece of clothing originally limited to the workers in Japan. In Tenrikyo this has become casual uniform that followers wear. In the back of each coat reads in Chinese characters or a romanized counterpart, "Tenrikyo." On the side flaps of the jacket reads the individual church name of the follower. During the morning and evening services, the followers wear this apparel to demonstrate their unity with the other members of the community. This *happi* jacket is also worn during *hinokishin* activities.

where organization is created. The customary structures that separate individual beings because of one hierarchical principle or another are broken down since a distinction is not supposed to exist at this place: returning "children" are all equal in the eyes of the "Parent" who awaits them. The symbolic economy of the phrase "welcome home," although many may not perceive it as such, suggests this particular understanding.

A third symbol is the kind of action that one perceives, as well as takes part in, at this special place. Communal aspirations are experienced once the pilgrimage begins: the bond, the exclusiveness of the group, and the anti-structuring of ordinary experience. These are but major characteristics of the liminal stage. There is no doubt that a communal aspect of togetherness and helping one another are culminated at this sacred place. Such manifestation is made evident through a type of devoted labor, *hinokishin*, and while taking part in it, the attitude that was the impetus for engaging in it is likely to also be reaffirmed through it.

The literal meaning for *hinokishin* is "daily contribution" and ideally one does it consistently. *Hinokishin* signifies expressing the joy of being kept alive by God the Parent. As mentioned, it is a result of the providence of God the Parent that one is able to function as one does. It is done with gratitude to God the Parent and done without greed toward oneself. From such a perspective, God the Parent accepts as *hinokishin* any activity that is done with these two salient points in mind. To be sure, the term *hinokishin* also appears in the dance text (Song III, 8; Song VII, 1; Song XI, 2; Song XI, 3; Song XI, 4). In this sense, such activity becomes consecrated action especially if it is done at this special place.

A typical sort of *hinokishin* done at the main sanctuary at Jiba is the cleaning of the sanctuary corridors. One will certainly notice many cleaning the sanctuary corridors on their knees when walking from one sanctuary to another. Such cleaning is not an obligatory enactment but one that is grounded on sincere devotion. In many cases, groups of people will be seen to take part in the corridor cleaning while singing the songs for the service.[10] There is little room to doubt that this aspect of this pilgrimage is part and parcel of the spirit of *communitas*.

Once the pilgrim returns home, however, s/he is never the same. The pilgrim returns to the ordinary structures of everyday life with an awareness that a positive tension exist between structure and anti-structure—bringing back some of the euphoria of the anti-structuring into the structure itself. At

---

[10] It is to reminded that those who take part in this type of *hinokishin*, whether it be young or old, man or woman, or head minister or follower, all get down on their hands and knees. This position is a marker of equality as well as demonstrating the importance of humility. One scholar examines this as a ritual process (Reader 1995).

first, the transformation—the religious experience of the physical body—assists the pilgrim in returning to the patterns of ordinary life. Yet once such patterns begins to become too demanding s/he can make another pilgrimage to "the original home" in the hopes of restructuring once again the already structured world.

Yamato in Context

Yamato, as we have seen, is a topic which arises a number of times in the dance text (*Yorozuyo*, 4; Song I, 8; Song V, 8) and coincidentally, the same nonverbal symbolic pattern for this particular theme, namely, "mountain," is also deployed a number of times with different verbal symbolic patterns (Song VIII, 8; Song IX, 8; Song XII, 8). The world view perspective of Yamato within the ritual dance text was underlined in the previous chapter. The importance of Yamato is in its spatial category with regard to other referents found in the intertextual domain. Here, a brief historical description will be adjoined in the attempt to refine the setting so that some observations in relation to the emotional and psychological meanings it carries—the ethos—will be made.

Prior to becoming a nation-state we find that the Japanese archipelago initially consisted of many small kingdoms. According to "scanty" compilers of the *Nihonshoki* concerning the origin of the country, Emperor Jimmu established his dynasty in the Yamato region in an arbitrary year since the writers were in search of a national history modeling the more civilized China (Sansom 1958, 42). In contrast to these chronicles, the *Kojiki* accounts of a mythical Amaterasu, the Sun Goddess, who sends her grandson Ningi to rule the earth. It was Ningi's grandson, Jimmu, who became the first emperor. These records, however, become more reliable after 400 AD despite its "naive mythology and historical tradition from earlier eras which throw a great deal of light on primitive Japanese beliefs" (Reischauer 1962, 30). What is important to underline, however, is that both texts refer to Yamato as the seat where civilization began.

According to ancient Chinese texts, however, there was once a kingdom known as Yamatai and for centuries this was thought to be identical with the early Yamato region (Kitagawa 1989, 308). Both the latter Eastern Han dynasty (25–220) and the Kingdom of Wei (220–265) in China document the situation in neighboring Japan. They depict Japan with a hundred states and acknowledge an hereditary ruler in the state of Yamatai. It is also of note, too, that they testify to a situation of chaos and disorder, when, a female besieged the population in shaman-like manner and restored order in the later half of the second century. The records state her name was Pimiko or Himiko but more importantly is that authority rested on magico-religious ability—despite gender—from such early times onwards.

162

Recent scholars have found through archeological evidence, however, that Yamatai and Yamato were not identical (Kitagawa 1966, 4–6). Accordingly, it was discovered that Yamatai was perhaps located closer to northern Kyushu than that of the actual Yamato borders. There are two basic reasons for this claim. First, there is marked evidence that Yamatai prospered before the Tenno clan—the emperor's lineage—a clan that is the same as Yamato. Second, the description of Yamatai in the *History of the Kingdom of Wei*, a document written in the third century AD, suit areas of Kyushu more than the Yamato district (Kitagawa 1966, 6). With all probability, then, Kyushu prevails as the area from which civilization begins in Japan but settled in later years within the borders of Yamato. In short:

> One of the claims which, according to its own misty tradition, moved up the Inland Sea from an earlier home in Kyushu, finally settled in the small Yamato Plain not far from the eastern end of the Inland Sea. There it grew and prospered, establishing off shoots in new areas and absorbing other clans, until it had won a vague suzerainty over all of central and Western Japan and even over parts of southern Korea. . . . The suzerainty of the Yamato clan within Japan did not extinguish the autonomous rights of the other clans, but the priest-chief of the Yamato group became the chief among clan chiefs, and the special cultus of this clan became the principal cultus of the whole land (Reischauer 1962, 14).

Although scholars nowadays agree that the Kyushu theory is most probable, they draw such claims through archeological evidence and written historical accounts. They do not, however, exactly mention the reason why people established themselves in Yamato in the first place. For some, Yamato may have been the ideal setting for agricultural life and this may give us a clue on why the early people settled in that area:

> Yamato is blessed with an almost year-round harvest of grain and fruit; in spring, there are bamboo sprouts, citron, strawberries and peaches; in summer numerous varieties of melon, pears and mushrooms; in autumn, mushrooms again, persimmon, chestnut and apples in addition to the rice harvest, while the winter orange, though perhaps less famous than its southern, Wakayama counterpart, is still no less tasty. *No doubt it is because Yamato is a good place to live in that it has a long history being lived in* (Bownas 1963, 135; emphasis added).

Bownas goes on to further illustrate the religious impact of the Yamato region throughout its vast historical period. A given place may have precisely a long history yet this does not necessarily mean that it will automatically be considered a special "sacred" place by its habitants. Some places become the center of civilization and remain simply its political seat while reserving a peripheral place as its religious center. Other places, on the other hand, become the political as well as the religious center of a particular country since the polity may rely on the power of the sacred to uphold its general tenets. Yamato, it seems, was just that. It is most likely that Yamato was simply an exceptional place where the cradle of civilization, the seat of its political administration, and its disposition for special religious meaning during varying historical periods resulted in it becoming an extraordinary place.

This takes our inquisitive in demonstrating how this particular structure of meaning is still being marshaled in sources that depict Tenri city. We read:

> Tenri city nestles under the hills in the heart of Yamato, the cradle of Japanese culture. About six miles to the north lies Nara, Japan's first capital and home of Buddhism in Japan. Less than a mile away to the east stands Isonokami Shrine, the 'Shrine Above the Stone,' the supposed site of court and administration during the reign of the Emperor Sujin in the first century BC, and the possessor of a sacred sword given, according to tradition, to the Emperor Jimmu by the Sun Goddess. To the west, about six miles away, is Horyuji, the oldest existing Buddhist temple in Japan, built by Prince Shotoku in AD 607 (Bownas 1963, 134).

It is indeed true that the history of a particular place imparts particular meaning to what it signifies in the present. This is true for the Japanese who have always interacted with the sacred in the hopes of having such interactions be acknowledged by the sacred so as to actualize the ideal course of nature. It was a conviction that agricultural produce could easily be destroyed by divine intervention. The Japanese have learned to come in contact with the sacred through magico-religious rituals of one sort or another. The ideal outcome of such ritualizations would of course be that the sacred manifest themselves positively and for the betterment of the people. One simply has to remember the connotations *kami* has within the religious discourse of the villagers. What follows, then, is that if the given climate and nature of events demonstrates to be ideal for its people, the interaction portrayed by the local people cannot be underscored. In short, a given climate as well as its natural manifestation is but a reflection of the people's attitudes and their interplay with the sacred. This, of course, has had more meaning in the past—especially to an agricultural community—than it signifies in the present.[11]

---

11 "The fertility of the rice crop, the due onset of the rains, the occurrence of storms, sickness, fire and accident, all these lay in the gift of the inhabitants of the other world beyond the barrier. Even today, although in intellectuals circles in Japan an aggressive secularism tends to be the rule, the belief still persists among many sections of the community that the causes of all calamity in

In a perspective that is in line with the above paradigm, a number of photographs in Tenrikyo publications of the four seasons at the Home of the Parent are semiotically portrayed as depicting the ideal of each season: snow in the winter; cherry blossoms in spring; the warmth of summer; and red leaves in autumn. All images, however, elicit not only the ideal season itself but also the ground on which this religious setting is founded upon. That is, these images depict a special religious place with a climate that only the most efficient rituals could possibly bring about to the place.

A few examples will be cited to illustrate this point. In a recent pamphlet introducing the Tenrikyo teachings to its Italian audience photographs of the four seasons of Oyasato, the Home of the Parent, are vividly portrayed with captions describing it as so (Tenrikyo Overseas Mission Department 1993). The English monthly published by the former Tenrikyo Overseas Mission Department (and presently the Tenrikyo Overseas Department), *Tenrikyo*, dedicates a portion of its news report in photograph form that candidly portrays the ideal of that particular season. Another example is found in the annually published *Photo Diary*, a journal with pictures of Tenrikyo events that give a relatively high priority to the seasons at Jiba. In the first pages of a publication dedicated to the Mikagura-uta, the Songs for the Service (Yamamoto 1988), the natural aesthetic qualities of Yamato province are found.

These examples are not meant to be exhaustive but enough to illustrate our point. The reason behind demonstrating such aesthetically bent images in these publications is due to the paradigmatic interplay between nature and the sacred throughout tradition. In other words, the climate for agriculturally based people is something which mirrors the power of the divine and the populace must interact in some ways with the divine in order to obtain benefits from it. This particular perception of the coherence between nature and the sacred continues even to this day—consciously or not—in the minds of the Tenrikyo community.

From these observations we can draw out a few interesting points. The first is that Yamato, with its special historical emphasis as the cradle of Japanese civilization, becomes the location for the primordial Japanese being. Religious dogma from Tenrikyo scriptures state a similar story of primordial beings but with reference to a special ritual and particular hexagonal stand to prove it. Where the historical chronicles speak of a mythical goddess sending her grandson, the Tenrikyo creation story speaks of a chaotic condition

---

human life lie in the spiritual realm" (Blacker 1975, 21).   Further we find: "In both wheat culture and rice culture, the staple farm products are regarded as sacred in themselves or as the gift of a superhuman being. Therefore, farm work is also regarded as a sacred action or rite and not merely productive labor. At the end of each agricultural task, various magico-religious rituals are performed in order to ensure the favorable course of the ripening of wheat or rice plants (Hori 1968, 21).

transformed into an ordered one by a monotheistic god and more precisely, at a particular spot of the same province. In brief, then, the historicity of Japanese civilization is combined with a particular sacred narrative to create a new symbolic meaning for those versed in both.

Historical records can prove what influences Yamato has had throughout the history of its people. This is then bound with the teachings of Nakayama Miki and renders it all the more nostalgic to "return home" for many. This twofold dimension of an historical tradition with one that is novel creates a new one set apart from the rest of the world. This is what may configure in the ethos when the term "Yamato" appears in the dance text.

An Indexing Principle

Recent studies into this disparate category for analysis have been quite effective not only in realm of Japanese studies but also in general areas of self, social order, and language as well. In fact, an entire volume has been dedicated to recent theories concerning the nature of the *uchi/soto* distinction (Bachnik and Quinn 1994). Scholars of Japanese studies have made this inside/outside (*uchi/soto*) distinction popular. Of note are the pioneering contributions made by two of them (Lebra 1976; Doi 1973).

The aim here would be first to recapitulate a general view of this theory therefore elaborating on this contrasting pair. If Japanese culture rests its social interaction upon this axiom, then, an interpretation in light of these categories of the ritual dance would be suitable for an anthropological bent study of it. In other words, it will be argued that dancing the Teodori creates *uchi/soto* distinctions for social relations and becomes a persuasive argument in the analysis toward depicting a thicker view of its context.

Uchi/Soto: A Definition

In the Japanese language the word *uchi* can carry one of the following two meanings. One is a definition that means "inside" in all of its conventions. The other meaning defines the word as "we," "us," "our group," "me," "'my group," and "I." *Uchi* is identified further with another term, *ie*, literally translated as household or family, and specifically refers to one aspect of the *ie* which is usually the living members of the household (Bachnik 1983; Smith R. 1985). *Uchi* in this case, then, speaks of social life in terms of "us," "our group," and "this generation." In fact, when referring to Japanese group organization, one Japanese anthropologist (Nakane 1970) speaks of *uchi* as being very much related for the existence of group organization in Japan.[12]

---

[12] One scholar, upon commenting on the notion of group identity, says: "It should therefore come as no surprise that there is a corresponding emphasis on distinctiveness of each group.

In retrospect, *soto* is a juxtaposition of the *uchi*. As *uchi* means inside, *soto* means outside in all of its conventional use. When one speaks of their *uchi* it is only in reference to *soto* that *uchi* carries any meaning. In general, then, one can see that *uchi* differentiates from *soto* and thus creates and defines boundaries for social interaction. The *uchi* as "we," "us," "our group," or "me" places a discourse of disparate terms between, on one pole, "the self," and on the other pole, "the other." In semiotic parlance the *uchi* becomes the "zero point of discourse" as one scholar has put it (Bachnik 1994). Here is where the distinction plays with our contentions.

The link between self and society introduces a number of equally important paired terms that give specific meaning in such a setting. For example, Doi Takeo highlights the *uchi/soto* distinction as categories found only in Japanese individuals (Doi 1986). His psychological bent analysis includes such opposition as the *ura* "in-back" versus the *omote* "in-front." This *ura/omote* distinction is quoted as being the two-tiered consciousness of the Japanese. Appropriately within the proximity of our discussion, *ninjo* "the world of personal feelings," versus *giri* "social obligations," have proven to be running along the same principle as the *uchi/soto* continuum. Doi became acknowledged internationally when he published a volume concerning his distinction between *amaeru* and *amaekasu* (Doi 1973). He aligns *amaeru* (indulgence or passive acceptance of love) with *uchi* and contrarily, gives further meaning to *amaekasu* (permitting indulgence or giving active love) through the spectacle of *soto*. In another parallel, social psychologist Lebra considers the *uchi/soto* and *omote/ura* very important in her studies concerning "situationalism" in Japanese culture and behavior (Lebra 1976).

Recent studies on *uchi/soto* distinctions demonstrate further interesting lines of inquiry of a multidisciplinary mold. One source reports that the usage of these paired words have been utilized in political hierarchy, large enterprise, small enterprise organization, family/household organization, marriage, health and illness, and religion (Bachnik 1994, 7). Architecture, too, can also define *uchi/soto* distinctions. As Hendry notes every Japanese house, no matter how small, will partition space with sliding paper doors. This is manifested in order to distinguish an inside area with an outside area. This spatial feature of inside/outside is metaphorically applied in its everyday usage: the inner area of the home is usually laid out for the closer members of the household whereas the outer areas will be for guests and visitors (Hendry 1983; 1993; Kondo 1990). We wish here to use this paired term for the ritual dance.

It is within these closed spheres of Japanese society that we find the clearest evidence for exclusivity—what "we" of our group know and do is unlike what "they" of their group believe and practice. It is for the newly recruited members of any group to master the details of its unique heritage" (Smith R. 1983, 94).

Another principle that is closely related to the *uchi/soto* dichotomy is the suggestive and interesting notion of wrapping. Anthropologists have dedicated an entire volume to the notion of the Japanese culture as "wrapped culture" (Ben-Ari et al., eds. 1990). A major proponent of this theory is anthropologist Joy Hendry who has singly taken this perspective by dedicating an entire volume justly entitled, *Wrapping Culture* (Hendry 1993). These scholars argue that not only are gifts wrapped in Japan—as one would find in the west—but that every day items are layered in one wrapping form or another. These scholars have taken it upon themselves to discover the broader implications of the phenomena.

Hendry in particular notes that in Japan one is bound to leave a store, even the most conventional type, with a purchased item enclosed in extravagant wrapping paper, which is then perhaps inserted in a box, and finally, put into a bag to be carried home. From an insider's experience-near point of view, wrapping demonstrates to others the process of being polite and a way of showing proper care and etiquette. Yet what Hendry sees is that the wrapping phenomenon is simply a part of a larger whole found not in the minds of the people but as a meaning structure for the Japanese people. Not only are materials wrapped in packaging invested with special gift-like qualities, but space is even given sacred qualities by placing rooms, for example, within rooms that are enclosed by a courtyard that lie inside a larger compound.

> At the most extreme level, the symbolic pinnacle of Japanese society, the Imperial Court, is perhaps accorded such high value because of its virtual lack of contact with the outside world. In Tokyo, the Imperial Palace is wrapped, just like the ancient castles were, in layers of gardens and moats, so that it is practically invisible from the surrounding streets. The inside is not open to general visiting, but some of the castles are, and these suggest that figure at the top of the hierarchical structures were further enveloped by elaborate arrangements of sliding doors and screens, all objects highly valued in Japanese culture (Hendry 1989, 629–30).

Wrapping is allocated to the vestments—a type of body wrapping—dressed by the imperial family for an auspicious occasion as a wedding. Wrapping in communication through layers of polite language, *keigo* in Japanese, honors the recipient. In the same manner, social gatherings are wrapped through use of confining interactions to formal introductions, without much content, hence insulating those interacting. A further example in the domain of Shinto can be found in the ritual wrapping exemplified in the heavy rope that wraps a Shinto shrine, a transition from the transcendent to the mundane to the transcendent, or the other way, from the highly polite and formal to the mundane (Hendry 1993).

At stake in this theory of wrapping, then, is the analysis of the *uchi/soto* continuum. Wrapping cannot be seen merely as a cover-up but as a social activity with meaning that can be analyzed. Two modes of analysis for meaning can be used: one that focuses on the core or center and the other which focuses on the activity of wrapping itself. In other words, the mode of analysis focuses on one or the other, namely, the inner or the outer areas (*omote/ura*, *soto/uchi*, or *giri/ninjo*). Hendry argues that for the Japanese, wrapping in polite language, ritual, dress, hierarchy, and so on, is itself linked to meaning. Her approach entails the claim that the core (inside) is *linked* to the wrapping (outside) yet not simply as a thing but as an almost literal embedding of the contents (the material) itself whether of a gift or of a talk. The argument, then, lies not only in prospect of a partial consideration of the core or simply the paired opposite of the wrapping activity but that which consists of both the material and the wrapping: the one without the other does not have meaning. The point is both the wrapping (*soto*) and its material object (*uchi*) become, as the Zen proverb goes, one and the same. The heart of the matter becomes not of focusing on one aspect to understand the meaning of that part per se, but rather, through focusing on one particular aspect as such—whether the wrapping or the material—the other, naturally becomes, to break with the metaphor, an unwrapping process in understanding the whole.

A more concrete example of how the notion of *uchi/soto* as well as how the above mentioned wrapping theory works to define boundaries of social interaction is explained in detail in an ethnographic description of small business enterprise (Kondo 1990). The author describes one pleasant occasion spending the afternoon with the mother of her host family when, the daughter of the host family and her two children—a boy of five and a girl merely able to toddle—pay the family a visit. As Kondo accounts:

> [T]he mother and I watched as the boy played with his sister, and chanted her first name—Kaori—as she toddled about the room. Charmed by the little girl's tentative efforts at walking, I joined in with a "Kaori." The little boy turned to glare at me. "You shouldn't say that. That's rude. You should say 'Kaori-*chan*.' You're not one of us." I was embarrassed by my gaffe, and stunned by his vehemence. Most of all, I realized that in-group/out-group distinctions must be of enormous cultural importance, for here was a child of five who had already mastered the process of drawing linguistic distinctions between *uchi* and *yoso* [*soto*] (Kondo 1990, 143).

This example describes not only a representation of the *uchi/soto* axiom and the wrapping construct at work but in particular, how linguistic markers in their everyday use become the index to which boundaries are drawn. What has come to be called "noun suffixes" has been argued as linguistic markers (Bachnik 1982). Noun suffixes such as "–*sama*," "–*san*," "–*kun*," and "–*chan*," are used according to order of politeness and distance. Even a small boy of five—despite the uncomfortable reaction of the anthropologist—is able to distinguish this. Through his use of simple everyday language the little boy was able to define the boundary between his collective self, *uchi*, and the consolidated other, *soto*. In this case his younger sibling was part of this collective "us" and the anthropologist was an abstract foreign element considered in the boy's world view as "them."

In terms of the wrapping element, as in this example, when a person summons another, s/he must always use one of the "noun suffixes" unless the person being called is an impending member of the *uchi*, as between siblings or between husband and wife. In other words, a name is always wrapped with a prefix to indicate the social distance—or closeness—between the person being called and the caller. Furthermore, it isn't that this noun prefix has any meaning per se, but carries meaning when linked with the name in which it is placed. Certainly the contextual element demonstrates the importance of how words must be placed and when.

The work of one Japanologist brings forth enhanced light on the *uchi*/*soto* dichotomy with respect to the organization of power based on Shinto thought (Rosenberger 1994). Accordingly, there are at least two manifestations of sacred power in Shinto: an outer power that is authoritative and differentiated and an inner one that is harmonious and centralizing. The manifestations of these powers are portrayed in a cyclical relationship like the seasons of the year reflected in a transforming tree. The inner manifestation views the tree as turning inwards upon itself during the winter to strengthen the roots and for returning to its primordial essence for future spawning. The outer manifestation views the tree in its outward growth during the spring and summer, demonstrating its command of the tree's energy into various compartments such as the branches, flowers, and leaves. Yet using the tree as a metaphor is very suggestive in representing a clarified view of the extent in which the *uchi*/*soto* axiom pervades even in the sacred realities of the Japanese:

> This metaphor for the power of the universe helps us to understand the nature of *soto* and *uchi* and the way that they interrelate. Like the sacred power, *soto* and *uchi* are ways of relating to others and the world that are transformations of a single process of life . . . . *Soto* is a centrifugal force pushing people and groups outward into social configurations that must relate with others . . . . *Uchi* is a centripetal force pulling people and groups inward toward likeness and generative reproduction (Rosenberger 1994, 100).

We would like to cite another example of everyday inside and outside elements. The Japanese are very much concerned with washing certain body parts throughout the day. In particular, the hands, the feet, and throat are given special hygienic care upon re-entering the home. The Japanese will immediately rinse away their throats and wash their hands upon re-entering the home. The feet should be kept clean since the feet touch the ground of the outside world. In other words, emphasis on washing these parts results because:

> [T]hey are the parts of the body that are the passages to outside or where the body us in contact with the outside; the hands touch outside objects, the feet touch the ground, and the throat is where outside air goes into the body (Ohnuki-Tierney 1984, 28).

Ohnuki-Tierney's persuasive insight within the Japanese perception toward hygiene for which her study is dedicated argues that the *uchi* aspect—the inside—becomes a symbol of purity whereas the *soto* aspect—the outside—becomes a symbol of impurity. In other words, her argument in Japanese hygienic practices originate from:

> [A] basic Japanese symbolic structure which is expressed as: inside : outside :: above : below :: purity : impurity. Put more precisely, they represent a symbolic correlation between two sets of spatial categories: inside:outside :: above:below whose meaning is purity : impurity (Ohnuki-Tierney 1984, 31).

The *uchi/soto* distinction is a powerful and persuasive tool for analyzing things constructed in the very context that it was developed in for its use creates and defines boundaries for social interaction. Further, as the notion goes, this axiom brings together other concentrated methods such as the one described in "wrapping." Other anthropologist have given such distinctions new meaning in the parameters of a pure/impure dichotomy and hence closer to the vocabulary used in religious symbolism. In the next section some of the *uchi/soto* distinctions that are found in the dance text are pointed out, namely the distinctions produced and proliferated through the performance of the Teodori. To do this, some examples will be illustrated in order to support the claim that social reality is being defined and redefined through the performance of the Teodori.

Uchi/Soto Markers Portrayed in the Teodori
The Ritual Attire

The first significant marker of the *uchi/soto* continuum is the outer layer of the wrapped body: the ritual attire. The black apparel is marked with the former Nakayama family crest that symbolize unity in that all who perform the service—and that would include those who dance the Teodori—are now simply part of one symbolic family. Such a family is embodied in universal fraternity where people join in to live the joyous life. The vestment is one symbolic measure that demonstrates the unifying attitude toward such a goal. Since a description of the clothing was given in the chapter two there is no need to further pursue along these lines of inquiry. Yet one can also see how this connects with the previous argument concerning the "wrapping" theory.

One author argues members of the imperial family don themselves in layers of wrapped vestiges so as to heighten their sacred quality (Hendry 1989; 1993). She argues that in order to fully understand this distinction one must of course see how its historical construct has influenced the making of such layers. Layered dress was a symbolic design that demonstrated the social status of the imperial family: more layers denoted higher sacrality. On the other hand, those wearing simple two-layered kimono clothing in retrospect were representative of the common people. This particular black-colored type of two-layered clothing, however, was considered in the times of Nakayama Miki formal attire and was vested for special occasions by the peasantry. For this special occasion, one such as the ritual dance, this formal attire had to be incorporated by the early followers. This is what stuck to this very day.

In contrast to the service performers we have the audience membership. The audience, for the most part, is constituent of the church membership yet, for some reason or another, do not wear the formal service attire. They usually wear the *happi* jackets explained earlier. This separation indicates social distance among participants. The language used by those wearing these special vestments are transformed simply because one becomes conscious of the clothes they are wearing. Not only are bodies wrapped in a particular type of apparel but the manner in which one speaks as a result of the worn vestments also become wrapped. Speaking becomes, to break with the metaphor, wrapped with polite language so as not to offend others for to do so would render the situation—the ritual time—without respect. An example will serve to illustrate this point.

The followers who gather prior to the service come to help with the preparations. As already mentioned, they busily prepare by doing their share of *hinokishin*, action that springs forth from gratitude. At the same time, however, there are those who converse with one another and share recent household events. Yet once the preparatory process is done and the time comes to wear the service performing attire—the *otsutome gi*—the mood that once characterized the church premise transforms into a solemn event. The perceptions of clothing themselves induce certain moods and motivations that are characterized by reverence, respect, and holiness although the actual service has not yet commenced.[13]

There is also a difference of ritual costume between men and women. The *kimono* apparel for males is considerably comfortable for both legs can theoretically stretch out very far. This is equally valid for the arm movements. This enables the male dancers to move about without restrictions or limitations. In dancing, for example, the nonverbal symbolic pattern for "mark line" is executed with both knees bent forward, perching close to the ground floor and is the only part of the ritual dance where performers must squat. For the male dancer this is done with ease, not only because of the ritual garb that is open for such movement but also because male dancers are usually stronger in strength than their female counterpart. Needless to mention, this particular nonverbal symbolic pattern requires more physical strength and balance than other movements. On the other hand, the female dancer must squat down with knees pointed inwardly and the distance of their feet must be situated together—a very awkward and uncomfortable position. From this particular position, however, balance and strength are required not only in the process of squatting down but also in the movement toward returning to one's original position.

One writer has demonstrated that among elements in Japanese dance such as movements, gender roles, and organization of dance forms, costumes utilized during these dances also reflect part of Japanese culture (Valentine 1986). In other words, he argues that the restricting and limiting movements apparent in the female dancer's costume, although underling that it is not the only element, mirrors a Geertzian *model of* and a *model for* womanhood in Japanese society. Part of his impression on Japanese dance, when performed by a woman goes as follows:

> Movement of the legs and feet are dainty and again inward turning: this restraint may be seen as conditioned by female costumes, yet costume can itself be viewed a further document. Costume is indeed an important part of *nihon buyo* [Japanese dance] performance, and the long sleeves characteristically worn for female dance roles are used further to emphasize inwardness and passivity: the sleeves may be closed in on the body almost as body doors, and they extend the slack passivity of the gently swaying arm, giving an impression of elegance and frailty (Valentine 1986, 124).

---

[13] This can be more vividly experienced when the monthly service is performed in a large church. In such a case, all service performers walk into the worship hall together from an adjacent room and when doing so, the audience do not talk with one another but simply bow to demonstrate a nonverbal symbolic gesture of respect to them. Thus the dichotomy of service performer/non service performer is strengthened.

Concentrating on the notion of the kimono alone, there appear to be four dominant motions of nonverbal behavior among women who wear the kimono apparel, namely, adjusting the sides, alignment of the tips of fingers and toes, handling an object with both hands, and hiding one's mouth (Ikegami 1991). Although these nonverbal behavior patterns can also be traced among gender wearing western attire, the author argues that the restrictive nature of the kimono influences and regulates nonverbal behavior in women.

The same argument applies to the notion of the female Teodori dancer. When walking from one place to another, women performers appear inward and passive through use of both hands close to the body or covering the mouth when talking. The distinction between the male and female during the ritual dance is quite apparent. Even though the movements and gestures are exactly the same for both genders there is a restricted sense of movements among female participants. In retrospect, then, although the costume as marker can distinguish between *uchi* and *soto*, between dancers and non-dancers, there is a further distinguishable element among dance performers themselves. This lies on the divergent ideals of gender relations in the Tenrikyo construct. This is related to a broader discourse for it presupposes constituents of what it means to be a female, and likewise for a male, with respect to the teachings themselves. From this perspective, then, the wearing of the ritual garb is seen as having a contextually meaningful import.

Hierarchy and Authority

Another marker that shapes *uchi/soto* distinctions lies in the performers of the ritual dance. There are other members besides the dancers such as the instrumentalists and singers who are part of the community of performers. Members who know the basic movements are asked to dance while others, who are less familiar and although belonging to the church, will not. This is simply due to the difficulty of mastering all the basic movements of the dance.[14] In other words, since the dancing is the main "text" of the monthly service those who are able to dance on the upper dais represent a hierarchical embodiment. Semiotically speaking, the hand movements to the dance are at "center stage" where the six dancers appear immediately in front of the altar that symbolically represent the highest order of authority in the teachings,

---

[14] Many followers practice not only the dance but also the musical instruments that accompany it as well in order to perfect the complete performance of it. Yet these efforts are taught as a manifestation of the participant's own sincerity. In other words, it is through one's sincerity in action, and not through one's cognitive knowledge of it, that one perfects the movements to the hand dance and the precise performance of the musical instruments.

174

namely God the Parent.[15] The singers sing and the instrumentalists create a tune to accompany such songs. Therefore, the instrumentalists and singers can be perceived as second order participants during the performance of the monthly service and the dance can be conceived of possessing primary import.

Between the dancers themselves, for instance, there is a hierarchy of social relations. As we have already mentioned, namely the seated service, the head minister of the church sits in the middle with his spouse sitting in his or her immediate proximity for the first part of the service. An illustration of the position where each member takes during the first part of the ritual dance is offered in figure 11 below.[16]

Figure 11. Position of dancers and their community status

| next male member | senior male member | Head minister and spouse | senior female member | next female member |

This setting, with the head minister and his or her spouse in the middle of "center stage," suggests not only that they are at the core of the community of believers but by situating them at center stage during this important gathering of faithful gives them, as well as others, a concrete incentive for the believing of it. These two persons portray a *model for* the members of the socially perceived church community: if anyone in the church congregation is to carry out a particular project it should be executed by these two persons prior to anyone else. Such ideal is not only carried out in everyday life but naturally more so in ritual where both world view and ethos lend each other its respective meaning.

The responsibilities of the couple, especially of the head minister, are enormous. We find the following description of an ideal head minister:

---

[15] This point occurred to the author while speaking with members at the Tenrikyo Mission Center in Europe during two summer visits in 1995 and 1996. In association with the notion of demonstrating one's sincerity by mastering the dance, a twofold representation is portrayed by dancing in front of the main altar, i.e. in front of God the Parent and also, by being observed as the center of attention by those who have assembled from behind.

[16] In the case that the head minister is a woman, she will sit opposite of where a male head minister would sit. The next member in seniority will sit closer to the center if a head minister does not have a spouse.

> As the core of a church, the head minister should be well aware of the weighty responsibility with which he or she has been charged. The head minister is to seek an ever deeper understanding of the teachings and put them into practice as a pioneer of the path of single-hearted salvation (Tenrikyo Missionaries Association 1993, 90–91).

In particular, the duty of a head minister can be summarized in the following way.

> The duties of a head minister of such a church are to be ever mindful of the origin, to seek a deeper understanding of the truth of the teachings, to settle the mind, and, with sincerity, to *teach* and *guide* the followers, taking the *lead* at the forefront of the Path. Then the followers, influenced by the head minister's virtue, will progress in spiritual growth, becoming harmonious and united. Thus, the teachings come to bear fruit (Tenrikyo Church Headquarters 1993a, 71; emphasis added).

Teaching, guiding, and leading are at stake. The performance of the Teodori itself solidifies efforts in trying to achieve such ideals despite the fact that they are often difficult requisites for anyone to execute. Moreover, for the head minister who is to take lead, s/he is literally the primary figure in the performance; the semiotic value at least portrays him or her as so. That is, as the primary figure in the execution of the service, s/he realizes that s/he must be the one who is convinced of it in order to teach it to others. In so doing, one act lends meaning to the other and vice versa, creating in both an aura of factuality for the believing of it.

When Guests Attend

The positioning of the head minister and what social relation it denotes becomes clearer when a guest speaker is invited to attend a monthly service. Since the invited person is, after all, a guest, s/he will be part of the Tenrikyo community. The reason for the invitation is to give a talk to the congregation after the ritual dance is over, usually to encourage members for even further spiritual growth. At times, Church Headquarters will organize pastoral visits. In such cases, those sent to visit churches are part of administrative headquarters or a head minister of a local church with ample experiences to convey to a church congregation other than his or her own. On rare and special occasions, the leader of Tenrikyo, Nakayama Zenji, or the previous one, Nakayama Zenye, appear as very important guests. Yet the concern here is what attire these guests wear and where they sit while the church celebrates a monthly service. By answering this we can see how the *uchi/soto* distinction—with the dancing of the Teodori at the context—becomes one such indexing principle.

176

On more than one occasion the author has personally witnessed guests at a various number of church congregations located in parts of Japan, Europe, and the United States. As we have mentioned earlier, guests identify themselves with another church and are often head ministers themselves of an "other" local Tenrikyo church, an "internal other." Although quite knowledgeable in the ritual dance, they are not asked to perform the dance with the welcoming congregation. In other words, they simply participate by observing the ritual dance, not simply as part of the worshippers in the hall, but as the internal "other."

The clothes these guests wear attest to the portrayal of coming from a socially constructed external church community. As we have said, clothing is an important indexing factor for the *uchi/soto* continuum. Those who wear ritual attire define their social position as belonging to the church community. Those wearing the ritual garb to perform the dance indicate to others of their participation at the local church and signifies connotatively, perhaps, a deeper conviction of the Tenrikyo teachings. The audience, too, have their own attire and this is usually the *happi* jackets mentioned. Yet summoned guests do not wear the *happi* jacket or the attire for the ritual dance. They usually wear western fitted formal wear—suit and necktie for example—for the occasion. On special auspices occasions, for example, there are guests who arrive wearing the traditional Japanese vestment worn for celebratory occasions such as a wedding. Despite the variation, however, this simply demonstrates the distinctiveness of a guest, the *soto*, from the church membership, the *uchi*. Such orchestrations of the symbolic economy of the vestments are markers in their own right of an *uchi/soto* distinction. Once again, these are in terms of the local situation where the local church membership constitutes one body and those from the outside, despite their deep relationship with the religion, constitute the other. Where this contrast can be likened to one of black and white there is another symbolic code in the positioning of where these guests, with respect to the others, are seated.

Depending on space availability the guests have a special seat reserved for them throughout the service. Usually, however, it is up-front and near the upper dais. If the dais is large enough some guests are allowed to sit on top of the dais while the performance of the service takes place. Although the proximity to the dais is emphasized the position along such proximity is situated in the periphery. In other words, the guests are seated to an off-centered angled area of the congregation. This positioning demonstrates a symbolic system that parallels with the principle of an *uchi/soto* configuration.

Figure 12. Places where guests are seated at a local church service

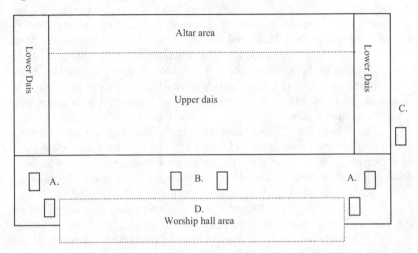

In figure 12 above, locations A, B, and C are befitting areas where local churches reserve seating for guests. Both A and B are frequent. C, on the other hand, is a special seating arrangements made when there is enough room near the lower dais. Usually, however, this orchestration is reserved when the spiritual leader of Tenrikyo, Nakayama Zenji, or the previous one, Nakayama Zenye, are invited to a local church for a very special occasion. Yet despite the frequency or the reasons behind such seating, the configuration is meant only to demonstrate one particular point: the pattern is that guests will not mix in with the other members of the congregation. This area for the congregation membership has been marked as area D.

The consequences of such seating arrangements and clothing are such that they symbolically represent indexes of an *uchi/soto* distinction. Guests are more than qualified to perform the ritual dance with the congregation yet they are not asked to nor are they obliged. Further, their clothing holds significance: they may wear such attire within their own respective churches but not at a church where they would be attributed as guests. In this manner the entire congregation consolidates their own position as members of the church and are able to demonstrate a unity to the "*soto*" outside element—one of the primary scopes of the performance of the service in the first place. This contrast becomes more apparent through the symbolic measures that have been mentioned and it is through such measures that the members themselves identify with the local church in solidifying loyalty to their social Tenrikyo group.

178

When the Teodori is Performed in Public

It is not always, however, that the Teodori is performed in a church setting for a monthly service. The Teodori is from time to time danced on a street corner—without the usual ritual garbs or use of the nine musical instruments. One musical instrument, however, is utilized and it is the wooden clappers to maintain a constant rhythm for the dancing. This type of performance is carried out prior to delivering a speech concerning the teachings of Tenrikyo. It can also be performed immediately after singing the songs to the service while walking through the city's sidewalks. When it is done in this way, the group carries a banner with the name of God the Parent, Tenri-O-no-Mikoto, written on it. In effect, this banner hoisting is a type of missionary conduct for Tenrikyo followers. Members are simply "leaving behind only the fragrance," or spreading the word of God to the general public by dancing the Teodori on a busy street corner, as described in Song VII, 1. It just may be an exaggerated form of the Teodori performed at a monthly service.

This method of missionary work originated during the days of Nakayama Miki. It is reported that Miki sent her youngest daughter, Kokan, to Osaka in 1853 in order to preach the name of God the Parent. Kokan was at that time a young girl of seventeen years and embarked on propagating the teachings outside the confines of the small village. Kokan, along with three others, carried a banner with "Tenri-O-no-Mikoto" inscribed in Chinese characters and proclaimed loudly, "*Namu Tenri-O-no-Mikoto, Namu-Tenri-O-no-Mikoto*" to the beat of the wooden clappers (Nakayama Y. 1986b, 8; Tenrikyo Church Headquarters 1996, 25–27). This has since come to be called, *kamina nagashi*, spreading the name of God.

Modern day practices have blended the performance of the ritual dance and, with a loudspeaker, propagate the teachings that is more conventionally known as the street preacher approach in missionary work. Yet it is through these experiences, especially through the dancing of the Teodori on a street corner, that provide an index of what this section intends to clarify: an *uchi/soto* distinction. This ritual dance becomes most distinguishing here since it is overlapped in the context of a modern day setting. It is obvious that *uchi/soto* distinctions are enhanced and portrayed here since the street corner is not where one often witnesses such an act.

The symbolic movements that are carried out in front of the general public by the Tenrikyo missionaries tell themselves—implicitly as well as to the onlookers—that they belong to a particular religious community. This religious community, in a very symbolic way, is communicating words of encouragement to themselves: the performers of the dance are in actuality solidifying their cohesiveness—their identity as missionaries—through action in such a context. This cohesion found among the well-structured dance movements therefore distinguish the inside *uchi* group—the dancers—from the outside *soto* group—the general public. There is thus a threefold layer of meaning when dancing the Teodori in such a context.

On one level, performers are simply telling themselves that they are carrying out the will of God by propagating in public an important ritual of the religion. The moods and motivations that stem from such a performance involve, as we have mentioned, a heartfelt acknowledgment that they are doing exactly what Nakayama Miki told her daughter to do many years ago. In other words, by propagating in public through dance form the words of God the Parent, the dancers re-enact a "sacred story" in their missionary lives: such performances give meaning to the performers themselves. On the second level, however, they undoubtedly have a message to expound since the participants are engaged in missionary work. Connotatively, then, the task set out by the performer is to recruit members. Those possessing the ritual knowledge (Jennings 1982) belong to an *uchi* group and those who may come in contact with the teachings through the dancing consist of a *soto* group. To extend the argument, and as implied earlier, the *uchi* implies purity whereas *soto* implies impurity. (Ohnuki-Tierney 1984). The dance becomes an attempt by the purified dancing assembly to extend and demonstrate their cleanliness to the defiled non-dancing public. Ideally, then, the pure intend to purify those who are impure through a dance that consists of the *uchi* in reaching out towards the *soto*. Action defined in such a context demarcates a line between the performers, the Tenrikyo dancers, and the non-performers, the general public.

On a third level, the text itself with its various missiological nuances holds special meaning. When dancing in public, while it is true perhaps anywhere, the dancer is confronted with a general aura of feeling that what s/he is actually doing is in actual reality what God the Parent would like most: spread the fragrance of the teachings. Yet dancing in a public corner has its psychological effects, which, for the most part, first time participants are hesitant to do. Despite the initial phase, however, once the dancer is able to identify with the other members of the gathered assembly, s/he is able to concentrate more upon the meanings of the ritual dance. And in such a text, it follows, we find many references to why the dancer is moving about in public: the text itself reminds the public performers of a *model of* cosmic reality and a *model for* social reality. In such a way, then, the dancers on a street corner are those who have committed themselves to single-hearted salvation so highly valued in the framework of the Tenrikyo teachings.

The dance text therefore imparts special missiological meaning, not for the onlookers who do not know of the Tenrikyo religion, but more for those who are engaged in single-hearted salvation. Although from an objective point of view, the dancing of the Teodori on a busy street corner is quite inappropriate, even out of place, it is certainly not so for the dancing missionary. Through the performance of the Teodori in the general public, the missionary is filled with strength by the performance of it. Such strength is transmitted not only through the dance text itself but because the interplay between *uchi* and *soto* coincides with it as well since it holds missiological meaning.

One theologian, Fukaya Tadamasu, gives us an insight as to why the missionary is so dependent on the songs for the service, especially with respect to the psychological impetus it imparts after a difficult day in the mission. According to him, the songs of the Mikagura-uta give the missionary a practical spirituality to work with when on the path of single-hearted salvation.

> After an unsuccessful day of missionary effort one walks a weary path alone homeward-bound, and he sings the Mikagura-uta to himself and finds that fear and weariness disappear. The life of Oyasama and the hardships of early followers come to mind. Tears issue forth and strength arises in the heart. Such experience, I believe, any one who has taken part in missionary work will have had (Fukaya 1978, 5).

For any missionary, then, the verbal symbolic patterns of the ritual dance are important. Meaning is given to the missionary who is exhausted and tired from the endeavor in single-hearted salvation simply by singing the text: it provides encouragement by recalling the intertext. Yet without its special significance—without providing the necessary ethos for the missionary—there would be no room for the believing of it. In other words, the verbal symbolic patterns create certain moods and motivation that socially consolidates with its cosmological building thereby giving encouragement and the drive to continue. What verses exactly provoke these moods and motivations? Some verses encapsulate an ethos for the missionary. With the repeated performance of the Teodori by the missionary with other missionaries, then, this ethos becomes a shared one that unifies membership thereby creating an even stronger bond for those found within.

There are certain textual strategies used in underlining the notion of those who are part of the socially constructed inside group. One major motif used for making such a distinction is in the verbal symbolic movement of comprehending the will of God. The word "understand" often appears as a marker to posit this dichotomy. Further, reference is made to those who doubt such understanding. We find:

> Though I have searched through myriad generations of this world, there is no one who understands My heart. (Yorozuyo, 1); It is natural, for it has not been explained. It is not unreasonable that you know nothing.

(Yorozuyo, 2); The human heart is a deeply doubting thing. (Song VI, 1); Although you are performing the Service here, there is no one who understands My heart. (Song IX, 9); The human heart does not understand truth easily. (Song X, 1); Until this time, of everyone, there is not one person who has understood My heart. (Song XI, 9).

There is also reference made to matters regarding faith. As one missionary has already demonstrated, missionary work is not an easy job that is often characterized by "others" who challenges the missionary's point of view (Fukaya 1978). Such provocations can be characterized by greed. Needless to mention, however, this becomes quite discouraging for the missionary who is characterized also by human weaknesses. The following words that imply a motive to continue, a message that attempts to rouse upon a particular disposition, are found. For instance, we find:

With effort you have followed and come this far; the true salvation begins from now. (Song III, 4); Always ridiculed and slandered, still I shall work remarkable salvation. (Song III, 5); No matter what people say, God is watching, so ease your mind. (Song IV, 1); Night and day performing the service; to the neighbors it must be noisy and annoying. (Song IV, 4); No matter how many steps of faith you have taken, do not let your heart become mistaken. (Song VI, 7); Yet still you must have faith; if your heart is wrong, start anew! (Song VI, 8); Because you have come this far in your faith, you must see at least one good result. (Song VI, 9); Strike away a greedy heart! Resolutely determine your heart! (Song VIII, 4); I see that in the world's heart greed is mixed throughout. (Song IX, 3); If you have greed, please give it up, because God cannot accept it (Song IX, 4).

At a different level, the verbal symbolic patterns make reference to the idea of group solidarity as well as the idea that one person alone cannot do it all by him or herself. The missionary is in need of others as others are in need of the missionary. Yet also important in such a formation is that God does not use force for the assembling of such people together. These ideals, too, are constituents of a particular ethos, one which proves to be effective for the missionary when building boundaries through the performance of the ritual dance.

If you believe, let us bind together in a fellowship. (Song V, 10); I do not say forcibly, "Do this or that"; it depends on each person's own heart. (Song VII, 6); No matter how long you continue to hesitate, it cannot be done by yourself. (Song VIII, 5); You should not forcibly prevent anyone, no matter who, if his heart is willing. (Song XI, 6); I do not say forcibly, "Come!" All, step by step, will follow and come (Song XII, 6).

Finally, another aspect of the text can be categorized which speaks of a connection being made between the words of God and the missionary's own action. That is, God appeared to explain everything yet it depends on the missionary to spread it to the world so that salvation can be realized, not only in one particular place, but throughout the world over. The missionary is seen as the "landing strips" for God to work. In this sense, then, the missionary is asked to rely on the words of God so that s/he can carry it out in concrete form and in doing is asked to watch closely on the workings of God. Such building blocks in providing a disposition for the missionary once again signifies the claim that the Teodori establishes boundaries of an *uchi* and *soto* kind.

> This time, God has appeared in the open, and explains all things in detail. (Yorozuyo, 3); All you close to me, watch God's acts and accomplishments! (Song IV, 3); Not only in Yamato, I shall go to other countries also to save. (Song V, 8); Clapping our hands through this wide world, with a penny or two we go to save. (Song IX, 1); I shall wipe out suffering; so lean wholly on the mind of God! (Song IX, 2).

An Emphasis on the *Uchi* Aspect

The works of some authors who utilize the *uchi/soto* indexing principle to map out social reality in a Japanese context were examined above. This dichotomy for the analysis has been useful in drawing attention to the import of group orientation. It has also proven to be a useful means to underline a common ethos that is consolidated through the Teodori and professed by the community of followers who believe in it. Examples have been limited in the performance of the monthly service and in the performance of the Teodori on a busy street corner, one performance reflecting the other. The aim was to depict how these two poles relate to one another in context and emphasis was centered on the *uchi* aspect with respect to the *soto*. In other words, the dichotomy was examined with respect to the connection one body, the *uchi*, has with other, the *soto*. Through these configurations, then, it was seen how this process reaffirms, tightens, and consolidates group awareness.

Now we will proceed into concentrating solely on the *uchi* aspect with relation to its social context, namely behavior patterns with respect to cosmology. The analogy of the wrapping metaphor is helpful here since we shall endeavor to analyze the gift itself rather than, as it has been demonstrated so far, illustrating the relationship between the wrapping and the gift. The following section is then considered as an extension of this context-oriented conceptual framework.

Observations were made to establish the relationship between inside and outside groups and how boundaries are drawn. As suggested, dancers of the Teodori constitute the inside *uchi* group. This particular frame of reference was made only because the "others" render themselves as *soto* groups. In particular, it was held that each group is distinguished, isolated, and highlighted during the ritual dance. Further, the important point of "belonging to a group," although not mentioned in this particular manner, was indicated: who belongs to what group serves as the means of differentiating between groups. In other words, the sense of belonging to a group has its social implications insofar as it hold meaning for the individual to be part of that particular group. But the consequences of such implications lead us to a further inquiry on how the individual within such a group behaves in context. Geertz claims "thick description" for any kind of text—including context—to be highly productive yet he leaves little clues on how one can analyze a context given that such a context owns a particular cosmology. To further deepen the notion of the inside/outside dichotomy, then, we will search for an answer in the work of the British anthropologist Mary Douglas.

A Context-centered Approach: The Work of Mary Douglas

We have mentioned Mary Douglas's contributions within the framework of certain points in our analysis, namely with respect to Japanese notions of purity and danger.[17] Yet her theoretical positions are well adapted for the Japanese context for anthropologist Valentine notes:

> Indeed Japan is relevant to Douglas's argument, not only because of its highly developed idea of purity and pollution, but also because of its emphasis of social form and boundaries, and its accompanying exploration and utilisation of ambiguity, notably in religion and the arts (Valentine 1990, 38).

One of her major theoretical contribution is what she coins as the grid/group theory. *Natural Symbols* (1970), which focuses on this theory, is an elaborated form of a chapter found in her previous volume *Purity and Danger* (1966). Yet, as one theorist notes, the second edition of *Natural Symbols* (1973) and its original utilize different approaches for he argues that the difference is so great that it can be considered two totally distinct theoretical paradigms.[18]

---

[17] We have cited her work in the previous section concerning the meaning of symbolic inversions. Notions of openings and closings of the physical body, however, in relation to its social body have also been elaborated by a another anthropologist (Ohnuki-Tierney 1984).

[18] One sociologist (Spickard 1989) notes a variation in her use of grid/group theory. In her original *Natural Symbols* (1970), one finds this version showing resemblance between cosmology and individual society. Yet *Natural Symbols* (1973) argues to concentrate on cosmologies as accountability devices. In other words, where the former version is concerned with symbolism, the later version is concerned with social control. *Cultural Bias* (1978) returns to the original thesis. Douglas is, however, less inclined to ask questions concerning the relationship between ritualized

In order to avoid methodological complications, however, we adhere to her original version concerning symbolism rather than social control since it is here that Douglas's analysis is useful. The grid/group theory, when properly used, focuses on cosmological notions that are then related to context, the particular aim of this section. According to Douglas such grid/group dimension provides a means of classifying social relations—with special emphasis on the social environment—to cosmology. The theory is designed to correlate particular kinds of symbolic structures with social variables since cosmologies are produced that structurally mirrors social relations (Douglas 1970, 67). Prior to extending this conception to the ritual dance a few words will be mentioned concerning the backdrop of this theory.

Symbolic Boundaries

For Mary Douglas, cultural classification in social life is to assume the presence of symbols that demarcate boundaries or lines of division. Order will not materialize without a symbolic system. It follows that social life is governed to a certain extent by symbols that have the power to order and classify. What Douglas is in search for, then, is the position of these symbolic compositions. In other words, her theory focuses on location within context. To illustrate this, we refer to her *Purity and Danger* (1966) where she argues that what is "clean" and what is "dirty" depends on a system of classification and the location of the matter within the system. A practical illustration is a pair of athletic shoes that are left on top of a dinner table: the athletic shoes in themselves are not considered "dirty" but when lying on top of a dinner table the set up is "dirty," almost repelling, in modern society. The point here is the notion of things "out of place" stems from only a particular context.

Social relations also have their own boundaries and tiers. Individuals can be seen to cross boundaries and become matter that, as in the case of dirt, result in reaction from those who are within their respective perimeters. There rises an opportunity to either "clean up the mess" by penalizing such actions that do not conform or put the object back into his/her correct location. Yet at other times classification rules are transformed in order to create a need to bring the community closer together. For our aims, then, the process of bringing the community closer together is but part of forming a more coherent *uchi*.

Douglas borrows restricted and elaborated codes from the field of linguistics to further expand her insights (Douglas 1970, 19–36). A restricted code in linguistics is one that confines and bounds an individual to speak in a

---

religions and body symbolism on the one hand with differing types of societies on the other. Instead she perceives cosmologies as ideas which seem to be part of the natural order but aims to demonstrate that they are strictly a product of social interaction.

very narrow mode, such that, only his or her group is able to comprehend the meaning. Linguistic theorists have proved, argues Douglas, that conversation is a mediating principle in which such group sentiments are confirmed. In other words, the commonly taken for granted assumptions are utilized in order to decode a particular message. This brings to surface a presupposed distinctive view of the world and would thus mean that it also reaffirms the group's boundaries when one converses with another. A common example of this can be drawn out from the realm of a university lecture. One who is proficient in making a lecture at a university uses distinct and specialized phrases that would perhaps be impossible to render meaningful for an outsider who is not part of the university. Contrarily, then, when a restricted code is not used, an elaborated code is put to use in conversation. This would imply that those conversing in elaborated code would have less coherence of group identity and will tend to possess higher individual identity. An elaborate code, for example, is used when speaking with strangers on the street for particular directions. A requisite to encode the message would imply an adequate understanding of the language that does not necessarily have to be as technical as, lets say, a university lecture. From this Douglas argues for two things: the greater the group's level of solidarity, the more restricted the linguistic code; the lower the group's level of solidarity, the more elaborated the linguistic code.

A few words on ritual in general should be made in connection with the claims made above. Seeing ritual as a condensed form of communication, as that of a linguistic code sending a message to someone, Douglas likens rituals to a set of restricted codes (Douglas 1970, 21). Her theory would retain that rituals are important in communities with closed social groups that use restricted codes in linguistic and symbolic communication. Further, Douglas elicits that rituals would be more prevalent in societies where emphasis is on hierarchical position rather than individual identity and that a general consensus could be found to uphold such a system (Bell 1992, 177–178). Together with this insight, as we shall examine later, it is worthwhile to keep in mind the importance of the physical body in ritual since it is here that Douglas's insights imparts deeper meaning for our endeavors.

Such notions of boundaries and confines are employed by Douglas to establish a theory based on how groups themselves create such lines and what rules demarcate one individual from another within a group. Such a theory may seem imposing and generalized but nevertheless proves helpful in isolating various groups with various cosmologies. For Douglas, group means the boundary that a people have erected between themselves and the outside world. Grid, on the other hand, are the other social markings and responsibility of authority employed to limit how people behave with one another. In Douglas's own words:

186

All I am concerned with is a formula for classifying relations which can be applied equally to the smallest band of hunters and gatherers as to the most industrialised nations. All we need to know is the way in which these relations are structured according to two independently varying criteria which I have called grid and group. Group is obvious—the experience of a bounded social unit. Grid refers to rules which relate one person to others on an ego-centered basis (Douglas 1970, viii).

By isolating the level of group coherence (high or low) with the amount of internal rules governing action of each individual within the group (high or low), the array of social structures that parallel with particular cosmologies can be made. In other words, this process is an extension of the polarizing of sociological thought between individual and group behavior. What she attempts to do is use both sources in order to demonstrate two dimensions within a given context: grid for individual and group for dimensions of social incorporation. With this we come up with a horizontal plane that represents group and a vertical one that represents grid in Figure 13.

Figure 13. Grid and group quadrants   **Figure 14. Detailed grid and group**

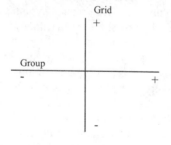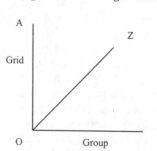

The horizontal dimension of the same schema—group—express the range of low association to tightly knit closed groups. The further we go on the line from left to right the more bounded, permanent, and inescapable the social group. The vertical dimension in this schema—the grid—focuses on an individual's obligation. That is, it relies on the set of rules engaging a person in reciprocal transaction. Douglas then draws out a detailed graph in the above manner, Figure 14, to simplify the notions of cosmology. In her own words, she describes the detailed grid and group in the following manner:

Z is the direction of maximal involvement of the individual in formalised social interaction. OB is in the direction of maximum group organisation. Moving along the line to B, group becomes a more and more effective principle of organisation and so it imposes group-focuses roles upon its

187

members: stratification, leadership and sub-groupings will develop. OA goes towards the maximum for ego-centered categories of behavior and the minimum for restraints of group. Somewhere near zero is the minimum for either kinds of social variable (Douglas 1970, 60).

Douglas asserts that this theory is applicable for any society—whether in the industrial or the so-called "primitive." In order that it may cut across social classes within such contexts, she makes the hypothesis concerning the relationship between the physical body and the social body. Her presumption is that the more value people place on social constraints the more value they place on symbols of bodily control. This, then, lends meaning to the grid/group theory and this will surely affect the outcome out how rituals are performed.

Douglas hypothesizes that it is the human body that is the natural symbol of all societies. This source is employed in the hopes comparing various societies or differing social groups. The varying attitudes of the human body will yield varying constructs of social structure and therefore will coincide in various ways with how rituals are perceived and carried out. This is her original contribution. Perceiving the human body through a particular cosmological lens will indeed influence social interaction—bridging a cosmology to context. Her main hypothesis concerning the physical body itself is twofold. First she sees that there is a drive to reach consonance on all levels of experience so that the body is coordinate with other media and controls. The idea is that social systems limit the use of the body as a medium of expression. Certain generalizations are made by becoming aware of how a community views the physical body. In short, this is to insinuate that the world view with respect to the physical body among a given community will draw its meaning accordingly on the values it has of the social body. This can be further confirmed through an observation of religious rituals that are executed within the pertinent community. Here lies our point of concern.

In demonstrating her hypothesis, Douglas elaborates on the attitude toward trance in two neighboring African tribes, the Dinka and the Nuer (Douglas 1970, 74–77). Trance, she says, concerns the way the human body is dissociated and that it should be considered in light of her discussion on formality and informality.[19] In other words, a person in trance usually is out

---

[19] Douglas argues: "A study of anti-ritualism must focus on the expression of formality and informality. It seems not too bold to suggest that where role structure is strongly defined, formal behavior will be valued. If we were to proceed to analyse a range of symbolism under the general opposition of formal/informal we would expect the formal side of every contrasted pair to be valued where role structure is more dense and more clearly articulated. Formality signifies social distance, well-defined, public, insulated roles. Informality is appropriate to role confusion, familiarity, and

of control, so to speak, and body movements are unrestrained. This would have broader implications for the community since what she argues is that the way a community values the physical body lends appropriate meaning to the social body.

Douglas's own example is that the Dinka see trance as beneficent. She also finds that they have a weak structure of society, namely, that the Dinka are high on grid (individual obligation for group) and low on group (group coherence). For her this is no surprise since it springs from the notion of their perception of the human body during trance. On the other hand, the Nuer see trance as dangerous. She also notes that they possess a strong structure of their society, namely that they are high on group (group coherence) yet low on grid (individual obligation for group). It follows that they are closed knit and see value in a controlled human body—a human body that attempts to reach consonance at all levels. All of this, however, is traced to the perception of the human body and this perception is related very much to the patterns found in the social world.

Types of Cosmologies

Ultimately for Douglas, then, the physical body is the "natural symbol" that becomes the key in understanding how a group behaves in a given context with the given cosmology. It is through an analysis of the human body that gives meaning on how to look at a given social context with respect to its governing structures. Such governing structures—the cosmology—may be bold and generalized but conjectures that there are four to point out. They are based on the physical body and are:

> [A] relatively unbounded, unstructured system (neither grid nor group), a bounded, otherwise unstructured system (grid alone), a bounded structured system (grid and group) and structure but unbounded (grid without group) (Douglas 1970, 160).

Further, and perhaps closer to our notion concerning religion and rituals, one finds her commenting that resembles much of what we have said so far concerning the attitudes of the human body found within the significance given to the Tenrikyo ritual dance:

> [T]he religious emphasis would be expected *to treat the body as the focus and symbol of life*. We would expect to find positive themes of symbolic nourishment developed to the extent that the social body and the physical body are assimilated and both focus the identity of individuals a *structured, bounded system* (Douglas 1970, 160; emphasis added).

---

intimacy. Body control will be appropriate where formality valued, and most appropriate where the valuing of culture above nature is most emphasised" (Douglas 1970, 71).

It is without doubt that the Tenrikyo ritual dance actualizes a bounded and well-structured embodiment. That is, the community of Tenrikyo faithful is classifiable to be both high on grid and high on group: they yearn for "maximal involvement of the individual in formalized social interaction." It is in the performance of an orderly type of ritual—controlled and composed—that lends meaning to the social context. In other words, the view of the body seen benignly in ordered form will result in possessing a strong social structure, namely, a strong value placed on group. This would be equal in implying the notion of high group and high grid on the grid/group diagram as we have already sustained.

A few observations will be made through notions that have been brought up through Douglas's framework. That is, since her grid/group theory hinges on the primary importance of how a particular community perceives the physical body, the endeavor will be to examine with particular attention how the Tenrikyo cosmology views it. In so doing, we hope to further provide the background on why Tenrikyo believers are charted high on both grid and group.

Meaning of the Physical Body in Tenrikyo

The use of the body—the physical body—in attracting new converts into the Tenrikyo community, then, places an immediate effect into the social dimension of the community. Claims here will be based on the assumption that the attitude which one has towards the body and how it is understood, especially when it is not functioning properly, are consequently reflected in the social structure of its world. In chapter two, emphasis was placed on how the human body represents the providence of God the Parent and as well as how it is considered part of the microcosm/macrocosm dichotomy. Certainly, this dichotomy relates well with our study. To fully understand why a person has been afflicted is to probe into what an illness means and how it comes about on the human body. In other words, the attitude one holds toward the human body will also influence the way in how the social community is perceived. The point of departure is the ailing body: what does illness mean according to Tenrikyo scripture and, if what we have been arguing until now is correct, how does this reflect in the social body? The following elaboration, then, is based on the hypothesis that unhealthy social relationships will result in unhealthy physical bodies, thus upholding the mirror reflection between the social and physical bodies.

Illness

There is ambiguity on this subject since on the one hand, the Sazuke is meant for curing an illness yet, on the other hand, it is written in scripture that illness does not exist. The main theological thrust of this tenet separates mind from body. The two are considered separate from one another yet, as we shall see later, there is an intricate interdependence between the two. To begin with, then, Tenrikyo scriptures postulate that the mind belongs to the individual yet the human body is that which is on loan. We read the following in scriptures:

> All human bodies are things lent by God. Do you not know the free and unlimited workings of God? (Ofudesaki: III, 26); All human bodies are things lent by God. With what thought are you using them? (Ofudesaki: III, 41); With human beings: the body is a thing lent by God, a thing borrowed. The mind alone is yours. (Osashizu: June 1, 1889).

Since it is an entity that is on loan to human beings by God the Parent, the human body is granted as a perfectly functioning object. That is to say, the human body, being something that is on loan to the human mind by a perfect being as God the Parent, is something that cannot but function properly. Yet this is not the case. There are times when the human body does not function properly. The answer to the question, "Why does the human body become afflicted in the first place?" can perhaps provide a clue to the answer to such a mystery. In a nutshell, the answer lies in the Tenrikyo teaching that "the mind alone is ours."

Illness and the Mind

It is through the physical body that God the Parent is made manifest and it is the mind which "resides" in such a body that ego-oriented desires are fulfilled. Our true self—the mind—has been endowed with a body and through the medium of the body we come to know the workings of God.[20] Yet when the body is not in an operative form, then, it is taught that the mind has deviated from the proper use of it. In other words, there is direct correlation between the way the mind—the perceptions and attitudes of it—with the wholeness of the body. Miki uses "dust" as a metaphor for the improper use of the mind. The Ofudesaki states:

---

[20] Here we use "self" for the Japanese term *kokoro*: Other connotations of *kokoro* are "heart" or "mind," as we have argued thus far. It includes will and emotion. A new religions scholar (Hardacre 1986) notes that the *kokoro* is not the sum of these faculties but differs distinctively from person to person according to personality traits, dispositions, and aesthetic sensibilities. The Japanese, she argues, make a distinction between one's spirit and flesh and attributes the *kokoro* to the spirit. The *kokoro* includes the soul but is not identical to it since the soul continues to exist after death but the *kokoro* does not. The *kokoro* is contrasted with the ego when selfish desires and negative nuances are the import of discourse. Yet what is comes down to is: "The notion of the *kokoro* is a hallmark of Japanese culture, and it is the central pillar of the world view of the new religions" (Hardacre 1986, 19). A concise volume (Rosenberger, ed. 1992) offers a multi-disciplinary perspective on the notion of Japanese self.

Looking all over the world and through all ages, I find no one who is evil. (I, 52); Among all humankind, there is no one who is evil. It is only a bit of dust stuck on. (I, 53); There is nothing at which should be called illness. It is only because there are paths of the mistaken mind.(III, 95); These paths are miserliness, covetousness, self-love, greed, and arrogance. They are the dusts. (III, 96).

Verse III, 95 demonstrates that there is nothing called illness—in the eyes of God the Parent—and when the body is suffering it is a sign that the mind is on a mistaken path. In order to find relief, or in allowing room to alleviate oneself from physical suffering, the workings of God the Parent must be liberated in the body. It is the mind itself that blocks such free and unlimited workings in the body.[21] One scripture further dictates: "God rides on the mind and works. As long as the mind is firm, God will ride the mind and work freely and unlimitedly" (Osashizu, October 2, 1898). The focal point, then, in all endeavors is the working of the individual mind. And to sweep the mind of dust is of salient importance when describing how one may fix the ailing human body.

The Sazuke healing ritual appears to free one from an illness through the stroking of the area that is affected. This may be so in appearance for the touching of the hands over the area needing to be cured requires bodily contact. It seems as though special power is vested in the hands which result in the healing yet this is not so. As mentioned, the transformation of the mind—replacing the mind—is but the springboard from which miracles such as the ones we have cited earlier leap forward. It is the mind that enables God to completely work in the body after it has been accepted. If the afflicted person changes perceptions and thoughts so as to accord them with God the Parent, free and unlimited workings take place. Although replacing the mind is indispensable for the wholeness of the body, the way in which we see concrete transformations occur in the social world will help in seeing the relation between the human and social bodies.

We cannot admit that the mind has really made a change for the better without demonstrating the change of heart in the social world: action in everyday life is proof of an internal transformation. It is in the relationships of everyday life that truly attest to the transformation of the mind. To illustrate this point, the following examples are provided in order to see how particular

---

[21] One missionary likened this twofold aspect, the unlimited workings of God the Parent on the one hand, and with the workings of it in the human body on the other, to that of trying to move a car parked on a hill with the brakes locked (Kontani 1993). No movement will result since the brakes are applied, no matter how much one attempts to move forward. In this case, the mind of joy is the car with the brakes having been released. If the mind can find joy, then, the unlimited workings of God the Parent will function thoroughly in the human body.

instances of illnesses depict the notion of reciprocal reflection between social body and physical body.

The Afflicted Physical Body, The Afflicted Social Body

A few examples of how illnesses are interpreted will illustrate just how the human body is portrayed as but part of the social body. Let us take as an example any type of illness that is associated with the skin. The person who is afflicted surely feels in need of some sort of alleviation from suffering. In order to restore the body to its original functioning form, at least within the Tenrikyo interpretations given to such afflictions, one must replace the mind that caused such an illness to take root in the first place. This would mean to change the way the person has perceived things prior to the illness, usually meaning to clear the mind from "dusts."

The interpretation in this particular case would be that such sickness results from the person unable to "join" with others in his or her own community—in the person's social world—causing the mind to accumulate "dust." In this instance it is important to recall the providence of skin on the human body originates from *Kunisazuchi-no-Mikoto* and this embraces "joining in general." In other words, the misfortune is perceived as a sign that the person afflicted is not able to recognize the importance of the interconnectedness of individuals with others. The advise to the afflicted person by the missionary is to become more open in "connecting" with others as well as to help others "connect." A change of relationships in his or her life occurs by seeing the human body as a symbol of the social body. It is as if the ailing social body is taken as the ailing human body, and the only remedy would be to transform the mind in accord with the notion of remedying a healthier social body. In order to do just this, scriptures dictate, one must change perceptions of the mind so as to transform how one "joins" with others.

Another example cited quite often among the interpretations of the human body—in the event of an illness—is the interpretation given to those with injuries to the head. As in the English language, the term "head" is often taken as the person responsible or leader of a particular group. In order to take the responsibility of such a post, however, the person must demonstrate that s/he is qualified to remain at the "top" of the organization, usually confirming such position through both competence and performance. The leader of the group is usually one who stands on top of others, so to speak, and has the role of being responsible for their subordinates. On a parallel, then, a person who is afflicted in the head demonstrates that such an ability is at stake, namely that the person has become too proud and must be quick in changing it. Furthermore, since the "head" is interpreted also as "standing on top of others" this would mean s/he has become arrogant: there is need of the person to return to the bottom to become "low" and humble. The reader is reminded that arrogance is a form of dust. As a result, then, there would automatically be a transformation not only of mind but also of social relations: the missionary will most likely suggest to the afflicted person to become humble with respect to others. This is but one of many examples in demonstrating how the body symbolizes social hierarchy and what connotations it has within the larger discourse of religion and society.

Broader Implications

Certainly the two examples mentioned are not the only sources for demonstrating this point. If we were to make a list at the numerous interpretations of illnesses we may just find that the human body is but a mirror relation of the social body.[22] In retrospect, then, this would confirm the world view of the human body representing a microcosm and the world at large as the macrocosm. Further, if we shift the wording of Douglas's "human body is a reflection of the social body," Tenrikyo jargon and interpretation—although unaware of the social implications of such terminology—would apply it more vigorously by saying "the human body is a reflection of the social universe." Harmony with the self, with the body, with the social order, and with the cosmos is, as Hardacre argues, the main principle on which this can be founded (Hardacre 1986).

The Tenrikyo community perceives the human body as something that is on loan by God the Parent, as dictated in normative scripture. Through the specific functioning of various aspects of God the Parent's providence the human body is portrayed as a living symbol of it. That is, the physical body is perceived as a symbol of the divine nature of all things present in the universe. The perfect working of the physical body is simply a reflection of the perfect working of the social body inasmuch as these social relations are reflected in the physical body. What this implies is that the use of the mind—the attitudes and perception—towards others and carried out *with* others is of paramount importance. In what follows is that through an affliction of the human body, the workings of the physical body that deteriorate, is simply a sign as that depicts a faulty and unjust relationship with others. Once again, this gauge would not function without the social interaction of the individual. It places a

---

[22] Others include the following: legs problems = not filial to one's parents; respiratory problem = unable to speak nicely of others; heart problems = unable to accept things with heart as they are; eye problems = inclinations of adultery or always with an eye on the opposite sex; nose trouble = critical of others; back pain = non supportive of parents. One hears such interpretations while assisting the administration of the Sazuke. Fukaya Tadamasu is most famous for his numerous healing accounts. One of his famous publications (Fukaya 1986) contains medical, scriptural, and missionary references concerning a wide variety of illnesses. His remedy is for the most part replacing the mind but implicitly argues for action-oriented responses in one's visible social world.

high emphasis on one's social interaction as well as placing a high emphasis on group cohesiveness. As such, we find that the community of Tenrikyo dancers grade high both on grid and group, vectoring toward the Z in Figure 14.

Two brief observations can be made with respect to the discussion above. One is that if the Teodori performers rank high on both grid and group they will obviously possess a well-bounded structured system springing from a cosmology that the human body is the symbol for life. There is a sense of belonging to a particular bounded group and rules that regulate interactions between individuals are manifold. Drawing from the discussion on the physical body, for example, an individual who becomes sick and belongs to a community of Tenrikyo believers is one means of organizing group solidarity and so of mustering up support for the ill. In Douglas's own words, the "group will tend to make a public show of admiration for the courage of infirm individuals, to announce bulletins on progress and to seek out causes and responsibility for ill-health as a matter of general concern" (Douglas 1978). That is, although an illness may hold an interpretation for the individual who is sick—as implied above—a matter of general concern for the group also becomes clear. The second observation is a consequence of the first. If the Teodori is taught to people that do not share the same idealized grid and group characteristics, it will certainly yield negative results. Seen in this fashion, then, the meaning of the Teodori will vary for people possessing differing perceptions of the human body—knowledge of the body that is not in line with the Tenrikyo teachings. This view would hold true with respect to propagating the Tenrikyo teachings in differing regions and having the Teodori as a means of expressing joyous group celebration. The first step, if this grid/group theory were of any missiological relevance, would be to focus on the meaning of the human body as a symbol of life that will then correlate with a perspective which will give importance to the general notion of rituals. This will surely facilitate meaning given to the performance of the Teodori for particular region.

CONCLUSION

More than a hundred and twenty years have elapsed since Nakayama Miki began to teach her disciples the Teodori. It was this shared activity, a scene of encounter (Keane 1997), that materialized as the principle means of portraying the main thrust of her teachings with the body. Accordingly, where Tenrikyo missions were established, the performance of the Teodori was, and still is, its most vital event for the establishment. In fact, the life of the community of believers is based on the performance of the Teodori—so crucial is its performance. Joy, harmony, and unity are expressed through the ritual dance and as such the Teodori depicts a *model of* cosmic reality and a *model for* social reality. At present, hundreds of thousands of followers are able to dance the thirteen songs Nakayama Miki put together through the will of God.

The point in having Nakayama Miki as the Shrine of God was to teach humankind the purpose of its existence: to live a life filled with joy. One means of teaching how to live joyously was through the Teodori. Her intent in teaching the Teodori was to symbolically portray its joyous and festive meaning at one and the same time. Her aim did not stop there. She also added that if humankind were able to discover joy, God, too, would also rejoice. That is, if the performance of the Teodori is done joyfully, then, God will also find reason to be joyful. In the final analysis, then, if humanity is able to live the Joyous Life, God too, will also take delight. By so doing, not only is the Joyous Life the aim and scope of humankind's existence it is also to be collectively shared with its original Parent. Such sharing is modeled in the performance of the Teodori inasmuch as its performance gives joy to the Parent.

In making a few concluding remarks, then, the same position as Geertz is assumed in that any sort of anthropological analysis will always be open-ended. One aim of this study was to exercise a constructive effort in understanding the "other." In doing so, the basic components of the ritual dance were mapped out by relying on the conceptual framework of a particular interpretive anthropology. For the remainder of this concluding section, then, more justice would be made to the anthropological method by offering a few suggestions concerning the ritual dance with its pertinence to other systems. In other words, we shall reflect upon the meaning of the Teodori for a modern pluralistic setting. These closing remarks will hopefully assist in further research concerning the ritual dance for the future.

Teodori in a Modern Pluralistic Setting

A process known as secularization, where, true meaning is lost in activities springing from a purely religious consciousness, characterizes the present world. From a sociological point of view, religion stands in the periphery of the social system and the functioning of society depends more on rationalized agencies than on the supernatural in a secularized world. The reason for such decline in religious consciousness is due in part by the development of attitudes in empirical matters. Space does not allow us to go into the particular details of its causes but science has played a major role in transforming the nature of the way we think: it has enhanced the awareness of gearing nature and organizing it for the well-being of humanity. Religious symbols, therefore, have lost their dynamic power because new assumptions about the way we perceive the world have unraveled old ones. They have become items for decoration or other dull insignificant object that lie around in the one's home or stored away from everyday view.

As such, then, the Teodori should appear to be unfitting in the secularized world since the meaning of the Teodori rests entirely on an understanding of religious symbols. The Teodori consists of connecting one religious symbol to the other since, as maintained throughout this investigation, it is a primarily a text consisting of such combinations. Yet through use of the many religious symbols portrayed in the Teodori—the origin, the seed, the fertile field, the carpenter, to name only a few—the community of believers are able to remind not only themselves of the need of religious symbols but are also able to transmit this reliance to others. It is as if the dancers are expressing themselves to the modern pluralistic world about the indispensable nature of symbols. In that which follows, we shall like to draw attention to one particular symbol, namely the symbol of origin, and provide an account of it so as to link it with the question of "play" that has been lost in the modern pluralistic setting. We shall also propose a missiological reflection concerning the Teodori as it crosses cultural and societal boundaries.

Returning to the Origin

One of the major tenets of the Tenrikyo world view is a return to the origin. In its denotative sense, this signifies to always have the origin of all beginnings fixed, and therefore settled, in the mind. That is, followers are continuously reminded of the reason for the creation of humanity, where such creation took place, who had the predestination to reveal such an origin, and what takes place in order to commemorate such origin. Indeed, when the origin remains fixed in the mind dispositions arise for a Tenrikyo member: spreading joy to others about the origin; participating in the local church's activities; and of course, renewing such tenets through the dancing of the Teodori. At stake is a consideration of the connotative meaning of this last perspective, namely "returning to the origin" during the dancing of the Teodori.

At the outset of this reflection, it was suggested that the modern pluralistic setting is one permeated with a secular perspective. There are some areas of religious life that have become weary in this regard where, in extreme cases, religion becomes an instrument to advance secular vantage points. In a sense, religious consciousness possesses a twofold ambiguity: it is perceived less meaningful with respect to the secular perspective and yet there are those living in the contemporary setting with deep religious convictions. The communities of Tenrikyo believers are not isolated away from the modern pluralistic setting but instead are part of it. They are not enclosed in their own fortresses but rather are inserted in the modern world: they live *in* and *among* people of a heterogeneous sort. In other words, the community of believers shares some of the meanings and values of its secularized world despite possessing a religiously bent consciousness that might situate them in the periphery. This tension between one perspective and the other is always present, especially when employment or education takes the believer into a world where the priority of religious symbols loses its leverage. Paradoxically, this is where the meaning of "returning to the origin" has greatest impact.

A believer who lies in the periphery of the society finds tension building up between its own world view and that of the modern pluralistic setting. For the follower, there is need to liberate oneself from the increasing individualistic and highly structured secular society. The faithful will certainly find a place to release such tension at a local Tenrikyo church where, among other things, a common world view and ethos are shared and realities appear to be all the more coherent. Moreover, the ritual dance, which is based upon these realities, is performed. A return to the original meanings and values of being a follower of Tenrikyo occurs in and through the performance of the Teodori: a return to the origin of one's individual faith takes place. This idea of returning to one's root, or core, is of vital importance yet the meaning lies in returning, not only to the origin in some nostalgic literal past, or a futuristic making of a new origin, but the origin of the present with regard to the "here and now" setting. Such an origin in the present signifies that renewal is being made and such restoration is important for the vitality of the community of believers living in the modern pluralistic setting. A different way of putting it is through an analogy. The dancer is vital for dancing as God is vital for creation: the perfect hand movements of the Teodori portray the perfect creation of humankind at the time of origin. Yet for the faithful, this becomes the source of energy to carry on in everyday life. Such imagery provokes an almost playful quality of the origin to which we shall now direct our attention.

Time set apart from ordinary time in attending a local church's service, to return to an origin, can be perceived as a playful event. One major proponent of play, Johan Huizinga, associates it intimately with creation and with creativity. One example is the play of light that causes mirages of double images it is implicit in wordplay (Huizinga 1970). He perceives play as bringing something into being which has never existed before by changing and re-shaping boundaries of cultural phenomena and thus resonates with origin: the play activity is the basis of civilization. Seeing that play was salient in the classical Greek period, he attributes play in the following mode: play stepping out of real life and into a temporary sphere; play as taking place in a marked off space; play assuming a culturally fixed and ordained form; play creating order and is order; and play constituting elements of repetition and alternation (Huizinga 1970). Accordingly, the Teodori can certainly be seen in light of these modes with the symbol of "returning to the origin" at its matrix.

A different attribute of play is that it is essentially "untrue" since it is something not taken seriously, that which is make-believe and inauthentic (Bateson 1972). This is so in the sense that reality in such a mood denotes messages that are nonexistent. Given its imaginary sense, then, we often speak of play as "unserious," or acting like "little children," or a primitive "not yet fully human." Inherent in play is a childlike quality which is further characterized by time set apart from the ordinary and can be juxtaposed to what we call "work." Work involves bodily movement that may or may not be formidable to the natural modalities of the human body. One works in order to make a living: one is paid a certain amount of money in return for a certain type of skilled service. As opposed to play, work is serious in character and certainly authentic in the sense that its general mood denotes things which are very much "really real." Work cannot escape the influence of the modern pluralistic setting where material concerns are encouraged and religious ones subjugated. Work in the modern setting has taken a totally different meaning from that which was once characteristic of religious work. Religious work entailed serving to maintain the world created by God and paying creation back for the life one has received. The denotative meaning in work always rested in the acknowledgment of the creative source as supreme. Needless to say, the concept of work as "earning one's bread" originally derived from a religious perspective where one receives "just returns."

Seen in light of a religious perspective, modern people in the pluralistic setting have lost the sense of the original meaning of work since gratitude that was once an attribute of work no longer is the primary motivation for it. Further, not only do symbols lose their meanings in the modern pluralistic setting but individual habits are stimulated, not by how one can serve others, but how one can take advantage of others. In other words, people become more concerned with egocentric needs rather than a concern for the other: a permanent, serious, unrestrained rigid perception develops where living beings become buried in their own stead. Seen from this extreme instance, the rigid structures of work are highly contrasted with the flow of play. In this sense it parallels with the "anti" of the ordinary structures of everyday life in a modern pluralistic setting and play becomes a source of leveling out the inflexibilities found in it. Through play, then, all structured categories are destablilized.

Ritual studies scholars remind us of the importance of play in ritual. After asserting that ritualization, decorum, ceremony, liturgy are constituents of ritual, one ritual studies scholar lists celebration as one final code for what he coins as ritual necessity (Grimes 1979). Yet the celebratory aspect of ritual is one for which there is no end for its major attribute is that of play. He illustrates a cynical yet recurring episode that transpires during religious liturgies:

> In our robes and other drapes of holiness we are always something of a clown. Our shabbiness is comic, but since it is on ritual occasions typically overpowered by finery, the comedy is seldom evident . . . . Our robes are always too big; the pleats are a stylized cover-up for our undersize. We are incapable of absolute belief and total sincerity, and his/her holiness does not need our struttings and smoke. So liturgical "work" transcends itself, becomes its own opposite, in moments of celebrative play and performance. Despite the obvious opposition of holy work and play, in all liturgy a note of playfulness, fictionality, and drama arises. When this note is fully sounded we name the ritual a celebration (Grimes 1979, 137).

The all too often rigid structures of modern life can become heavy and bitter at times, especially in the contemporary pluralistic setting. Yet confronting the demands of work, its "anti," the notion of play, paves its way. Through a playful ritual structure, playing and playfulness, inflexible forms begin to unbind and deconstruct. Through religious rituals that are characterized by a playful celebratory mood, an individual is capable of experiencing a transformation since the experience is juxtaposed with the normality of everyday life.

The performance of the Teodori appears to possess a playful structure to help in the endeavor to return to the original cause of all things. With these preliminary insights, it is suggestive that there exists a playful perspective of it if it is ever to be considered a true ritual celebration. In other words, ideas that accord significance to celebration in this modern pluralistic can further deepen this work/play dichotomy world by utilizing the performance of the Teodori for its data.

Different Settings for the Missions

A concern that has occurred to any missionary involved in foreign missions is the vernacular of the ritual dance itself: can the verbal symbolic patterns be altered to accommodate the receiving culture so that a dynamic unity between the mother church—the Jiba—and the local culture be realized? Once again this itself can become another theme that can stand on its own. Here, however, we offer a few reflections; these are suggestions at most that may help further induce missiological conversations. As the question suggests, it has been reiterated that the ritual language of the Teodori is too foreign to a receptive audience and that it has become a barrier for missionary work. The debate, however, can be seen from two perspectives. One view wants change. The other is convinced that human beings should not tamper with a divinely inspired dance. Both shall be examined briefly.

One of the first things that a missionary will do is invite a perspective follower to a local church's monthly service where the Teodori is performed. In rare cases, the prospect will return for a future monthly service and therefore stabilize the relationship with members of the religion. In most cases, however, the majority of them never return. Missionaries attempt to seek answers to the reasons why there is this negative turnabout. In deliberations with perspective newcomers, they claim that the ritual language is simply too foreign: participation for them is difficult because of the unfamiliar language. They are in search of something that is closer to "home" and an impersonal ritual does not seem to do the job. When speaking about the ritual language, the referent is the language of the verbal chanting rather than its transcultural symbolic value spoken about earlier in this section. Simply put, there are people who do not understand the Teodori at face value. Missionaries who urge for change argue that just as language is constituent of a culture, the language of the ritual dance is also constituent of a culture. A performance of the ritual dance would simply mean that a newcomer, despite pertaining to one particular culture, must forget his or her own culture and adapt quickly to a Japanese one. Adherents wanting change point their finger at Church Headquarters's refusal to incorporate local cultures with their own one. In understanding the conglomeration of the religious symbols portrayed in the ritual dance, one must first obtain access to the cultural key to unlock it. This point is has been stressed throughout the study. Many are simply turned off because they are without the keys or the codes to interpret it. Missionaries working in local cultures want change but are not granted permission to construe a different type of ritual dance other than what has been passed down from one generation to the next.

There is a different group of missionaries who uphold an opposite view to the suggestion proposed above. The words themselves that are vested in the ritual dance are the precise reason why people are so attracted to it. One example will illustrate this point. At the many gatherings for world peace, the Teodori is seen executed by members of the European Tenrikyo community. Comments by the audience are suggestive for they remark that the representation of the dance best describes the religious structures necessary for world peace. Once again, the power of religious symbols is perceived at work despite discrepant cultural meanings. That is, one who is religiously receptive can discover the underlying meanings of the dance despite the cultural barrier—that is, despite the barriers of both the verbal and nonverbal symbolic patterns. Further, there have been times where onlookers have inquired about the meanings of the dance as insinuated in the performance of the Teodori on the street corner. This is despite the Teodori being performed in a country totally foreign to the Japanese setting. These are but two illustrations that demonstrate how religious symbols transcend their own indigenous structural meaning and encompass a broader universal one.

Perhaps a reason behind the attraction to the ritual dance despite its alien language is simply *because* of its depiction in such an impersonal form. More often than not, however, the Japanese themselves are prone to ask questions about the *Japanese* meaning of the dance: some portions of the verbal symbolic patterns are incomprehensible even for the indigenous follower. Surveying other religious vernaculars in Japanese religiosity, Shinto prayers are read in a language of worship developed centuries ago. Although they are often memorized by heart, Buddhist sutras are not in Japanese at all (Kitagawa 1987, 229). This may tell us something about the importance of ritual language in the Japanese setting. That is, meaning of a prayer for the layperson is not found in the content of the language but in the manner in which it is said. As one scholar has pointed out, the Japanese language elicits a wrapped structure and more so when communicating on a sacred level (Hendry 1993, 65). This demonstrates that the power of words are found not in the content of the words themselves but in the form in which they are read, chanted, sung, or shouted (Blacker 1975, 93). This may also cast a clue as to why ritual language can be so pleasing to a given audience: the incomprehensible and mysterious formulations are very attractive for the observer. One parallel can be found in Noh dramas that are rich in symbolic meaning yet possessing a language that is certainly beyond any reasonable logic.

It is not our endeavor here to decide which of the two modes, the view that supports alteration or the view that supports the power of words, is better for the community of believers. Further studies will perhaps assist and point toward new directions. Advocates who insist on altering the vernacular are pressed by considerations of a truly contextualized and inculturated religion. These proponents point at the Tenrikyo Korean Church where the ritual language of the Teodori has been adapted to its own local setting. They observe how the Korean Church is on a constant rise. The similar cultural codes found between the Japanese and Korean cultures have facilitated this adaptation. Other places should also be able to change the ritual language to match its own if it has been proven successful in a different region. On the other hand, however, there are those who insist that the Teodori conveys deep religious meaning to the local culture because of its mysterious power of the ritual language itself. A person who is sensitive to the symbolic values of the ritual dance will naturally recognize its religious significance. Surely enough, a performance in public of the ritual dance can be rejected at face value for the modern pluralistic setting. Yet the Teodori tends to be more meaningful for a different audience who recognizes the deeper structures of the dance, as in a religious gathering for world peace. An experiment of translating the Teodori across cultures, then, is needed. Something must be done to accommodate the two growing trends in the hopes that the ritual dance possesses significance in as many diverse cultural settings without disrupting the original intent of procreating joy to others. That something should not begin at an official level but should, if anything, begin from the local members themselves.

When making observations about the ritual language of the Teodori something concerning its counterpart, the ritual behavior, should also be mentioned. It has been maintained throughout this study that the verbal and nonverbal symbolic patterns constitute the text—the Teodori. Without one or the other constituent of the text, then, the Teodori would not exist as a whole. In other words, it is the combination of these signs that compose our textual substance: one without the other would obfuscate the integrity of the Teodori. Adherents who want to alter the ritual language want to do just that: change its verbal symbolic patterns to match the prefabricated nonverbal symbolic ones. One must then realize that a whole new text is being constructed if alterations are made. Here lies the perplexity of change. This point must be kept in mind when mingling with the idea of transforming the symbols of the text.

A parallel along this line can be made concerning the priority placed on the dancing form rather than the dancing content. Here, once again, a mission-based problem is confronted since the dance should be correctly taught from one person to another in order for it to be performed communally.

204

How the Teodori is taught can be problematic with respect to the varying settings it is to be performed.

There is a saying, "entering through form," in the Japanese setting. This is most applicable when teaching someone a hobby, a skill, and even a sport. The formulation of one's outer aspects in acquiring a new skill is quite salient and highly valued. Three examples are worth mentioning. One example is in the martial arts, where *kata*, or form, is the basis in which the offensive and defensive moves emerge. Without the basic *kata* structure, then, a judoist will not be promoted onto higher levels of training: the *kata* is most fundamental of all. With time, however, other judo techniques such as how to defend oneself from a particular attack, for example, naturally arises through the *kata*. Another example can be found in the Japanese tea ceremony (Kondo 1985). A tea ceremony teacher will not say much to a student: it is up to the student to observe the teacher in the correct mode and simply pattern after the bodily movements. The teacher offers no rationale to the student as to why certain forms are done in one way and not in another. The entire ceremony, in fact, is highlighted by a profusion of nonverbal symbolic patterns that requires a student to be most receptive to bodily forms rather than its content. A third example can be illustrated by remarking how one is taught to meditate in a Zen manner. Zen meditation emphasizes the posture of the body: knees bent, back straight, with neck and head naturally aligned together. Such a position for many is unnatural and questions on certain dogmatic issues concerning Zen Buddhism would be more stimulating than withstanding the bodily pain experienced in this most awkward position. The point in illustrating these examples is that it is often taken for granted that one learns by way of the body, and not through intellectual positing (Kadowaki 1982). This is especially true with respect to the "stuff" deriving from Japan. Yet learning by way of the body is not the way all cultures go about its training. The procedure of "entering through form" will be a difficult endeavor to carry out unless one is essentially disposed at bracketing one's conceptualizations.

Parallel to this, however, is teaching the Teodori to someone who does not share the same "entering through form" ideal. Posing questions why certain movements are done in one way and not in another are difficult ones that challenge the pedagogy in the missions. Unsatisfactory responses are indeed a trait when having to bend over backwards to learn through the body. The Teodori is taught with emphasis on its bodily form rather than its qualitative meaningfulness especially when it crosses cultural borders and into a new setting. This will certainly have an effect at a different level of the performance of the Teodori since Miki herself taught limp hands while dancing the Teodori portray a mind that is undisciplined (Tenrikyo Church Headquarters 1996, 71).

The aim in addressing this discussion lies in the importance of learning with the body without altogether forgetting a conceptualization of the theories that go with it. In other words, the dialectic of a mind-body concern when learning the dance is an important dichotomy not only while learning the dance structures but also when performing it, too. There is no need to disagree that one cannot learn only through the body but rather that it is an important feature of the ritual dance to be able to do so. On the other hand, however, simply learning with the intellect is not enough and this would especially hold true for those who adhere solely to theoretical pursuits. One is reminded about the theory of driving a car or that of riding a bicycle: theoretical frameworks are necessary but the "actual doing of it" compliments the entire procedure. Both body and mind must combine for the execution of it.

The discussion about the human body in this study evolved around the Tenrikyo meaning placed on creating the human body, the divine providences in the human body, "healing" the human body, and perceiving the human body as a corollary of the social body. Yet the aspect of the body in relation to the mind during the actual dancing of the Teodori has not been deepened. In other words, how the mind and body becomes unified during the ritual dance seems to be an important aspect of completing the dance. This theme, one of subjective consciousness, should bring about a different pursuit in perceiving the mechanics of the Teodori—driving toward deeper levels of inquiry. The tone in which this type of research naturally requires an examination into the transformative powers of the subject during the dance and how one's mind becomes unified with one's body—if it ever takes place.

The underlining intention of this study has been to apply an interpretive anthropological method to the Teodori and it is hoped that this has contributed in understanding the meaning and dynamics of the Tenrikyo ritual dance. The vision for the future, then, is that more studies of this sort will continue. As these concluding pages suggest, studies concerning an understanding, for example, of a psychological perspective while dancing the Teodori is open for investigation. Another approach is to view the Teodori as play and relate this factor with other religious systems of different times and different places, such as the Greek ritual dances mentioned in the introduction. Further, studies concerning particular cultures and their attitude to rituals can be made use of in order to see if these varying localities will be open to accept the Teodori as a means of a joyous portrayal of living. The field concerning future studies on the ritual dance is indeed open. This present study has been a modest attempt toward one sound direction.

206

GLOSSARY

The original terms are italicized. Bold-faced characters in the explanation signify the English usage of the term. In retrospect, bold-faced characters do not appear in the explanation when the original term is used in English.

Besseki　　　　　　　　　　別席

a series of nine lectures given in order to receive the Sazuke. The **Besseki lectures** are held only at the Home of the Parent.

Hinokishin　　　　　　　　　ひのきしん

any action or word that is done without greed for oneself and with gratitude to God the Parent for being able to do it. Hinokishin is an external expression of gratitude and joy salient in the life of a Tenrikyo follower.

Honseki　　　　　　　　　　本席

refers to Iburi Izo, the most important disciple of the foundress. This term also refers to the precise locus when the Sazuke is bestowed upon a follower as the **main seat**.

Kashimono, karimono　　　　かしもの・かりもの

the teaching of **a thing lent, a thing borrowed**. According to Tenrikyo doctrine, the human body is a thing lent to human beings by God the Parent. Thus, it is taught that humankind has borrowed the body from God the Parent.

Jiba　　　　　　　　　　　　ぢば

the Jiba is the place where humankind was first conceived.

Kanrodai　　　　　　　　　かんろだい

a thirteen-tiered wooden hexagonal stand approximately two and a half meters in height that marks the Jiba. The Kanrodai stands in the center of the main sanctuary.

Kyōkai　　　　　　　　　　教会

a Tenrikyo local **church**

Kyōkai honbu　　　　　　　教会本部

Church Headquarters. The administrative headquarters that is located in Tenri, Nara, Japan.

Mikagura-uta　　　　　　みかぐらうた

　　the Mikagura-uta, *The Songs for the Service* was written by Nakayama Miki. It is
　　divided in two parts: the かぐらのうた (*Kagura no uta*), the Songs for the Kagura
　　and the てをどりのうた (*Teodori no uta*), the Songs for the Teodori. The
　　Mikagura-uta is considered one of three Tenrikyo scriptures. English versions have
　　been translated by Church Headquarters since 1967. Its seventh edition was printed
　　in 1999.

Moto no ri　　　　　　元の理

　　the **Truth of Origin**. The Tenrikyo story of how human beings and the world were
　　created by God the Parent.

Nakayama Miki　　　　　　中山みき

　　the name of the foundress of Tenrikyo. Nakayama Miki was born on April 18, 1798
　　and withdrew from physical life on January 26, 1887. She is considered everliving
　　to Tenrikyo adherents.

Obiya yurushi　　　　　　をびや許し

　　the **Grant of Safe Childbirth**. This is the first of many grants that attracted the
　　minds of the early followers to Oyasama.

Ofudesaki　　　　　　おふでさき

　　the 1,711 poems written in *waka* style by Nakayama Miki. The Ofudesaki is
　　considered one of three Tenrikyo scriptures. An English version of the Ofudesaki
　　has been translated by Church Headquarters since 1971. A revised edition was
　　published in 1993.

Osashizu　　　　　　おさしづ

　　the words of God the Parent revealed from the most part through the mouth of the
　　Honseki, Iburi Izo, from 1887 to 1907. Accordingly, it consists of seven volumes.
　　The Osashizu is considered one of three Tenrikyo scriptures. So far no complete
　　translation of the Osashizu exists. The exception is a selection from this scripture to
　　instruct those who become head ministers.

Otsutome gi　　　　　　おつとめ着

　　the ritual apparel that is worn for a monthly service by service performers. The
　　service garment is also the outfit worn when one receives the Sazuke as well as the
　　apparel worn by the bride and groom in a traditional Tenrikyo wedding ceremony.

Oyasama　　　　　　教祖

　　the honorary name given to the foundress, Nakayama Miki. Oyasama signifies
　　"beloved parent."

Oyagami　　　　　　親神

　　God the Parent.

208

Oyasato   親里

the **Home of the Parent**. Refers to the area around which the Jiba is located.

Oyasato-yakata   おやさとやかた

the quadrangle building complex that will enclose the precinct of the Jiba 2,850 feet on each side. The **Oyasato-yakata building complex** commenced in 1954 and the completed sections presently house follower's dormitories, various education institutions, administrative offices of Church Headquarters, the Besseki lecture halls, and a hospital.

Sazuke   さづけ

a grant bestowed upon a follower that enables him or her to pray for the sick. Oyasama through the Shinbashira bestows the Sazuke upon a follower after completing the nine Besseki lectures.

Shūyōka   修養科

a three-month **Spiritual Development Course** held throughout the year at the Home of the Parent.

Taisai   大祭

a **grand service**. Monthly services held in the months of January and October are considered grand services since they commemorate the beginning of Tenrikyo (October) and when Nakayama Miki withdrew from physical life (January). Where the former is referred to as the autumn grand service, the latter is referred to as the spring grand service. Church Headquarters conducts its grand services on January 26 and October 26, respectively.

Tasuke ichijō   たすけ一条

single-hearted salvation. たすけ一条の道 (*tasuke ichijō no michi*), the path of single-hearted salvation, consists principally of performing the service and administering the Sazuke.

Tenri   天理

a city in Nara Prefecture, Japan, where the spiritual and administrative center of Tenrikyo is located. The population of Tenri is approximately 60,000.

Tenrikyo   天理教

literally, "teaching of divine wisdom," it is a Japanese new religion founded by Nakayama Miki in 1838. The community of believers performs the Teodori as its vital ritual dance. There are approximately three million followers in Tenrikyo.

Tenri-O-no-Mikoto   天理王命

God the Parent, **Tenri-O-no-Mikoto**, is God of Origin, God in Truth.

Teodori   てをどり

often translated as **the dance with hand movements**, it is the ritual dance based on the second part of the Mikagura-uta which was composed by the foundress of Tenrikyo, Nakayama Miki. The Teodori is actively performed at local Tenrikyo churches.

Tsukinamisai 月次祭

a **monthly service**. It is a Tenrikyo service held on a monthly basis at local Tenrikyo churches that primarily consists of the complete performance of the Mikagura-uta.

Tsutome つとめ

the Tenrikyo **service** but has many referents. Among them is the Kagura Service, a service performed only around the Jiba. The same service is referred to as the Salvation Service, the Kagura Service, and the Joyous Service. In addition to a monthly service, daily services are conducted at both church headquarters and local churches. These daily services are the 朝づとめ (*asa zutome*), the morning service and the 夕づとめ(*yū zutome*), the evening service.

Yattsu no hokori 八つのほこり

the **eight dusts** of the mind. Nakayama Miki used the metaphor of "dust" to describe the murkiness of the mind when it is used self-centeredly. In particular, she spelled the following types of dust: miserliness, covetousness, hatred, self-love, grudge-bearing, anger, greed, and arrogance.

Yōkigurashi 陽気ぐらし

the **Joyous Life**. The model way of living for Tenrikyo followers. It is also the purpose and goal of humankind's existence.

Yōboku ようぼく

literally "useful timber" and refers to those who have received the truth of the Sazuke. Yoboku generally refers to a Tenrikyo missionary.

BIBLIOGRAPHY

General Bibliography

Adshead, Janet, ed. 1988. *Dance Analysis: Theory and Practice*. London: Dance Books.

Agency for Cultural Affairs, ed. 1972. *Japanese Religions*. Tokyo: Kodansha International.

Allison, Anne. 1994. *Sexuality, Pleasure, and Corporate Masculinity in a Tokyo Hostess Club*. Chicago: University of Chicago Press.

Asad, Talal. 1982. Anthropological conceptions of religion: Reflections on Geertz. *Man* (n.s) 18: 237–259

Ashkenazi, Michael. 1991. Anthropological aspects of the Japanese meal: Tradition, internalization, and aesthetics. In *Rethinking Japan* vol. 2, eds. Adriana Boscaro, Franco Gatti, and Massimo Raveri, 338–349. Sandgate: Japan Library.

Babcock, Barbara A. 1980. Reflexivity: Definitions and discriminations. *Semiotica* 30(1–2): 1–14.

_____, ed. 1978. *The Reversible World: Symbolic Inversion in Art and Society*. Ithaca: Cornell University Press.

Bachnik, Jane M. 1982. Deixis and self/order reference in Japanese discourse. *Working Papers in Sociolinguistics* 99:1–36.

_____. 1983. Recruitment strategies for household succession: Rethinking Japanese household organization. *Man* (n.s.) 18: 160–182.

_____. 1994. Uchi/soto: Challenging our conceptualizations of self, social order, and language. In *Situated Meaning: Inside and Outside in Japanese Self, Society, and Langauge*, eds. Jane M. Bachnik and Charles J. Quinn, 2–37. Princeton: Princeton University Press.

Bachnik, Jane, and Charles J. Quinn, eds. 1994. *Situated Meaning: Inside and Outside in Japanese Self, Society, and Language*. Princeton: Princeton Universtiy Press.

Bakker, Jan Willem. 1988. *Enough Profundities Already: A Reconstruction of Geertz's Interpretive Anthropology*. Utrecht: Rijksuniversiteit Utrecht.

Banton, Michael, ed. 1966. *Anthropological Approaches to the Study of Religion*. London: Tavistock.

Barker, Eileen. 1989. *New Religious Movements: A Practical Introduction.* London: HMSO.

Barker, Eileen, James A. Beckford, and Karel Dobbelaere, eds. 1993. *Secularization, Rationalization, and Sectarianism. Essays in Honour of Bryan R. Wilson.* Oxford: Clarendon Press.

Barthes, Roland. 1957. *Mythologies.* Paris: Édition du Seuil.

_____. 1973. *Le Plaisir du Texte.* Paris: Édition du Seuil.

_____. 1982. *Empire of Signs.* New York: Hill and Wang.

Bateson, Gregory. 1972. *Steps to an Ecology of Mind.* San Francisco: Chandler.

Baum, Gregory. 1980. The sociology of Roman Catholic theology. In *Sociology and Theology's Alliance and Conflict,* eds. David Martin and John Orme Mills, 120–135. New York: St. Martin's Press.

Beardsley, Richard K. 1965. *Village Japan.* Chicago: Chicago University Press.

_____. 1970. *Japanese Sociology and Social Anthropology.* Ann Arbor: University of Michigan Press.

Beattie, John H. M. 1966. Ritual and social change. *Man* (n.s) 1: 60–74.

Befu, Harumi. 1971. *Japan: An Anthropological Approach.* San Francisco: Chandler.

Bell, Catherine. 1992. *Ritual Theory, Ritual Practice.* Oxford: Oxford University Press.

Ben–Ari, Eyal, Brian Moeran, and James Valentine, eds. 1990. *Unwrapping Japan: Society and Culture in Anthropological Perspective.* Manchester: Manchester University Press.

Benedict, Ruth. 1946. *The Chrysanthemum and the Sword.* Boston: Houghton Mifflin.

Berger, Arthur Asa. 1984. *Signs in Contemporary Culture. An Introduction to Semiotics.* New York: Longman Inc.

Berger, Peter L. 1961. *The Precarious Vision.* Garden City, NY: Doubleday

_____. 1967. *The Sacred Canopy: Elements of a Sociological Theory of Religion.* Garden City, NY: Doubleday.

_____. 1969. *A Rumor of Angels.* New York: Anchor Books.

Berger, Peter L., and Thomas Luckman. 1966. *The Social Construction of Reality: A Treatise in the Sociology of Knowledge.* New York: Viking Press.

Bernard, Charles André. 1984. *Teologia Simbolica.* Roma: Edizioni Pauline.

Bernstein, Gail Lee. 1983. *Haruko's World: A Japanese Farm Woman and Her Community.* Stanford: Stanford University Press.

_____, ed. 1991. *Recreating Japanese Women.* Berkeley: University of California Press.

Berreby, David. 1995. Unabsolute truths: Clifford Geertz. New York Times Magazine, 9 April 45–47.

Bertelli, Sergio, and Monica Centanni, eds. 1995. *Il Gesto.* Firenze: Ponte alle Grazie.

Blacker, Carmen. 1975. *The Catalpa Bow: A Study of Shamanistic Practices in Japan*. London: Allen and Unwin Ltd.

_____. 1991. Rethinking the study of religions in Japan. In *Rethinking Japan* vol 2, eds. Adriana Boscaro, Franco Gatti, and Massimo Raveri, 237–241. Sandgate: Japan Library.

Blacking, John, ed. 1977. *The Anthropology of the Body*. London: Academic Press.

Blacking, John, and Joan W. Kealiinohomoku, eds. 1979. *The Performing Arts: Music and Dance*. The Hague: Mouton.

Blackwood, Robert T. 1964. *Tenrikyo: A Living Religion*. Tenri: Tenrikyo Overseas Mission Department.

Bloch, Maurice. 1974. Symbols, song, dance, and features of articulation: Is religion an extreme form of traditional authority? *European Journal of Sociology* 15: 55–81.

_____. 1989. *Ritual, History, and Power: Selected Papers in Anthropology*. London: Athlone Press.

Blondeau, Anne–Marie, and Kristofer Schipper, eds.1988. *Essais sur le Rituel*. Louvain: Peeters Press.

Bodiford, William. 1992. Zen in the art of funerals: Ritual salvation in Japanese Buddhism. *History of Religions* 32(2): 146–164.

Boon, James. 1972. *From Symbolism to Structuralism: Lévi–Strauss in Literary Tradition*. New York: Harper and Row.

_____. 1982. *Other Tribes, Other Scribes: Symbolic Anthropology in the Comparative Study of Cultures, Histories, Religions, and Texts*. Cambridge: Cambridge University Press. '

Boscaro, Adriana, Franco Gatti, and Massimo Raveri, eds. 1991. *Rethinking Japan*. 2 vols. Sandgate: Japan Library.

Boudewijnse, Barbara H. 1990. The ritual studies of Victor Turner: An anthropological approach and its psychological impact. In *Current Studies on Rituals: Perspectives for a Pscychology of Religion*, eds. Hans–Gunter Heimbrock and Barbara H. Boudewijnse, 1–17. Amsterdam: Rodopi.

Bownas, Geoffrey. 1963. *Japanese Rainmaking and Other Folk Practices*. London: George Allen and Unwin Ltd.

Brack, Clairette, ed. 1993. *Dance and Research: Proceedings from the International Congress Dance and Research, Brussels, Belgium 2–6 July 1991*. Louvain: Peeters Press.

Burns, Tom. 1982. *Erving Goffman*. London: Routledge.

Casal, Ugo A. 1958. Salt. *Monumenta Nipponica*14(1–2): 61–90.

_____. 1960. The lore of the Japanese fan. *Monumenta Nipponica*16(1–2): 53–117.

_____. 1967. *The Five Festival of Ancient Japan: Their Symbolism and Historical Development*. Tokyo: Sophia University Press.

Clarke, Peter B., and Jeffrey Sommers, eds. 1994. *Japanese New Religions in the West*. Sandgate: Japan Library.

Clifford, James, and George E. Marcus, eds. 1986. *Writing Culture: The Poetics and Politics of Ethnography*. Berkeley: University of California Press.

Cohen, Anthony P. 1985. Symbolism and social change: Matters of life and death in Whalsay, Shefland. *Man* (n.s.) 20: 307–324.

Collins, Mary. 1976. Ritual symbols and the ritual process: The work of Victor W. Turner. *Worship* 50(4): 336–346.

Cornell, John B. 1970. Japanese social stratification: A theory and a case. *Monumenta Nipponica* 25(1–2): 107–135.

Cornille, Catherine, and Valeer Neckebrouck, eds. 1992. *A Universal Faith? Peoples, Cultures, Religions and the Christ*. Louvain: Peeters Press.

Crapanzano, Vincent. 1980. *Tuhami: Portrait of a Moroccan*. Chicago: University of Chicago Press.

Crump, Thomas. 1992. *The Japanese Numbers Game: The Use of and Understanding of Numbers in Modern Japan*. London: Routledge.

Culler, Jonathan. 1983. *Barthes*. Glasgow: Fontana.

————. 1992 [1981]. *The Pursuit of Signs*. London: Routledge.

Dale, Peter N. 1986. *The Myth of Japanese Uniqueness*. London: Croom Helm.

D'Aquili, Eugene G., Charles D. Laughlin Jr., and John McManns, eds. 1979. *The Spectrum of Ritual: A Biogenetic Structural Analysis*. New York: Columbia University Press.

Davies, J. G. 1984. *Liturgical Dance. An Historical, Theological and Practical Handbook*. London: SCM Press.

Davis, Martha, and Janet Skupien, eds. 1982. *Body Movement and Nonverbal Communication. An Annotated Bibliography, 1971–1981*. Bloomington: Indiana University Press.

Davis, Winston. 1980. *Dojo: Magic and Exorcism in Modern Japan*. Stanford: Stanford University Press.

————. 1992. *Japanese Religion and Society*. New York: State University of New York Press.

De Coppet, Daniel, ed. 1993. *Understanding Rituals*. London: Routledge.

De Napoli, George A. 1987. Inculturation as communication. In *Inculturation – Working Papers on Living Faith and Culture IX: Effective Inculturation and Ethnic Identity*, ed. Arij A. Roest Crollius, 71–98. Rome: Centre "Culture and Religions" Pontifical Gregorian University.

Denny, Federick Mathewson. 1987. Hands. In *The Encyclopedia of Religions*, ed. Mircea Eliade, VI: 188–191. New York: Macmillan Press.

Doi, Takeo. 1973. *The Anatomy of Dependence: The Key Analysis of Japanese Behavior*. Tokyo: Kodansha International.

————. 1986. *The Anatomy of Self*. Tokyo: Kodansha International.

Dolgin, Janet, David S. Kemnitzer, and David M. Schneider, eds. 1977. *Symbolic Anthropology: A Reader in the Study of Symbols and Meanings*. New York: Columbia University Press.

214

Doroszewki, W. 1933. Quelques rémarques sur les rapports de la sociologie et de la linguistique: Durkheim et F. de Saussure. *Journal de Psychologie et Pathologie* 30: 82–91.

Douglas, Mary. 1966. *Purity and Danger*. London: Routledge and Kegan Paul.

_____. 1970. *Natural Symbols: Explorations in Cosmology*. New York: Random House.

_____. 1971. Deciphering a meal. In *Myth, Symbol, and Culture*, ed. Clifford Geertz, 61–81. New York: Newton.

_____. 1973. *Natural Symbols: Explorations in Cosmology*. 2nd ed. New York: Vintage Books.

_____. 1975. *Implicit Meanings: Essays in Anthropology*. London: Routledge and Kegan Paul.

_____. 1978. *Cultural Bias*. London: Royal Anthropological Institute.

_____. 1979 [1964]. The abominations of Leviticus. In *Reader in Comparative Religion: An Anthropological Approach,* eds. William A. Lessa and Evon. Z. Vogt, 149–152. New York: Harper and Row.

_____. 1989. The background of the grid dimension: A comment. *Sociological Analysis* 50(2): 171–176.

Durkheim, Emile. 1965 [1915]. *Elementary Forms of Religious Life*. Translated by J. W. Swain. New York: Free Press.

Dwyer, Kevin. 1982. *Moroccan Dialogues: Anthropology in Question*. Baltimore: John Hopkins University.

Earhart, Byron H. 1970. *The New Religions of Japan: A Bibliography of Western Language Material*. 2nd ed. Tokyo: Sophia University Press.

_____. 1987. *Gedatsu–kai and Religion in Contemporary Japan: Returning to the Center*. Bloomington: Indiana University Press.

Edwards, Walter. 1989. *Modern Japan Through Its Weddings: Gender, Person, and Society in Ritual Portrayal*. Stanford: Stanford University Press.

Ellwood, Robert S. Jr. 1974. *The Eagle and the Rising Sun: Americans and the New Religions of Japan*. Philadelphia: Westminster Press.

_____. 1982. *Tenrikyo: A Pilgrimage Faith*. Tenri: Tenri University Press.

Estepa, Pio. 1992. The comic sacred: A socio–cultural semiotics of a Pende joke rite. Doctoral diss., Pontifical Gregorian University.

Evans–Pritchard, E. E. 1928. The dance. *Africa* 1: 446–462.

_____. 1940. *The Nuer*. Clarendon: Oxford University Press.

_____. 1965a [1937]. *Witchcraft, Oracles, and Magic Among the Azande*. Oxford: Clarendon Press.

_____. 1965b. *Theories of Primitive Religion*. Oxford: Clarendon Press.

Featherstone, Mike, ed. 1992. *Cultural Theory and Cultural Change*. London: Sage Publications.

Firth, Raymond. 1973. *Symbols: Public and Private*. London: George Allen and Unwin LTD.

Fischer, Edward. 1973. Ritual as communication. In *The Roots of Ritual*, ed. James D. Shaughnessy, 161–184. Grand Rapids, MI: William B. Eerdman Publishing Company..

Fischer, Michael M. 1977. Interpretive anthropology. *Reviews in Anthropology* 4(4): 391–404.

Friedland, LeeEllen. 1987. Dance: Popular and folk dances. In *The Encyclopedia of Religions*, ed. Mircea Eliade, VI: 212–221. New York: Macmillan Press.

Fujii Keiichi, and P. D. Perkins. 1940. Two ancient Japanese dances. *Monumenta Nipponica* 3(1): 314–320.

Fukaya, Tadamasu. 1976. *A Commentary on the Mikagura–Uta, the Songs for the Tsutome*. Tenri: Tenrikyo Overseas Mission Department.

_____. 1983. One truth: The principle of unification and salvation of the human world. *Tenri Journal of Religion* 17: 44–70.

_____. 1986. *Mijo Satoshi: Yamae no Ne o Kiru*. [Advise on Afflictions: Severing the Root of Illness]. Tenri: Yotokusha.

Fuss, Michael. 1998. Tenrikyo: Il pellegrinaggio verso le origini. *Religioni e Sette nel Mondo* 14 (2): 12–32.

Fuss, Michael A. ed. 1998. *Rethinking New Religious Movements*. Rome: Pontifical Gregorian University Research Center on Cultures and Religion.

Galanter, Marc. 1989. *Cults: Faith, Healing, and Coercion*. Oxford: Oxford University Press.

Garon, Sheldon. 1986. State and religion in imperial Japan: 1912–1945. *Journal of Japanese Studies* 12(2): 273–302.

Geertz, Clifford. 1957. Ritual and social change: A Javanese example. *American Anthropologist* 59: 32–54.

_____. 1973. *The Interpretation of Cultures*. New York: Basic Books.

_____. 1983. *Local Knowledge*: *Further Essays in Interpretive Anthropology*. New York: Basic Books.

_____. 1984a. Culture and social change: The Indonesian case. *Man* (n.s.) 19: 511–532.

_____. 1984b. Distinguished lecture: Anti anti–relativism. *American anthropologist* 86: 263–278.

_____. 1985. Waddling in. Times Literary Supplement, 7 June 623–624.

_____. 1988. *Works and Lives: The Anthropologist as Author*. Stanford: Stanford University Press.

_____. 1995. *After the Fact: Two Countries, Four Decades, One Anthropologist*. Cambridge, MA: Harvard University Press.

Geertz, Clifford. ed. 1971. *Myth, Symbol and Culture*. New York: Norton.

Giglioli, Pier Paolo. 1990. *Rituale Interazione, Vita Quotidiana: Saggi su Goffman e Garfinkel*. Bologna: CLUEB

Gilday, Edmund T. 1993. Dancing with spirit(s): Another view of the other world in Japan. *History of Religions* 32(3): 273–300.

Goffman, Erving. 1959. *The Presentation of Self in Everyday Life*. Garden City, NY: Doubleday.

_____. 1967. *Interaction Ritual: Essays on Face–to–Face Behavior*. Garden City, NY: Doubleday.

Gorman, Frank H. J. 1990. *The Ideology of Ritual: Space, Time, and Status in the Priestly Theology*. Sheffield: JSOT Press.

Grapard, Allan G. 1982. Flying mountains and walkers of emptiness: Toward a definition of sacred space in Japanese religions. *History of Religions* 21(3): 195–221.

Grimes, Ronald L. 1975. Masking: Toward a phenomenology of exteriorization. *Journal of the American Academy of Religion* 43(3): 508–516.

_____. 1979. Modes of ritual necessity. *Worship* 53(2): 126–141.

_____. 1982a. *Beginnings in Ritual Studies*. Lanham, NY: University Press of America.

_____. 1982b. Defining nascent ritual. *Journal of the American Academy of Religion* 50(4): 539–555.

_____. 1982c. The lifeblood of public ritual: Fiestas and public exploration projects. In *Celebrations: Studies in Festivity and Ritual*, ed. Victor W. Turner, 272–282. Washington DC: Smithsonian Institute Press.

_____. 1985. *Research in Ritual Studies*. Metuchen, NJ: Scarecrow Press and The American Theological Library Association.

Hall, Edward T. 1969. *The Hidden Dimension*. Garden City, NY: Doubleday.

_____. 1973. *The Silent Language*. Garden City, NY: Doubleday.

Hamabata, Matthews M. 1990. *Crested Kimono: Power and Love in the Japanese Business Family*. Ithaca: Cornell University Press.

Hamaguchi, Esyun. 1985. A contextual model of the Japanese: Toward a methodological innovation in Japanese studies. *Journal of Japanese Studies* 11(2): 289–232.

Hamerton–Kelly, Robert G., ed. 1987. *Violent Origins: Walter Burkert, René Girard, and Jonathan Z. Smith on Ritual Killing and Cultural Formation*. Stanford: Stanford University Press.

Hanna, Judith Lynne. 1977. To dance is human. Some psychobiological base of an expression form. In *The Anthropology of the Body*, ed. John Blacking, 211–232. New York: Academic Press.

_____. 1979a. Movement towards understanding human through the anthropological study of dance. *Current Anthropology* 20: 313–339.

_____. 1979b. Toward a cross–cultural conceptualization of dance and some correlate considerations. In *The Performing Arts: Music and Dance*. eds. John Blacking and Joann W. Kealiinohomoku, 17–45. The Hague: Mouton.

_____. 1987 [1979]. *To Dance is Human: A Theory of Nonverbal Communication*. 2nd ed. Chicago: University of Chicago Press.

_____. 1988. *Dance, Sex, and Gender: Signs of Identity, Dominance, Defiance, and Desire*. University of Chicago Press.

_____. 1989. The representation and reality of religion in dance. *Journal of the American Academy of Religion* 56(2): 281–306.

217

Hardacre, Helen. 1982. The transformation of healing in the Japanese new religions. *History of Religions* 21(4): 305–20.

_____. 1983. The Cane and the Womb World. *Japanese Journal of Religious Studies*. 10(2–3): 149–176.

_____. 1984. *Lay Buddhism in Contemporary Japan: Reiyukai Kyodan*. Princeton: Princeton University Press.

_____. 1986. *Kurozumikyo and the New Religions of Japan*. Princeton: Princeton University Press.

_____. 1988. The Shinto priesthood in early Meiji Japan: Preliminary inquiries. *History of Religions* 27(3): 294–320.

Harris, Marvin. 1976. History and significance of the emic/etic distinction. *Annual Review of Anthropology* 5: 329–350.

Hashimoto, Taketo. 1979. The teaching of innen in Tenrikyo. *Tenri Journal of Religion* 13: 29–47.

_____. 1982. The Kagura Service: Its structure and meaning. *Tenri Journal of Religion* 15: 31–44.

Hawkes, Terence. 1985. *Structuralism and Semiotics*. London: Methuen Press.

Hayasaka, Masaaki. 1987. Tenrikyo under the structure of national Shintoism: Double faced aspects in the development of Tenrikyo doctrine during the lifetime of the Foundress. *Tenri Journal of Religion* 21: 9–38.

Headland, Thomas N., Kenneth L. Pike, and Marvin Harris, eds. 1990. *Emics and Etics: The Insider/Outsider Debate*. Newbury Park, CA: Sage.

Heimbrock, Hans–Gunter, and Barbara H. Boudewijnse, eds. 1990. *Current Studies on Rituals: Perspectives for a Psychology of Religion*. Amsterdam: Rodopi.

Hendry, Joy. 1986. The contribution of social anthropology to Japanese studies. In *Interpreting Japanese Society: An Anthropological Approach,* eds. Joy Hendry and Jonathan Webber, 3–13. Oxford: JASO.

_____. 1987. *Understanding Japanese Society*. London: Croom Helm.

_____. 1989. To wrap or not to wrap: Politeness and penetration in ethnographic inquiry. *Man* (n.s) 24: 620–635.

_____. 1993. *Wrapping Culture: Politeness, Presentation and Power in Japan and Other Societies*. Oxford: Clarendon Press.

Hendry, Joy, and Jonathan Webber, eds. 1986. *Interpreting Japanese Society: An Anthropological Approach*. Oxford: JASO.

Hinde, Robert A., ed. 1972. *Non–verbal Communication*. Cambridge: Cambridge University Press.

Hirano, Tomokazu. 1985. *Mikagura–uta Josetsu*. [Introducing the Mikagura–uta]. Tenri: Doyusha.

_____. 1995. *Moto no Ri o Horu*. [Unraveling the Truth of Origin]. Tenri: Doyusha.

Hodgens, Pauline. 1988. Interpreting the dance. In *Dance Analysis: Theory and Practice*, ed. Janet Adshead, 60–89. London: Dance Books.

Hofstee, Wee. 1986. The interpretations of religion—Some remarks on the work of Clifford Geertz. In *On Symbolic Representation of Religion*, eds. Hubertus G. Hubbeling and Hans G. Kippenberg, 70–83. Berlin: Walter de Gruyter.

Hori, Ichiro. 1968. *Folk Religion in Japan: Continuity and Change*. Translated and edited by Joseph Kitagawa and Allan Miller. Tokyo: University of Tokyo Press.

Hubbeling, Hubertus G., and Hans G. Kippenberg, eds. 1986. *On Symbolic Representation of Religion*. Berlin: Walter de Gruyter.

Huizinga, Johan. 1970 [1938]. *Homo Ludens: A Study of the Play–Elements in Culture*. New York: Harper and Row.

Iida, Teruaki. 1979. The meaning of religion in an age of crisis. *Tenri Journal of Religion* 13: 81–94.

_____. 1982. The eschatological thoughts and the historical view of Tenrikyo. *Tenri Journal of Religion* 16: 81–94.

_____. 1986. Idea of Evolution in the Creation Story. In *The Theological Perspectives of Tenrikyo: In Commemoration of the Centennial Anniversary of Oyasama*, ed. Oyasato Research Institute, 171–179. Tenri: Tenri University Press.

Ikeda, Shiro. 1996. Returning, rebirth, departure: The phenomenology of returning to *Ojiba*. *Tenri Journal of Religion* 24: 19–33.

Ikegami, Yoshihiko ed. 1991. *The Empire of Signs. Semiotic Essays in Japanese Culture*. Amsterdam: John Benjamin's Publishing Company.

Ikema, Hiroyuki. 1981. *Folk Dance in Japan*. Tokyo: National Recreation Association of Japan.

Immoos, Thomas. 1987. Shinto ritual and Catholic liturgy. *The Japan Missionary Bulletin* 41(4): 226–230.

Inoue, Akio. 1988. 'Signs coincided' and the way of 'divine model.' *Tenri Journal of Religion* 22: 1–14.

Inoue, Akio, and Matthew Eynon. 1987. *A Study of the Ofudesaki*. Tenri: Doyusha.

Ito, Lucy S. 1952. Kô: Japanese confraternities. *Monumenta Nipponica* 8(1–2): 412–415.

Jennings, Theodore. 1982. On ritual knowledge. *Journal of Religion* 62: 117–127.

Johnson, Mark. 1987. *The Body in the Mind*. Chicago: University of Chicago Press.

Kadowaki, Kakichi J. 1982. *Zen and the Bible: A Priest's Experience*. New York: Routledge and Kegan Paul.

Kaeppler, Adrienne L. 1978. Dance in anthropological perspective. *Annual Review of Anthropology* 7: 31–49.

Kaplan, David, and Robert A. Manners. 1972. *Culture Theory*. Englewood Cliffs: Prentice Hall.

Kealiinohomoku, Joann W. 1979. Culture change: Functional and dysfunctional expression of dance, a form of affective culture. In *The Performing Arts:*

Music and Dance, eds. John Blacking and Joann W. Kealiinohomoku, 47–64. The Hague: Mouton.

Keane, Webb. 1997. *Signs of Recognition: Powers and Hazards of Representation in an Indonesian Society*. Berkeley: University of California Press.

Keesing, Roger M. 1974. Theories of culture. *Annual review of anthropology* 3: 73–97.

_____. 1976. *Cultural Anthropology: A Contemporary Perspective*. New York: Holt, Reinhart and Winston.

_____. 1987. Anthropology as interpretive quest. *Current Anthropology* 28(2): 161–176.

Kelly, John C. 1981. *A Philosophy of Communication: Explorations for a Systematic Model*. London: The Centre for the Study of Communication and Culture.

Kertzer, David I. 1988. *Ritual, Politics, and Power*. New Haven: Yale University Press.

Kimball, Bruce. 1979. The problem of epistemology in Japanese new religions. *Tenri Journal of Religion* 13: 29–47.

Kisala, Robert. 1994. Contemporary karma: Interpretations of karma in Tenrikyo and Rissho Koseikai. *Japanese Journal of Religious Studies* 21(1): 73–91.

_____. 1994b. Social ethics and the Japanese new religions: The social welfare activities of Tenrikyo and Rissho Koseikai. *In New religious movements in Asia and the Pacific Islands: Implications for church and society: Proceedings of a conference sponsored by the Association of Southeast and East Asian Catholic Universities held in Manilla 10–13 February 1993*, edited by Robert C. Salazar, 31–45. Manilla: Social Development Research Center of De La Salle University.

Kishimoto, Hideo. 1967. Some Japanese cultural traits and religions. In *The Japanese Mind: The Essentials of Japanese Philosophy and Culture*, ed. Charles A. Moore, 110–121. Honolulu: East–West Center Press.

_____, ed. 1956. *Japanese Religion in the Meiji Era*. Translated by John F. Howes. Tokyo: Obunsha.

Kitagawa, Joseph M. 1966. *Religion in Japanese History*. New York: Columbia University Press.

_____. 1987. *On Understanding Japanese Religion*. Princeton: Princeton University Press.

_____. 1988. Some Remarks on Shinto. *History of Religions* 27(3): 227–245.

_____, ed. 1967. *The History of Religions: Essays on the Problem of Understanding*. Chicago: University of Chicago Press.

_____, ed. 1989. *The Religious Traditions of Asia: Religion, History, and Culture. Readings from the Encyclopedia of Religions*. New York: Macmillan.

Kobayashi, Kazushige. 1981. On the meaning of masked dances in Kagura. *Asian Folklore Studies* 40: 1–22

Kondo, Dorinne K. 1985. The way of the tea: A symbolic analysis. *Man* (n.s.) 20: 287–306.

_____. 1990. *Crafting Selves. Power, Gender, and Discourse of Identity in a Japanese Workplace*. Chicago: University of Chicago Press.

_____. 1992. Multiple selves: The aesthetics and politics of artisanal identities. In *Japanese Sense of Self*, ed. Nancy R. Rosenberger, 117–139. Cambridge: Cambridge University Press.

Kontani, Hisanori. 1993. *Shin Fufu no Hanashi, Kenko no Hanashi*. [Further Discourses on Married Couples and Health]. Tokyo: Ikeda Press.

Kuhn, Thomas S. 1962. *The Structure of Scientific Revolutions*. Chicago: University of Chicago Press.

Kurachi, Kazuta. 1986. Man and culture in the Tenrikyo story of creation. Translated by Carl Becker. *G –Ten* 14: 108–124.

La Fontaine, Jean S., ed. 1970. *The Interpretation of Rituals: Essays in Honour of A.I. Richards*. London: Tavistock.

Landowski, Eric. 1989. *La Société Réfléchie: Essais de Socio–Sémiotique*. Paris: Éditions du Seuil.

Lange, Roderyk. 1975. *The Nature of Dance. An Anthropological Perspective*. London: MacDonald and Evans LTD.

_____. 1977. Some notes on the anthropology of dance. In *The Anthropology of the Body*, ed. John Blacking, 241–252. New York: Academic Press.

Lawler, Lillian B. 1985 [1964]. *The Dance in Ancient Greece*. 3rd ed. Middletown: Wesleyan University Press.

Leach, Edmund. 1961. *Rethinking Anthropology*. London: Anthlone Press.

_____. 1970. *Claude Lévi–Strauss*. Glasgow: Fontana Press.

_____. 1972. The influence of cultural context on non–verbal communication in man. In *Non–verbal Communication*, ed. Robert A. Hinde, 315–342. Cambridge: Cambridge University Press.

_____. 1976. *Culture and Communication: The Logic by which Symbols Are Connected. An Introduction to the Use of Structural Analysis in Social Anthropology*. Cambridge: Cambridge University Press.

_____. 1979 [1964]. Anthropological aspects of language: Animal categories and verbal abuse. In *Reader in Comparative Religion: An Anthropological Approach*, eds. William A. Lessa and Evon. Z. Vogt, 153–166. New York: Harper and Row.

_____. 1982. *Social Anthropology*. Oxford: Oxford University Press.

_____, ed. 1968. *Dialectic in Practical Religion*. Cambridge: Cambridge Univerisity Press.

Leach, Edmund, and Alan Aycock. 1983. *Structuralist Interpretations of Biblical Myth*. Cambridge: Cambridge University Press.

Lebra, Takie Sugiyama. 1976. *Japanese Patterns and Behavior*. Honolulu: University Press of Hawaii.

_____. 1992. Self in Japanese culture. In *Japanese Sense of Self*, ed. Nancy R. Rosenberger, 105–120. Cambridge: Cambridge University Press.

_____, ed. 1974. *Japanese Culture and Behavior: Selected Readings*. Honolulu: University of Hawaii Press.

Leeds–Hurwitz, Wendy. 1993. *Semiotic and Communication: Sign, Codes, Cultures*. Hillside, NJ: Lawrence Erlbaum Associates.

Lesher, Margot D. 1978. The pause of the moving structure of dance. *Semiotica* 22: 107–126.

Lessa, William A., and Evon Z. Vogt, eds. 1979 [1964]. *Reader in Comparative Religion: An Anthropological Approach*. New York: Harper and Row.

Lévi–Strauss, Claude. 1963. *Structural Anthropology*. New York: Basic Books.

_____. 1970. *The Savage Mind*. Chicago: University of Chicago Press.

Lewis, Gilbert. 1980. *Day of Shining Red: An Essay on Understanding Ritual*. Cambridge: Cambridge University Press.

_____. 1986. *Religion in Context: Cults and Charisma*. Cambridge: Cambridge University Press.

Lienhardt, Godfrey. 1961. *Divinity and Experience: The Religion of the Dinka*. Oxford: Clarendon Press.

Luzbetak, Louis J. 1988. *The Church and Cultures: New Perspectives in Missiological Anthropology*. Maryknoll: Orbis Books.

Malinowski, Bronislaw. 1922. *Argonauts of the Western Pacific*. London: Routledge and Kegan Paul.

_____. 1967. *A Diary in the Strict Sense of the Term*. New York: Harcourt, Brace and World.

Manners, Roger A., and David Kaplan. 1968. *Theory in Anthropology: A Sourcebook*. Chicago: Aldine.

Manning, Peter. 1987. *Semiotics and Fieldwork*. Newbury Park, CA: Sage.

Marcus, George E., and Dick Cushman. 1982. Ethnographies as texts. *Annual Review of Anthropology* 11: 25–69.

Marcus, George E., and Michael M. Fischer. 1986. *Anthropology as Cultural Critique: An Experimental Moment in the Human Sciences*. Chicago: University of Chicago Press.

Marra, Michele. 1988. The development of *Mappo* thought in Japan (1–2). *Japanese Journal of Religious Studies* 15(1): 25–54; 15(4): 287–305.

Marras, Pino. 1982. Tenrikyo as mission: Reflections from outside. *Tenri Journal of Religion* 16: 73–80.

Marukawa, Hitoo. 1986. Religious circumstances in the late Tokugawa and the early Meiji periods. In *The Theological Perspectives of Tenrikyo: In Commemoration of the Centennial Anniversary of Oyasama*, ed. Oyasato Research Institute, 274–309. Tenri: Tenri University Press.

Maruyama, Masao. 1974. *Studies in the Intellectual History of Japan*. Translated by Mikiso Hane. Tokyo: Tokyo University Press.

Matsumoto, Shigeru. 1976. *In Quest of the Fundamental*. Tenri: Tenrikyo Overseas Mission Department.

_____. 1981. *Modern Society and Spiritual Maturity*. Tenri: Tenrikyo Overseas Mission Department.

_____. 1983. On the significance of Oyasama. How we should become close to her. *Tenri Journal of Religion* 17: 63–78.

_____. 1988. An approach to the truth of creation. *Tenri Journal of Religion* 22: 15–32.

Mayer, Fanny Higgin. 1969. Available Japanese folk tales. *Monumenta Nipponica* 24(1–2): 235–47.

_____. 1982. Japanese folk humour. *Asian Folkore Studies* 41(2): 187–99.

McGuire, Meridith B. 1987 [1981]. *Religion: The Social Context*. 2nd ed. Belmont, CA: Wadsworth Publication.

McKenna, John H. 1976. Ritual activity. *Worship* 50(4): 347–352.

McLeod, Norma. 1974. Ethnomusicalogical research and anthropology. *Annual Review of Anthropology* 3: 99–115.

Mead, Margaret. 1965. Ritual expression of the cosmic sense. *Worship* 40: 66–72.

Meynell, Hugo A. 1991. *An Introduction to the Philosophy of Bernard Lonergan*. 2nd ed. London: Macmillan Academic and Professional LTD.

Miller, Allan L. 1984. Ame no Miso–Ori Me (The heavenly weaving maiden): The cosmic weaver in early Shinto myth and ritual. *History of Religions* 24 (1): 27–48.

_____. 1987a. Japanese religions: Popular religions. In *The Encyclopedia of Religions*, ed. Mircea Eliade, VII: 538–545. New York: Macmillian Press.

_____. 1987b. Of weavers and birds: Structure and symbol in Japanese myth and folktale. *History of Religions* 26 (3): 309–327.

Moore, Charles A. 1967. The enigmatic Japanese mind. In *The Japanese Mind: Essentials of Japanese Philosophy and Culture*, ed. Charles A. Moore, 288–313. Honolulu: East–West Center Press.

_____, ed. 1967. *The Japanese Mind: Essentials of Japanese Philosophy and Culture*. Honolulu: East–West Center Press.

Moore, Robert L., and Frank Reynolds, eds. 1984. *Anthropology and the Study of Religion*. Chicago: Center for the Scientific Study of Religion.

Moore, Sally F., and Barbera G. Myerhoff, eds. 1977. *Secular Ritual*. Amsterdam: Van Gorcum.

Mori, Susumu. 1986. A study of three pilgrimages in Japan. *Tenri Journal of Religion* 20: 79–166.

_____. 1988. Religious studies and human understanding. *Studies of Worldviews* 1: 1–30

_____. 1995. The influence of historical trends in religious studies: Methodological change in the studies of the Tenrikyo religion by Christian missionaries and western scholars of religion. *Tenri Journal of Religion* 23: 67–104.

Morii, Toshiharu. 1990. *Kami·Ningen·Moto no Ri: Futatsu Hitotsu no Sekai*. [God·Man·Truth of Origin: The Two–in–One World]. Tenri: Tenri Yamato Bunka Kaigi.

Morioka, Kiyomi. 1975. *Religion in Changing Japanese Society*. Tokyo: University of Tokyo Press.

_____. 1977. The appearance of 'ancestor religion' in modern Japan: The years of transition from the Meiji to the Taisho periods. *Japanese Journal of Religious Studies* 4(2–3): 183–212.

Morioka, Kiyomi, and William H. Newell, eds. 1968. *The Sociology of Japanese Religion*. Leiden: E. J. Brill.

Moroi, Masakazu. 1953. *Seibun–iin*. [Posthumous Manuscripts]. Tenri: Doyusha.

Moroi, Yoshinori. 1963. *Hinokishin Josetsu, Tanno no Kyori*. [Introducing Hinokishin and the Doctrinal Teachings of Tanno]. Tenri: Doyusha.

_____. 1964. *Tenrikyo: Some Misconceptions Corrected*. Tenri: Tenrikyo Overseas Mission Department.

Morris, Brian. 1987. *Anthropological Studies of Religion*. Cambridge: Cambridge University Press.

Murakami, Shigeyoshi. 1980. *Japanese Religion in the Modern Century*. Translated by Byron H. Earhart. Tokyo: University of Tokyo Press.

Myerhoff, Barbara G. 1980. *Number Our Days*. New York: Simon and Schuter.

_____. 1982. Rites of passage: Process and paradox. In *Celebrations: Studies in Festivity and Ritual*, ed. Victor W. Turner, 109–135. Washington DC: Smithsonian Institute Press.

_____. 1990. The transformation of consciousness in ritual performance: Some thoughts and questions. In *By Means of Performance*, ed. Richard Schechner, 245–249. Cambridge: Cambridge Univeristy Press.

Myerhoff, Barbara G., and Jay Ruby. 1982. Introduction. In *A Crack in the Mirror: Reflective Perspectives in Anthropology*, ed. Jay Ruby, 1–35. Philadelphia: University of Pennsylvania Press.

Nakajima, Hideo. 1983. Between individuality and self–styled faith. *Tenri Journal of Religion* 17: 133–144.

Nakamura, Hajime. 1964. *Ways of Thinking of Eastern Peoples: India–China–Tibet–Japan*. Honolulu: East–West Center Press.

Nakamura, Kyoko Motomochi. 1981. Revelatory experience in the female life cycle: A biographical study of women religionists in modern Japan. *Japanese Journal of Religious Studies* 8(3–4): 187–205.

_____. 1983. Women and religion in Japan. *Japanese Journal of Religious Studies* 10 (2–3): 115–121.

Nakane, Chie. 1970. *Japanese Society*. Berkeley: University of California Press.

Nakayama, Shozen. 1957. *Koki no Kenkyu*. [A Study of the Koki]. Tenri: Doyusha.

_____. 1964. *Hitokotohanashi: Anecdotes of the Foundress and Her Disciples*. Tenri: Tenrikyo Overseas Mission Department.

Nakayama, Yoshikazu. 1979. *Mind and Body*. Tenri: Tenrikyo Overseas Mission Department.

_____. 1986a. *My Oyasama*. vol 1. Tenri: Tenrikyo Overseas Mission Department.

_____. 1986b. *My Oyasama*. vol 2. Tenri: Tenrikyo Overseas Mission Department.

Nakayama, Zenye. 1979. *Guideposts*. Tenri: Tenrikyo Overseas Mission Department.

_____. 1992. *Yorokobi no Hibi*. [Joyousness Day After Day]. Tenri: Doyusha.

_____. 1993. *Seijin e no Hibi*. [Growing Spiritually Day by Day]. Tenri: Doyusha.

Newell, William H., and Fumiko Dobashi. 1968. Some problems of classification in religious sociology as shown in the history of Tenri Kyokai. In *The Sociology of Japanese Religion*, eds. Kiyomi Morioka and William H. Newell, 84–100. Leiden: E. J. Brill.

Niida, Kenji. 1986. The legal environment surrounding the Foundress of Tenrikyo. In *The Theological Perspectives of Tenrikyo: In Commemoration of the Centennial Anniversary of Oyasama*, ed. Oyasato Research Institute, 310–357. Tenri: Tenri University Press.

Nishiyama, Teruo. 1981. *Introduction to the Teachings of Tenrikyo*. Tenri: Tenrikyo Overseas Mission Department.

_____. 1989. *Mikagura–uta no Sekai*. [The World of the Mikagura–uta]. Tenri: Tenri Yamato Bunka Kaigi.

Oesterley, W. O. E. 1923. *The Sacred Dance. A Study in Comparative Folklore*. Cambridge: Cambridge University Press.

Offner, Clark B., and Henry van Straelen. 1963. *Modern Japanese Religions: With Special Emphasis on Healing Techniques*. Leiden: E. J. Brill.

Oguchi, Iichi, and Hiroo Takagi 1956. Religious effects of social change during Meiji. In *Japanese Religion in the Meiji Era*, ed. Hideo Kishimoto, 319–334. Tokyo: Obunsha.

Ohnuki–Tierney, Emiko. 1984. *Illness and Culture in Contemporary Japan: An Anthropological View*. Cambridge: Cambridge University Press.

_____. 1987. *The Monkey as Mirror: Symbolic Transformations in Japanese History and Ritual*. Princeton: Princeton University Press.

_____. 1993. *Rice as Self: Japanese Identity Through Time*. Princeton: Princeton University Press.

Okely, Judith, and Helen Callaway, eds. 1992. *Anthropology and Autobiography*. New York: Routledge

Okubo, Akinori. 1985. *A Study of Social Welfare in Tenrikyo*. Tenri: Tenrikyo Overseas Mission Department.

Ooms, Emily Groszos. 1993. *Women and Millenarian Protest: Deguchi Nao and Omotokyo*. Ithaca: Cornell University East Asia Series.

Organizing Committee of "Tenrikyo-Christian Dialogue," eds. 1999. *Tenrikyo-Christian Dialogue*. Tenri: Tenri University Press.

Ortner, Sherry B. 1978. *Sherpas Through Their Rituals*. Cambridge: Cambridge University Press.

Ortolani, Benito. 1990. *The Japanese Theatre: From Shamanistic Ritual to Contemporary Pluralism*. Leiden: E. J. Brill.

Ota, Isao. 1988. *Historical Sketch of the Life of Oyasama*. Tenri: Tenrikyo Overseas Mission Department.

Oyasato Research Institute. 1987. The early stage of overseas mission in Tenrikyo. *Tenri Journal of Religion* 21: 49–54.

_____. 1988. The early mission of Tenrikyo in its early stage 2. *Tenri Journal of Religion* 22: 53–58.

Oyasato Research Institute, ed. 1986. *The Theological Perspectives of Tenrikyo: In Commemoration of the Centennial Anniversary of Oyasama*. Tenri: Tenri University Press.

Peacock, James L. 1986. *The Anthropological Lens: Harsh Light, Soft Focus*. Cambridge: Cambridge University Press.

Penner, Hans. 1985. Language, ritual, and meaning. *Numen* 32(1): 1–16.

_____. 1989. *Impasse and Resolution: A Critique of the Study of Religion*. New York: Peter Lang.

Perron, Paul, and Frank Collins, eds. 1989. *Paris School of Semiotics*. Amsterdam: John Benjamin's Publishing Company.

Piryns, Ernest D. 1994. New religious movements (1–2): A missiological reflection. *The Japan Mission Journal* 48(2): 123–140; 48(4): 265–277.

Pitts, Walter. 1988. Keep the fire burnin': Language and ritual in the Afro–baptist church. *Journal of the American Academy of Religion* 56(1): 77–97.

Pratt, Mary Louise. 1986. Fieldwork in common places. In *Writing Culture: The Poetics and Politics of Ethnography*, eds. James Clifford and George E. Marcus, 27–50. Berkeley: University of California Press.

Pérez Valera J. Eduardo. 1972. Towards a transcultural philosophy. *Monumenta Nipponica* 27(1): 39–64; 27(2): 175–89.

Rabinow, Paul. 1977. *Reflections on Fieldwork in Morocco*. Berkeley: University of California Press.

Rabinow, Paul, and William M. Sullivan, eds. 1979. *Interpretive Social Sciences: A Reader*. Berkeley: University of California Press.

Rappaport, Roy. A. 1967. *Pigs for the Ancestors: Ritual in the Ecology of a New Guinea People*. New Haven: Yale University Press.

Reader, Ian. 1991. *Religion in Contemporary Japan*. Honolulu: University of Hawaii Press.

_____. 1993. Recent Japanese publications in the new religions: The work of Shimazono Susumu. *Japanese Journal of Religious Studies* 20(2–3): 227–248.

_____. 1995. Cleaning floors and sweeping the mind: Cleaning as a ritual process. In *Ceremony and Ritual in Japan: Religious Practices in an Industrialized Society*, eds. Jan G. van Bremen and D. P. Martinez, 227–245. London: Routledge.

Reischauer, Edwin O. 1962. *Japan: Past and Present*. New York: Alfred A. Knopt.

Ricco, Mario. 1966. *Religione della Violenza e Religione del Piacere*. Firenze: Saggi.

Rice, Kenneth A. 1980. *Geertz and Culture*. Ann Arbor: University of Michigan Press.

Ricouer, Paul. 1971. The model of the text: Meaningful action considered as a text. *Social Research* 38: 529–562.

Roseberry, William. 1982. Balinese cockfights and the seduction of anthropology. *Social Research* 47: 1013–1028.

Rosenberger, Nancy R. 1992. Tree in summer, tree in winter: Movement of self in Japan. In *Japanese Sense of Self*, ed. Nancy R. Rosenberger, 67–92. Cambridge: Cambridge University Press.

_____. 1994. Indexing hierarchy through Japanese gender relations. In *Situated Meaning: Inside and Outside in Japanese Self, Society, and Langauge*, eds. Jane M. Bachnik and Charles J. Quinn, 88–112. Princeton: Princeton University Press.

_____, ed. 1992. *Japanese Sense of Self*. Cambridge: Cambridge University Press.

Royce, Anya Peterson. 1977. *The Anthropology of Dance*. Bloomington: Indiana University Press.

Ruby, Jay, ed. 1982. *A Crack in the Mirror: Reflexive Perspectives in Anthropology*. Philadelphia: University of Pennsylvania Press.

Sadler, A. W. 1969. The form and meaning in festival. *Asian Folklore Studies* 28: 1–16.

_____. 1970. O–kagura: Field notes on the festival drama in modern Tokyo. *Asian Folklore Studies* 29: 275–300.

Sakurai, Tokutaro. 1968. The major features and characteristics of Japanese folk beliefs. In *The Sociology of Japanese Religions,* eds. Kiyomi Moriaka and William H. Newell, 13–24. Leiden: E. J. Brill.

Sanders, Dale E. 1960. *Mudra: A Study of Symbolic Gesture in Japanese Buddhist Sculpture*. London: Routledge and Kegan Paul.

Sansom, Sir George. 1958–64. *A History of Japan*. 3 vols. Stanford: Stanford University Press.

Sasada, Katsuyuki. 1982. On hinagata, the divine model of Oyasama. *Tenri Journal of Religion* 16: 37–46.

Sasaki, Louise W. 1980a. The Tenrikyo sacred dance: The symbolic use of movement. *Tenri Journal of Religion* 14: 29–64.

_____. 1980b. *The Tenrikyo Sacred Dance: The Song Text and Dance Movements*. Tenri Journal of Religion 14 Supplement Volume. Tenri: Tenri University Press.

Sato, Koji. 1986. Salvation through Tenrikyo's service (Tsutome). In *The Theological Perspectives of Tenrikyo: In Commemoration of the Centennial Anniversary of Oyasama*, ed. Oyasato Research Institute, 155–170. Tenri: Tenri University Press.

Satoshi, Shionoya. 1979. Tenrikyo's future missionary work. *Tenri Journal of Religion* 13: 48–58.

Sawai, Yoshitsugu. 1986. The providence of God the Parent. In *The Theological Perspectives of Tenrikyo: In Commemoration of the Centennial*

Anniversary of Oyasama, ed. Oyasato Research Institute, 79–110. Tenri: Tenri University Press.

Schechner, Richard. 1989. *Between Theatre and Anthropology*. Philadelphia: University of Pennsylvania Press.

_____. 1993. *The Future of Ritual: Writings on Culture and Performance*. London: Routledge.

Schechner, Richard, and Willa Appel, eds. 1990. *By Means of Performance: Intercultural Studies of Theatre and Ritual*. Cambridge: Cambridge University Press.

Scholes, Robert. 1982. *Semiotics and Interpretation*. New Haven: Yale University Press.

Segal, Robert A. 1989. *Religion and the Social Sciences. Essays on the Confrontation*. Atlanta, GA: Scholars Press.

Seki, Keigo. 1968. Celebration of Hama–yama. *Asian Folklore Studies* 27(1): 1–18.

_____, ed. 1963. *Folktales of Japan*. Chicago: University of Chicago Press.

Serizawa, Shigeru. 1980. Mission as seen in the Ofudesaki. *Tenri Journal of Religion* 14: 22–28.

_____. 1981. *Ofudesaki Tsuyaku*. [An Interpretation of the Ofudesaki]. Tenri: Doyusha.

_____. 1983. Historical facts concerning self–styled beliefs in Tenrikyo and reflections upon our faith. *Tenri Journal of Religion* 17: 145–158.

Shankman, Paul. 1984. The thick and the thin: On the interpretive theoretical program of Clifford Geertz. *Current Anthropology* 25(3): 261–281.

Sheets–Johnson, Maxine. 1979. *The Phenomenology of Dance*. 2nd ed. London: Dance Books.

Shimazono, Susumu. 1979. The living *kami* idea in the new religions of Japan. *Japanese Journal of Religious Studies* 6(3): 389–412.

_____. 1981. Religious influences on Japan's modernization. *Japanese Journal of Religious Studies* 8(3–4): 207–223.

_____. 1986. The development of millennialistic thought in Japan's new religions: From Tenrikyo to Honmichi. In *New Religious Movements and Rapid Social Change*, ed. James A. Beckford, 55–86. London: Sage Publications.

_____. 1991. The expansion of Japan's new religions into foreign countries. *Japanese Journal of Religious Studies* 18(2–3): 105–132.

_____. 1993. From religion to psychotheraphy: Yoshimoto Ishin's Naikan or 'method of inner observation.' In *Secularization, Rationalism, and Sectarianism. Essays in Honour of Bryan R. Wilson*, eds. Eileen Barker, James A. Beckford, and Karel Dobbelaere, 223–239. Oxford: Clarendon Press.

_____. 1995. New new religions and this world: Religious movements in Japan after the 1970's and their belief about salvation. *Social Compass* 42(2): 193–205.

Sless, David. 1986. *In Search of Semiotics*. London: Croom Helm.

Smith, Brian. 1989. *Reflections on Resemblance, Ritual, and Religion*. Oxford: Oxford University Press.

Smith, Jonathan Z. 1978. *Map is Not Territory: Studies in the History of Religions*. Leiden. E. J. Brill.

_____. 1982. *Imagining Religion. From Babylon to Jonestown*. Chicago: Uninversity of Chicago Press.

_____. 1987. *To Take Place: Toward a Theory in Ritual*. Chicago: University of Chicago Press.

Smith, Robert. J. 1966. On certain tales of the Konjaku Monogatari as reflections of Japanese folk religions. *Asian Folklore Studies* 25: 221–233.

_____. 1983. *Japansese Society: Tradition, Self, and Social Order*. Cambridge: Cambridge University Press.

_____. 1985. A pattern of Japanese society: *Ie* society or acknowledgment of interdependance? *Journal of Japanese Studies* 11(1): 29–46.

_____. 1987. Gender inequality in contemporary Japan. *Journal of Japanese Studies* 13(1): 1–25.

Smith, Stephan R. 1994. The wrapped, the rapt, and the rapped: Considerations on models of Japanese society, Japanist, and stigmatized Japanese hot roders. *Review in Anthropology* 23(1): 21–34.

Spae, Joseph J. 1979. Missiology as local theology and interreligious encounter. *Missiology* 7(4): 479–500.

Spencer, Jonathan. 1989. Anthropology as a kind of writing. *Man* (n.s.) 24: 145–164.

Spencer, Paul. 1988. *The Maasai of Matapato. A Study of Rituals of Rebellion*. Bloomington: Indiana University Press.

_____, ed. 1985. *Society and the Dance: The Social Anthropology of Process and Performance*. Cambridge: Cambridge University Press.

Spickard, James V. 1989. A guide to Mary Douglas's three versions of grid/group theory. *Sociological Analysis* 50(2): 151–170.

Stocking, George W. Jr., ed. 1983. *Observers Observed: Essays in Ehnographic Fieldwork*. Madison: University of Wisconsin Press.

Strenski, Ivan. 1993. *Religion in Relation: Method, Application and Moral Location*. Columbia, SC: University of South Carolina Press.

Stroupe, Bart. 1983. Healing in the history of Tenrikyo, the religion of divine wisdom. *Tenri Journal of Religion* 17: 79–132.

Suzuki, Daisetz. 1972. *Japanese Spirituality*. Translated by Norman Waddell. Tokyo: Japan Society for the Promotion of Science.

Takahashi, Tomoji. 1986. *Great and Gentle Mother: Yoshi Nakagawa*. Translated by Ingrid Seldin. Tenri: Tenrikyo Overseas Mission Department.

Takahashi, Toshiyuki. 1988. Aperçu de la predication de Tenrikyô au Congo–Brazzaville. *Studies of Worldviews* 1: 31–38.

Takano, Tomoji. 1980. *Kami to Ningen no Aida*. [Between Human Beings and God]. Tenri: Doyusha.

_____. 1981. *The Missionary*. Translated by Mitsuru Yuge. Tenri: Tenrikyo Overseas Mission Department.

_____. 1985. *Disciples of Oyasama, the Foundress of Tenrikyo*. Translated by Mitsuru Yuge. Tenri: Tenrikyo Overseas Mission Department.

Tambiah, Stanley. 1985. *Culture, Thought, and Social Action*. Cambridge, MA: Harvard University Press.

Taylor, Charles. 1979. Interpretation and the sciences of man. In *Interpretive Social Sciences: A Reader*, eds. Paul Rabinow and William M. Sullivan, 25–71. Berkeley: University of California Press.

Tenrikyo Church Headquarters. 1976. *The Anecdotes of Oyasama, the Foundress of Tenrikyo*. Tenri: Tenrikyo Church Headquarters.

_____. 1985 [1967]. *The Mikagura–Uta, the Songs for the Service*. Tenri: Tenrikyo Church Headquarters.

_____. 1993a [1954]. *The Doctrine of Tenrikyo*. Tenri: Tenrikyo Church Headquarters.

_____. 1993b [1971]. *Ofudesaki*. Tenri: Tenrikyo Church Headquarters.

_____. 1996 [1967]. *The Life of Oyasama, the Foundress of Tenrikyo*. Tenri: Tenrikyo Church Headquarters

Tenrikyo Missionaries Association. 1993 [1976]. *Yoboku Handbook*. Tenri: Tenrikyo Church Headquarters.

Tenrikyo Overseas Mission Department. 1966. *Tenrikyo: Its History and Teachings*. Tenri: Tenrikyo Overseas Mission Department.

_____. 1979. *Tenrikyo Terms*. Tenri: Tenrikyo Overseas Mission Department.

_____. 1986a. *Honyaku Handbook*. Tenri: Tenrikyo Overseas Mission Department.

_____. 1986b. *The Teachings and History of Tenrikyo*. Tenri: Tenrikyo Overseas Mission Department.

_____. 1987. *Encounters With Salvation and Shuyoka Faith Experience Speeches*. Tenri: Tenrikyo Overseas Mission Department.

_____. 1990. *Selections from the Osashizu*. Tenri: Tenrikyo Overseas Mission Department.

_____. 1992. *The Otefuri Guide*. Tenri: Tenrikyo Overseas Mission Department.

_____. 1993a. *Rewarding Adventures*. Tenri: Tenrikyo Overseas Mission Department.

_____. 1993b. *Guida alla Dimora Parentale*. Tenri: Tenrikyo Overseas Mission Department.

_____. 1996. *The Path to the Joyous Life*. Tenri: Tenrikyo Overseas Mission Department.

_____. 1998. *Tenrikyo: The Path to Joyousness*. Tenri: Tenrikyo Overseas Mission Department.

Thwaites, Tony, Lloyd Davis, and Warwick Mules. 1994. *Tools for Cultural Studies: An Introduction*. Melbourne: Macmillian Education Australia.

Togi, Masataro. 1971. *Gagaku: Court Music and Dance*. Translated by Don Kenny. New York: Weatherhill.

Towler, Robert. 1974. *Homo Religiosus: Sociological Problems in the Study of Religion*. London: Constable.

Tracy, David. 1981. *The Analogical Imagination: Christian Theology and the Culture of Pluralism*. New York: Crossroad.

Tsushima, Michihito, Shigeru Nishiyama, Susumu Shimazono, and Hiroko Shiramizu. 1979. The vitalistic conception of salvation in Japanese new religions: An aspect of modern religious consciousness. *Japanese Journal of Religious Studies* 6(1–2): 139–161.

Turball, Colin. 1990. Liminality: A synthesis of subjective and objective experience. In *By Means of Performance*, eds. Richard Schechner and Willa Appel, 50–81. Cambridge: Cambridge University Press.

Turner, Bryan S. 1984. *The Body and Society*. Oxford: Basil Blackwell.

Turner, Victor W. 1969. *The Ritual Process: Structure and Anti–Structure*. Chicago: Aldine.

_____. 1973. The center out there: Pilgrim's Goal. *History of Religions* 12(3): 191–230.

_____. 1974. *Dramas, Fields, and Metaphors: Symbolic Action in Human Society*. Ithaca: Cornell University Press.

_____. 1977. Variations on a theme of liminality. In *Secular Ritual*, eds. Sally F. Moore and Barbera G. Myerhoff, 36–52. Amsterdam: Van Goreum.

_____. 1979 [1964]. Betwixt and between: The liminal period in *rites de passage*. In *Reader in Comparative Religion: An Anthropological Approach*, eds. William A. Lessa and Evon Z. Vogt, 234–243. New York: Harper and Row.

_____. 1982. *From Ritual to Theatre: The Human Seriousness of Play*. New York: Performing Arts Journal Publication.

_____. 1986. *The Anthropology of Performance*. New York: PAJ Publications.

_____, ed. 1982. *Celebrations: Studies in Festivities and Ritual*. Washington DC: Smithsonian Institute Press.

Turner, Victor W., and Edward M. Brunner, eds. 1986. *The Anthropology of Experience*. Urbana: University of Illinois Press.

Turner, Victor W., and Edith Turner. 1978. *Image and Pilgrimage in Christian Culture: Anthropological Perpectives*. New York: Columbia University Press.

Tyler, Stephen A. 1969. *Cognitive Anthropology*. New York: Holt, Rinehart and Winston.

Ueda Yoshinaru. 1982. *Tenri–O–no–Mikoto. What is the Character of God?* Tenri: Tenrikyo Overseas Mission Department.

_____. 1994. *Okagura no Uta*. [The Songs to the Okagura]. Tenri: Doyusha.

Umiker–Sebeok, Jean D. 1977. Semiotics of culture: Great Britian and North America. *Annual Review of Anthropology* 6:121–135.

Valentine, James. 1986. Dance space, time, and organization: Aspects of Japanese cultural performance. In *Interpreting Japanese Society: An Anthropological Approach*, eds. Joy Hendry and Jonathan Webber, 111–128. Oxford: JASO.

_____. 1990. On the borderlines: The significance of marginality in Japanese society. In *Unwrapping Japan: Society and Culture in Anthropological Perspective*, eds. Eyal Ben–Ari, Brian Moeran, and James Valentine, 36–57. Manchester: Manchester University Press.

van Bragt, Jan. 1992. Inculturation in Japan. In *A Universal Faith? Peoples, Cultures, Religions and the Christ*, eds. Catherine Cornille and Valeer Neckebrouck, 49–71. Louvain: Peeters Press.

van Bremen, Jan G. 1986. The post–1945 anthropology of Japan. In *Interpreting Japanese Society: An Anthropological Approach*, eds. Joy Hendry and Jonathan Webber, 14–28. Oxford: JASO.

van Bremen, Jan G., and D. P. Martinez, eds. 1995. *Ceremony and Ritual in Japan: Religious Practices in an Industrialized Society*. London: Routledge.

van Der Leeuw, Geradus. 1963. *Sacred and Profane Beauty: The Holy in Art*. Translated by David E. Green. New York: Holt, Rinehart and Winston.

van Gennep, Arnold. 1970 [1909]. *The Rites of Passage*. Chicago: University of Chicago Press.

van Straelen, Henry. 1957. *The Religion of Divine Wisdom*. Kyoto: Veritas Shonin.

Walters, Ronald G. 1980. Clifford Geertz and the historians. *Social Research* 47: 537–556.

Wheelock, Wade T. 1982. The problem of ritual language: From information to situation. *The Journal of the American Academy of Religion* 50(1): 49–71.

Wikstrom, Owe. 1990. Ritual studies in the history of religions. A challenge for the psychology of religion. In *Current Studies on Rituals: Perspectives for a Psychology of Religion*, eds. Hans–Gunter Heimbrock and Barbara H. Boudewijnse, 57–67. Amsterdam: Rodopi.

Wilson, Bryan, and Karel Dobbelaere. 1993. *A Time to Chant: The Soka Gakkai Buddhists in Britian*. Oxford: Clarendon Press.

Wuthnow, Robert, and James Davison Hunter. 1984. *Cultural Analysis: The Work of Peter Berger, Mary Douglas, Michel Foucault, and Jürgen Habermas*. London: Routledge and Keagan Paul.

Yamamoto, Masayoshi. 1988. *Mikagura–uta o Utau*. [Singing the Mikagura–uta]. Tenri: Doyusha.

Yamamoto, Takeo. 1981. *Faith, Sincerity, Joy*. Tenri: Tenrikyo Overseas Mission Department.

Yamazawa, Tametsugu. 1989. *Otefuri Gaiyo*. [Guide to the Otefuri]. 10th ed. Tenri: Doyusha.

Yoshida, Mitsukuni, and Tsune Sesoko, eds. 1989. *Naorai: Communion of the Table*. Hiroshima: Mazda Motor Corporation.

Zuesse, Evan M. 1975. Meditation on ritual. *Journal of the American Academy of Religion* 43(3): 517–530
_____. 1979. *Ritual Cosmos: The Sanctification of Life in African Religions.* Athens, OH: Ohio University Press.

Tenrikyo Bibliography Extract
Sources
Tenrikyo Church Headquarters. 1976. *The Anecdotes of Oyasama, the Foundress of Tenrikyo.* Tenri: Tenrikyo Church Headquarters.
_____. 1985 [1967]. *The Mikagura–Uta, the Songs for the Service.* Tenri: Tenrikyo Church Headquarters.
_____. 1993a [1954]. *The Doctrine of Tenrikyo.* Tenri: Tenrikyo Church Headquarters.
_____. 1993b [1971]. *Ofudesaki.* Tenri: Tenrikyo Church Headquarters.
_____. 1996 [1967]. *The Life of Oyasama, the Foundress of Tenrikyo.* Tenri: Tenrikyo Church Headquarters.
Tenrikyo Overseas Mission Department. 1990. *Selections from the Osashizu.* Tenri: Tenrikyo Overseas Mission Department.

Statements and Studies by Tenrikyo Adherents
Fukaya, Tadamasu. 1976. *A Commentary on the Mikagura–Uta, the Songs for the Tsutome.* Tenri: Tenrikyo Overseas Mission Department.
_____. 1983. One truth: The principle of unification and salvation of the human world. *Tenri Journal of Religion* 17: 44–70.
_____. 1986. *Mijo Satoshi: Yamae no Ne o Kiru.* [Advise on Afflictions: Severing the Root of Illness]. Tenri: Yotokusha.
Hashimoto, Taketo. 1979. The teaching of innen in Tenrikyo. *Tenri Journal of Religion* 13: 29–47.
_____. 1982. The Kagura Service: Its structure and meaning. *Tenri Journal of Religion* 15: 31–44.
Hayasaka, Masaaki. 1987. Tenrikyo under the structure of national Shintoism: Double faced aspects in the development of Tenrikyo doctrine during the lifetime of the Foundress. *Tenri Journal of Religion* 21: 9–38.
Hirano, Tomokazu. 1985. *Mikagura–uta Josetsu.* [Introducing the Mikagura–uta]. Tenri: Doyusha.
_____. 1995. *Moto no Ri o Horu.* [Unraveling the Truth of Origin]. Tenri: Doyusha.
Iida, Teruaki. 1979. The meaning of religion in an age of crisis. *Tenri Journal of Religion* 13: 81–94.
_____. 1982. The eschatological thoughts and the historical view of Tenrikyo. *Tenri Journal of Religion* 16: 81–94.
_____. 1986. Idea of Evolution in the Creation Story. In *The Theological Perspectives of Tenrikyo: In Commemoration of the Centennial*

Anniversary of Oyasama, ed. Oyasato Research Institute, 171–179. Tenri: Tenri University Press.

Inoue, Akio. 1988. 'Signs coincided' and the way of 'divine model.' *Tenri Journal of Religion* 22: 1–14.

Inoue, Akio, and Eynon Matthew. 1987. *A Study of the Ofudesaki.* Tenri: Doyusha.

Kontani, Hisanori. 1993. *Shin Fufu no Hanashi, Kenko no Hanashi.* [Further Discourses on Married Couples and Health]. Tokyo: Ikeda Press.

Marukawa, Hitoo. 1986. Religious circumstances in the late Tokugawa and the early Meiji periods. In *The Theological Perspectives of Tenrikyo: In Commemoration of the Centennial Anniversary of Oyasama*, ed. Oyasato Research Institute, 274–309. Tenri: Tenri University Press.

Matsumoto, Shigeru. 1976. *In Quest of the Fundamental.* Tenri: Tenrikyo Overseas Mission Department.

_____. 1981. *Modern Society and Spiritual Maturity.* Tenri: Tenrikyo Overseas Mission Department.

_____. 1983. On the significance of Oyasama. How we should become close to her. *Tenri Journal of Religion* 17: 63–78.

_____. 1988. An approach to the truth of creation. *Tenri Journal of Religion* 22: 15–32.

Mori, Susumu. 1986. A study of three pilgrimages in Japan. *Tenri Journal of Religion* 20: 79–166.

_____. 1988. Religious studies and human understanding. Studies of Worldviews 1: 1–30.

_____. 1995. The influence of historical trends in religious studies: Methodological change in the studies of the Tenrikyo religion by Christian missionaries and western scholars of religion. *Tenri Journal of Religion* 23: 67–104.

Morii, Toshiharu. 1990. *Kami·Ningen·Moto no Ri: Futatsu Hitotsu no Sekai.* [God·Man·Truth of Origin: The Two–in–One World]. Tenri: Tenri Yamato Bunka Kaigi.

Moroi, Masakazu. 1953. *Seibun–iin.* [Posthumous Manuscripts]. Tenri: Doyusha.

Moroi, Yoshinori. 1963. *Hinokishin Josetsu, Tanno no Kyori.* [Introducing Hinokishin and the Doctrinal Teachings of Tanno]. Tenri: Doyusha.

_____. 1964. *Tenrikyo: Some Misconceptions Corrected.* Tenri: Tenrikyo Overseas Mission Department.

Nakajima, Hideo. 1983. Between individuality and self–styled faith. *Tenri Journal of Religion* 17: 133–144.

Nakayama, Shozen. 1957. *Koki no Kenkyu.* [A Studyn of the Koki]. Tenri: Doyusha.

_____. 1964. *Hitokotohanashi: Anecdotes of the Foundress and Her Disciples.* Tenri: Tenrikyo Overseas Mission Department.

Nakayama, Yoshikazu. 1979. *Mind and Body.* Tenri: Tenrikyo Overseas Mission Department.

_____. 1986a. *My Oyasama*. vol 1. Tenri: Tenrikyo Overseas Mission Department.

_____. 1986b. *My Oyasama*. vol 2. Tenri: Tenrikyo Overseas Mission Department.

Nakayama, Zenye. 1979. *Guideposts*. Tenri: Tenrikyo Overseas Mission Department.

_____. 1992. *Yorokobi no Hibi*. [Joyousness Day After Day]. Tenri: Doyusha.

_____. 1993. *Seijin e no Hibi*. [Growing Spiritually Day by Day]. Tenri: Doyusha.

Niida, Kenji. 1986. The legal environment surrounding the Foundress of Tenrikyo. In *The Theological Perspectives of Tenrikyo: In Commemoration of the Centennial Anniversary of Oyasama*, ed. Oyasato Research Institute, 310–357. Tenri: Tenri University Press.

Nishiyama, Teruo. 1981. *Introduction to the Teachings of Tenrikyo*. Tenri: Tenrikyo Overseas Mission Department.

_____. 1989. *Mikagura–uta no Sekai*. [The World of the Mikagura–uta]. Tenri: Tenri Yamato Bunka Kaigi.

Okubo, Akinori. 1985. *A Study of Social Welfare in Tenrikyo*. Tenri: Tenrikyo Overseas Mission Department.

Ota, Isao. 1988. *Historical Sketch of the Life of Oyasama*. Tenri: Tenrikyo Overseas Mission Department.

Organizing Committee of "Tenrikyo-Christian Dialogue," eds. 1999. *Tenrikyo-Christian Dialogue*. Tenri: Tenri University Press.

Oyasato Research Institute. 1987. The early stage of overseas mission in Tenrikyo. *Tenri Journal of Religion* 21: 49–54.

_____. 1988. The early mission of Tenrikyo in its early stage 2. *Tenri Journal of Religion* 22: 53–58.

_____, ed. 1986. *The Theological Perspectives of Tenrikyo: In Commemoration of the Centennial Anniversary of Oyasama*. Tenri: Tenri University Press.

Sasada, Katsuyuki. 1982. On hinagata, the divine model of Oyasama. *Tenri Journal of Religion* 16: 37–46.

Sasaki, Louise W. 1980a. The Tenrikyo sacred dance: The symbolic use of movement. *Tenri Journal of Religion* 14: 29–64.

_____. 1980b. *The Tenrikyo Sacred Dance: The Song Text and Dance Movements*. Tenri Journal of Religion 14 Supplement Volume. Tenri: Tenri University Press.

Sato, Koji. 1986. Salvation through Tenrikyo's Service (Tsutome). In *The Theological Perspectives of Tenrikyo: In Commemoration of the Centennial Anniversary of Oyasama*, ed. Oyasato Research Institute, 155–170. Tenri: Tenri University Press.

Satoshi, Shionoya. 1979. Tenrikyo's future missionary work. *Tenri Journal of Religion* 13: 48–58.

Sawai, Yoshitsugu. 1986. The providence of God the Parent. In *The Theological Perspectives of Tenrikyo: In Commemoration of the Centennial Anniversary of Oyasama*, ed. Oyasato Research Institute, 79–110. Tenri: Tenri University Press.

Serizawa, Shigeru. 1980. Mission as seen in the Ofudesaki. *Tenri Journal of Religion* 14: 22–28.

_____. 1981. *Ofudesaki Tsuyaku*. [An Interpretation of the Ofudesaki]. Tenri: Doyusha.

_____. 1983. Historical facts concerning self–styled beliefs in Tenrikyo and reflections upon our faith. *Tenri Journal of Religion* 17: 145–158.

Takahashi, Tomoji. 1986. *Great and Gentle Mother: Yoshi Nakagawa*. Translated by Ingrid Seldin. Tenri: Tenrikyo Overseas Mission Department.

Takahashi, Toshiyuki. 1988. Aperçu de la predication de Tenrikyô au Congo–Brazzaville. *Studies of Worldviews* 1: 31–38.

Takano, Tomoji 1980. *Kami to Ningen no Aida*. [Between Human Beings and God]. Tenri: Doyusha.

_____. 1981. *The Missionary*. Translated by Mitsuru Yuge. Tenri: Tenrikyo Overseas Mission Department.

_____. 1985. *Disciples of Oyasama, the Foundress of Tenrikyo*. Translated by Mitsuru Yuge. Tenri: Tenrikyo Overseas Mission Department.

Tenrikyo Missionaries Association. 1993 [1976]. *Yoboku Handbook*. Tenri: Tenrikyo Overseas Mission Department.

Tenrikyo Overseas Mission Department. 1966. *Tenrikyo: Its History and Teachings*. Tenri: Tenrikyo Overseas Mission Department.

_____. 1979. *Tenrikyo Terms*. Tenri: Tenrikyo Overseas Mission Department.

_____. 1986a. *Honyaku Handbook*. Tenri: Tenrikyo Overseas Mission Department.

_____. 1986b. *The Teachings and History of Tenrikyo*. Tenri: Tenrikyo Overseas Mission Department.

_____. 1987. *Encounters With Salvation and Shuyoka Faith Experience Speeches*. Tenri: Tenrikyo Overseas Mission Department.

_____. 1992. *The Otefuri Guide*. Tenri: Tenrikyo Overseas Mission Department.

_____. 1993a. *Rewarding Adventures*. Tenri: Tenrikyo Overseas Mission Department.

_____. 1993b. *Guida alla Dimora Parentale*. Tenri: Tenrikyo Overseas Mission Department.

_____. 1996. *The Path to the Joyous Life*. Tenri: Tenrikyo Overseas Mission Department.

_____. 1998. *Tenrikyo: The Path to Joyousness*. Tenri: Tenrikyo Overseas Mission Department.

Ueda Yoshinaru. 1982. *Tenri–O–no–Mikoto. What is the Character of God?* Tenri: Tenrikyo Overseas Mission Department.

_____. 1994. *Okagura no Uta*. [The Songs to the Okagura]. Tenri: Doyusha.

Yamamoto, Masayoshi. 1988. *Mikagura–uta o Utau*. [Singing the Mikagura–uta]. Tenri: Doyusha.

Yamamoto, Takeo. 1981. *Faith, Sincerity, Joy*. Tenri: Tenrikyo Overseas Mission Department.

Yamazawa, Tametsugu. 1989. *Otefuri Gaiyo*. [Guide to the Otefuri]. 10th ed. Tenri: Doyusha.

Studies on Tenrikyo

Blackwood, Robert T. 1964. *Tenrikyo: A Living Religion*. Tenri: Tenrikyo Overseas Mission Department.

Bownas, Geoffrey. 1963. *Japanese Rainmaking and Other Folk Practices*, 131–140. London: George Allen and Unwin LTD.

Earhart, Byron H. 1970. *The New Religions of Japan: A Bibliography of Western Language Material*. 2nd ed. Tokyo: Sophia University Press.

Ellwood, Robert S. Jr. 1974. *The Eagle and the Rising Sun: Americans and the New Religions of Japan*. Philadelphia: Westminster Press.

_____. 1982. *Tenrikyo: A Pilgrimage Faith*. Tenri: Tenri University Press.

Fuss, Michael. 1998. Tenrikyo: Il pellegrinaggio verso le origini. *Religioni e Sette nel Mondo* 14 (2): 12–32.

Hori, Ichiro. 1968. *Folk Religion in Japan: Continuity and Change*, 217–246. Translated and edited by Joseph Kitagawa and Allan Miller. Tokyo: University of Tokyo Press.

Kimball, Bruce. 1979. The problem of epistemology in Japanese new religions. *Tenri Journal of Religion* 13:29–47.

Kisala, Robert. 1994. Contemporary karma: Interpretations of karma in Tenrikyo and Rissho Koseikai. *Japanese Journal of Religious Studies* 21(1): 73–91.

_____. 1994b. Social ethics and the Japanese new religions: The social welfare activities of Tenrikyo and Rissho Koseikai. *In New religious movements in Asia and the Pacific Islands: Implications for church and society: Proceedings of a conference sponsored by the Association of Southeast and East Asian Catholic Universities held in Manilla 10–13 February 1993,* edited by Robert C. Salazar, 31–45. Manilla: Social Development Research Center of De La Salle University.

Kurachi, Kazuta. 1986. Man and culture in the Tenrikyo story of creation. Translated by Carl Becker. *G –Ten* 14: 108–124.

Marras, Pino. 1982. Tenrikyo as mission: Reflections from outside. *Tenri Journal of Religion* 16: 73–80.

Nakamura, Kyoko Motomachi. 1981. Revelatory experience in the female life cycle: A biographical study of women religionists in modern Japan. *Japanese Journal of Religious Studies* 8(3–4): 187–205.

Newell, William H., and Fumiko Dobashi. 1968. Some problems of classification in religious sociology as shown in the history of Tenri Kyokai. In *The Sociology of Japanese Religion*, eds. Kiyomi Morioka and William H. Newell, 84–100. Leiden: E. J. Brill.

Offner, Clark B., and Henry van Straelen. 1963. *Modern Japanese Religions—With Special Emphasis on Healing Techniques*, 41–60. Leiden: E. J. Brill.

Oguchi, Iichi, and Hiroo Takagi 1956. Religious effects of social change during Meiji. In *Japanese Religion in the Meiji Era*, ed. Hideo Kishimoto, 319–334. Tokyo: Obunsha.

Reader, Ian. 1995. Cleaning floors and sweeping the mind: Cleaning as a ritual process. In *Ceremony and Ritual in Japan: Religious Practices in an Industrialized Society*, eds. Jan G. van Bremen and D.P. Martinez, 227–245. London: Routledge.

Ricco, Mario. 1966. *Religione della Violenza e Religione del Piacere*. Firenze: Saggi.

Shimazono, Susumu. 1979. The living kami idea in the new religions of Japan. *Japanese Journal of Religious Studies* 6(3): 389–412.

_____. 1986. The development of millennialistic thought in Japan's new religions: From Tenrikyo to Honmichi. In *New Religious Movements and Rapid Social Change*, ed. James A. Beckford, 55–86. London: Sage Publications.

Stroupe, Bart. 1983. Healing in the history of Tenrikyo, the religion of divine wisdom. *Tenri Journal of Religion* 17: 79–132.

Tsushima, Michihito, Shigeru Nishiyama, Susumu Shimazono, and Hiroko Shiramizu. 1979. The vitalistic conception of salvation in Japanese new religions: An aspect of modern religious consciousness. *Japanese Journal of Religious Studies* 6(1–2): 139–161.

van Straelen, Henry. 1957. *The Religion of Divine Wisdom*. Kyoto: Veritas Shonin.

Finito di stampare
nel mese di luglio 2001

presso la tipografia
"Giovanni Olivieri" di E. Montefoschi
00187 Roma - Via dell'Archetto, 10,11,12